Community Crime Prevention

Copyright 2019

3rd Edition

Published by: CreateSpace, North Charleston, SC

ISBN-13: 978-1718649118

Authored by: Jerrold G. Antoon, MS, CPP, RL, ICPS

All rights reserved. This publication is protected by Copyright. Reproduction by storage in a retrieval system, transmission in any form or by any means, electronic, mechanical, photocopying, recording, or likewise is prohibited without written permission from the author.

Physical Security Survey forms used in this textbook are available in Microsoft Word form at no cost to purchasers of this book. Survey forms may be altered to include the name of any hosting agency provided that the footer that is a part of the survey form remains intact. Requestors may contact the author at: Jerry.Antoon@gmail.com for an electronic copy.

Higher Education Instructors:

Please contact the author for instructor support materials in the form of PowerPoint presentations, quizzes, and exams. Materials are available at no charge with verification of college bookstore textbook requirement.

Author may be contacted at: Jerry.Antoon@gmail.com

Table of Contents

Additional Web Based Resources
NOTE: web sites may have changed since publication

Check Fraud
National Check Fraud Center:
http://www.ckfraud.org/

American Express, counterfeiting issues (type into their search engine)
http://www.americanexpress.com

Bank card Fraud
U.S. Federal Trade Commission, credit:
www.ftc.gov

Counterfeiting
U.S. Treasury Department Web Site and free materials:
www.moneyfactory.com

New York Federal Reserve Bank, publications on money:
www.newyorkfed.org

San Francisco Federal Reserve Bank, publications on money:
http://www.frbsf.org/federalreserve/money/index.html

U.S. Bureau of Engraving and Printing, publications and information on
counterfeiting and mutilated currency:
http://www.bep.treas.gov/

CPTED
Secured by Design
http://www.securedbydesign.com/

Projects for Public Places
http://www.pps.org/

The CPTED Page
http://www.thecptedpage.wsu.edu/

Glazing
US Glass Magazine:
http://www.usglassmag.com/

Intrusion Alarm Systems
Intrusion Sensor Technology Handbook
https://hsdl.org/?abstract&did=451638

Electronic Security Association
http://www.alarm.org/

Retail Theft
Annual Retail Theft Report
http://web.soc.ufl.edu/srp.htm
Store Security Tips

http://home.ica.net/~shoptheft/info.htm
Loss Prevention Magazine
http://losspreventionmedia.com/magazine/

Safes

Gardall, safe manufacturing company:
http://www.gardall.com/

Meilink, safe manufacturing company:
http://www.meilinksafe.com/

Schwab, safe manufacturing company:
http://www.schwabcorp.com/

Security Lighting

Dark Skies Organization
http://www.darksky.org

KIM Lighting
http://www.kimlighting.com/

Bieber Lighitng
http://www.bieberlighting.com/

Illuminating Engineering Society of North America
http://www.iesna.org/

Light Meters
http://www.omnicontrols.com/

Security and Loss Prevention Magazines

All of these magazines have on-line articles as well as free subscriptions to qualified subscribers. A qualified subscriber is any person who works in the security field either for a private company or as an independent security or crime prevention consultant (which all security and law enforcement students are). Simply create a business name when you subscribe and indicate yourself as a consultant.

Loss Prevention Magazine (LP Magazine)
www.lpportal.com

Security Magazine
http://www.securitymagazine.com/

Security Dealer and Integrator
http://www.securityinfowatch.com/magazine/Dealer

Access Control and Security Systems
http://securitysolutions.com/

Homeland Protection Professional
http://www.homeland1.com/homeland-protection-professional-magazine

Security Distributing and Marketing
http://www.sdmmag.com/

Security Management
www.ASISonline.org

Chapter One

Principles of Crime Prevention

Principles of Crime Prevention Performance Objectives:

- Describe the role of the law enforcement officer for smaller businesses
- Explain the role of the business owner in fighting crime
- Describe the conflict that can occur between law enforcement and the business owner
- Cite the three hats a law enforcement officer should wear regarding crime prevention
- Explain the concept of the criminal hat
- Explain the concept of the cop/prevention hat
- Explain the concept of the business owner hat
- Describe how societal limitations can influence a police officer's ability to think like a thief
- Explain why overcoming any aversion to criminal thoughts is required to be successful in crime prevention efforts

Introduction

This textbook in Business Crime Prevention is designed to assist both the business owner and the security or law enforcement professional in reducing crimes committed against brick and mortar businesses. Topical areas presented in this book are areas of common concern to any business. Each topical chapter presents both the inadequate security related issues and prevention techniques associated with the crime. The relevant partners in business security - owners, and either law enforcement or security consultants, will benefit from the contents of this book.

The law enforcement officer takes on the role of the security consultant in businesses that are too small to employ a security consultant. Small businesses are, by far, the majority of commerce in America. Therefore, it is important that both law enforcement officers and security consultants understand types of business crimes and how these crimes are perpetrated against businesses. Then, they should understand both relevant prevention methods and be able to articulate best prevention practices for that business based on local experience, geographic location, and type of property being protected. Law enforcement officers conduct this type of consultation as part of their regular law enforcement patrol duties.

The security professional does the same thing for businesses but on a larger scope and size. Security professionals will generally charge for their time and expertise. They are also more likely to be working with larger businesses or small chain stores. Like their law enforcement partners, security professionals will make security solution recommendations to the business owner based on what is perceived to be in the best interest of the client.

The partner in this war against crime is the business owner. He or she is the person who must choose the final solution to implement for each problem. However, without proper guidance, direction, and advice from either the trained law enforcement officer or the security professional the business owner may not even recognize a crime problem exists. Further, because crime prevention is not what their training, education, or experience has prepared them for, crime prevention solutions escape them. A well-trained security specialist or law enforcement crime prevention officer can assist the business in becoming aware of those prevention solutions and assist in making final solution decisions.

Conflict between business owners and law enforcement/security consultants can occur, however, when the prevention specialist fails to consider the impact of the prevention *cost* of a particular solution to an identified problem or vulnerability with that business. Any solution that will cost the business owner money affects the bottom line of all businesses. The cost issue is especially relevant to small business owners. If the business owner chooses not to implement a particular law enforcement recommended solution to a problem because of the cost the decision will affect the law enforcement officer in a negative manner. The officer can become frustrated with the lack of action on the part of a store owner and the resulting response by law enforcement may be a lack of future effort in educating businesses in crime prevention. The main issue is that the officer is not educated in looking at business costs versus profit margins. For example:

The law enforcement officer might suggest a $5000 prevention solution to a potential burglary issue at a business. In the mind of the officer this is a small price to pay to prevent a burglary. However, given the small profit margin of some businesses the cost may reflect a month's worth of profit. A business cannot justify one month of profits on just one potential loss aspect of their business. Consequently, without additional options, the owner does nothing, the officer gets frustrated, turning his/her back on the business and the criminal wins with an easy burglary. The root of the issue is a simple lack of understanding by the officer of basic business economics.

The final part of this chapter is designed to assist the officer and the security consultant in better understanding costs and profit margins as a basic component of business management to better prepare them to offer legitimate consultation advice to the small retailer or business entity.

Crime Prevention Business Considerations

The most successful law enforcement officer or security consultant involved in crime prevention should do three things every time they look at a business. They are;

- Think Like a Thief
- Think Like a Cop/Security Specialist
- Think Like a Business Owner

The first area, **"Think like a Thief'**, asks you to wear the hat of a criminal as you evaluate a building and business as a potential crime profit center. The burglar will look at a business and identify potential burglary entry points based on weak security areas. He will evaluate the business and its contents for the black-market value of the stolen goods when he later tries to sell those goods. The thief does not give any consideration of damage to a building, the lost peace of mind for the victim or customer disruption to the business. His or her only interest is the ease of entry and potential for non-detection. Likewise, the con artist or robber sees the business as their own source of money. If the law enforcement officer or consultant is able to mentally prepare him/her to look at a business through the eyes of these criminals they will be much more effective in their prevention role. It is no coincidence that the mindset of the best cop could also be the mindset of the best criminal. If you want to be successful in this area of law enforcement or security, constantly evaluate your environment for the opportunity to commit a crime. Always be alert to when and how you could be 'the thief'. Whenever you see a business building take a minute to analyze how you would burglarize or rob it. When you make a purchase think about how you could slip in a bogus check or bank card. One of the purposes of this book is to train the reader to constantly 'think like a thief' in order to put later prevention considerations into perspective. Consider that if one does not know or study his/her adversary you cannot fully expect to win the day or the battle.

The second area of consideration, **'Think like a Cop/Security Specialist'**, requires the reader to figure out exactly how to prevent the identified crime loss from occurring in the first place. The better you are at thinking like a thief the better you will be at identifying the solutions to stopping that thief. If you spotted an easily defeated door lock, valuables displayed behind inadequate glass, a visible bank bag being carried by an employee, or a check being accepted without the clerk giving it a second look, you have identified a crime risk that a criminal will readily spot. As a police officer or security professional your responsibility is to identify and communicate the security solution for these potential crimes. Some of the solutions require nothing more than education and policy implementation. Other solutions will require an investment in security hardware upgrades. Not having access to this educational material puts the retailer at a disadvantage. While they may know their retail product very well they know nothing about security. The criminal knows about weak security. You, wearing your professional prevention hat, are the bridge between what the criminal knows and how to stop the crime from occurring.

Much of what the reader learns in this book will educate them on what types of prevention methods are available to reduce the opportunity for loss to burglary, robbery, business document loss to fire, fraud and retail theft, as well as prevention methods for each loss. For law enforcement officers, studying and learning these techniques and procedures will benefit the business owner, increase public relations for their agency, make their community safer, giving additional meaning to the term 'Protect and Serve'. For the security professional, this concept reduces the direct losses to their client or employer which is exactly why they were employed in that position. This hat is the one that the reader will wear immediately after identifying the potential crime or loss.

The third and final area/hat, **'Think Like a Business Owner'**, has always been the least understood and least considered among police officers. Security/loss prevention specialists learn this concept more quickly as they are immersed in the business world. The lack of comprehension of this hat also accounts for the greatest frustration for law enforcement when businesses fail to implement law enforcement crime prevention recommendations. This hat, then, relates to the cost of the evaluators' suggested prevention methods. Many police officers and some security specialists become frustrated with business owners when their prevention recommendations are never implemented. This frustration is caused by the disconnect between business and law enforcement in particular. It is the business profit vs. cost-of-prevention factor that has eluded crime prevention specialists in the past. Officers and crime prevention specialists must learn that a potential $1,000 business crime loss cannot be fiscally reconciled against a $1,000 prevention cost suggestion. At this ratio the business owner sees the *potential* loss as just a wash over the very *real* cost of prevention. In other words, the $1000 loss is a 'maybe' risk. The same $1000 for prevention efforts is a definite loss to the bottom profit line. For the business owner this simply makes no economic sense and consequently nothing at all is done to correct the vulnerability. The resulting lack of basic fiscal understanding on the part of the crime prevention/security specialist results in frustration for both parties.

One of the purposes of this chapter and the remainder of the book is to educate the prevention specialist in business economics. Each solution presented ('cop') hat for every identified potential business loss ('criminal hat') should include the implementation of this third and final hat; to 'Think like a business owner'. The prevention specialist must ask him/herself what the best solution to a potential crime loss is when the reality of economics is figured into the equation. Looking at it from the business owner's point of view, the business owner would probably only be able to justify security enhancement spending at 10-20% of the total cost of the estimated losses (called the '10% rule'). If the total crime loss would appear to approach $5000, then your security improvement suggestions should not exceed $500 to $1000. This certainly limits prevention options but it does increase the likelihood that something will actually be done by the business owner. That, of course, is the goal of all parties involved: implementation of a solution. That is not to say that more expensive options approaching 25% or 30% could not be offered or even implemented, just that at least one of the options should include a 10-20% cost factor rule. Of course, policy suggestions to change employee behaviors would typically not cost anything to implement. These should always be recommended by the prevention specialist whenever appropriate.

It is only when all three hats are worn in succession that the best crime prevention/security solution for each potential loss/issue can be identified. Make sure it is a daily part of your employment routine whether you are in loss prevention or law enforcement.

Societal Limitations and Criminal Thinking

The average law-abiding individual is working with serious handicaps in trying to think like a criminal. First, there is a long-standing, ingrained sense of aversion to the idea of committing a crime, particularly a crime of violence. This is very often compounded in the minds of individuals desiring to serve society in the role of public or private peace keepers. Crime is not a part of this persons' daily intellectual activity and represents the darker side of human nature that he/she has been taught to avoid. Many readers can probably identify with a parent responding to a childhood incident like shoplifting with an admonition of "Don't you dare even THINK about doing anything like this ever again!" Thus, during a person's formative childhood years, he/she is taught to condemn all forms of antisocial behavior thinking. The resulting mindset makes it difficult for a police officer or security professional to completely alter their thought process and attempt to formulate the devious mind of a criminal.

The additional handicap that law enforcement and security professionals must overcome is that the very criminals that they are fighting against have probably had just the opposite view of the criminal thought process. Certainly, they spend more time at it. And as with all things, practice makes perfect. Additionally, criminals tend to gather in the same social circles contributing to the sharing of improved criminal methods to accomplish many of the same age-old crimes. How many police or security professionals spend as much time together discussing crime prevention and related cost efforts? Most social gatherings discuss the highlights of an apprehension or a chase. Prevention is not at the forefront of a professional's mind. Hopefully, this unit of instruction will allow additional consideration to trying to halt a crime problem rather than talking about it after the fact. Certainly, business owners would appreciate this.

It has frequently been said that criminals are stupid. While that could be true, it simply mirrors any other population groups of society. Some individuals and groups will always be more intelligent than others. And perhaps those criminals who are caught are just the less intelligent ones that are easily spotted by law enforcement or security professionals. Regardless, underestimating your adversary is never wise. Even in the criminal world there are individuals who excel at what they do best. The job of the protection professional is to be just that much better. Consider that every time a property crime occurs the criminal wins the battle and the police officer loses. Every officer should consider that a personal affront and take actions to prevent future losses wherever possible, working with the business owner to take corrective actions on identified vulnerabilities before the crime occurs.

Successful Crime Intervention

The methods of crime must be learned to best understand and formulate an attack and prevention against criminal activity. One of the best methods of learning crime is to study crime, real crimes. Study the way in which they were committed, why they were successful, or why they failed, and why the target was selected. What culmination of circumstances existed to bring about the crime? The successful study and understanding of crime and related behavior cannot be accomplished by mere imagination or logic, any more than you could hope to be a successful chemist by imagining how various elements might work together. The successful crime prevention or security professional must make a specific, determined, goal-oriented study of real crimes to understand criminals, their methods, their successes and failures, and most importantly, their mindset. Then he/she must continue to be aware of the latest crime trend to remain vigilant in their fight against it. This is fairly easy for law enforcement officers. There are plenty of crimes investigated by officers in the course of their duties. Take the time to study the crime scene and imagine the sequence of events during every investigation. Talk to other officers about their investigations and what they observed, then discussing how it might have been prevented. Ultimately, you will find yourself becoming a much better criminal investigator and much better at identifying future crime risks and vulnerabilities. The rest of the book is designed to give you the tools on how to prevent many of those crimes.

One last thought on this area as it relates to your own thinking. You must overcome the aversion to criminal thoughts if you hope to be successful in your prevention efforts. Making a conscious effort to think like a criminal while maintaining a posture of crime-free living is an easy transition for self-confident, law abiding individuals. Remember, like the criminal, practice makes perfect.

Successful Prevention Advice

The crime prevention/security profession is not unlike the medical profession when it comes to an understanding of medical drugs by the general public. Physicians and pharmacists have a clear understanding of what the drug can and cannot do. They understand the ailment it was made for, and they know the side effects of specific drugs. Unless the general public knows what questions to ask, they are at the mercy of their medical professional to tell them what they need. A good physician will take the time to explain everything about the medication to his/her patient before they leave the medical office.

When a crime prevention/security professional recognizes a crime opportunity and identifies several solutions to preventing the crime one of the errors commonly committed by the professional is to simply give them static advice. (Take this pill twice a day and the problem will go away). A prevention specialist who simply tells a client to install acrylic glazing, purchase a TL 30X6 safe, run a fingernail over the hologram of a bank card, install a motion detection alarm system, or any one of thousands of other prevention suggestions, *without explaining why*, runs the risk of ignored advice by the recipient and the danger of future criminal activity on the very issue originally observed. The general public only knows security issues from what they see on television. As much of what we see is media driven or simply Hollywood imagination the public has a misconception of what security can and cannot do. You have an obligation to explain the function, purpose, options, reasons, and even the downside for everything you recommend. A good prevention professional also asks questions that will inform them on any future plans of the business. If you discover that the business is moving to a larger building in 18 months you might not suggest strong physical security solutions which will cost them money that cannot be recovered when they move.

Law enforcement and security professionals in all occupations have an obligation to educate the public on what crime prevention means *before* a crime occurs. This gives the home or business owner time to digest the knowledge and apply the information to their own home or business without the stress of doing so after a crime. Attending business association luncheons, neighborhood watch meetings, Lions Clubs, Optimists, etc., or being a guest on a local radio show are great positive media opportunities and wonderful personal professional growth experiences that benefit both the individual and the community.

Chapter Two

Glazing

Security Glazing Materials Performance Objectives:

- Define glazing materials
- Describe and explain the applications of the three forms of safety glazing
- Describe the attributes of the three types of security glass
- Describe the applications of the three types of security glass
- Describe the attributes of the two types of security plastic glazing
- Describe the applications of the two types of security plastic glazing

Introduction

Glazing is defined as any translucent material designed to be used in a window frame. Translucent material allows light to penetrate. Transparent material allows see-through vision. Clear window glass is both translucent and transparent while many glass shower doors are only translucent. Security glazing is a product that combines the capability of transmitting light or vision for surveillance with the physical ability to withstand high energy impacts.

When a glass window is broken in a home the homeowner may repair it him/herself or call a glass company. Few glass company repair personnel and even fewer homeowners would do anything more than verify the type of glass originally in the window frame and replace it with the same thing. For most homes suffering a broken window this is logical. But to follow the same logic in replacing a broken business window is flirting with further loss. Let's examine why.

A broken residential window most often is caused by some accident. However, a broken business window is too frequently intentional. The broken window could be an act of vandalism or the entry point for a burglary. The burglary may have occurred because the store window was ordinary, non-security glass, easy to break and leaving a large access entry point. Unfortunately, too rarely in the clean-up and repair process is thought given to preventing a re-occurrence of the burglary. Thus, the glass that was so easily broken is re-installed with the same type of glass, the stolen merchandise is replaced in the same location and the business person continues their daily commerce. Thus, the circumstances for a repeat burglary have just been created.

For clarification purposes it may be important to understand that residential and commercial plate glass may not be the same. The manufacturing process is identical, however residential single glass panes are 1/8" thick and commercial window glass is ¼" thick. However, if the commercial glass is double pane insulated then it will be composed of two 1/8" pieces, the same as insulated residential windows. Intuition would tell you that the thicker the glass the more difficult it is to break.

Glazing as a Barrier

If glass is such a poor security barrier why do we even have glass in our businesses? Well, the reason lies with us. Who among us would shop at a major department store that had solid block walls with full steel doors? Customers expect to approach a store and be able to see inside. We expect to see lights, merchandise, and people. Without glass we would not feel welcome to enter. While it is a poor security barrier, most retailers without windows would suffer loss of customers. High-rise building owners would find few people willing to work in their buildings. So, while window glazing may be necessary for human acceptance, it need not be easily broken.

Standard Glazing

Standard glazing is glazing that is designed only to allow the passage of light and, in the context of transparent glazing, to allow the occupants to view the outside world. However, two problems exist with standard window glass. First, standard glazing breaks very easily. As a result, a liability situation may arise by someone accidentally tripping and falling through a window, sustaining personal injuries. This typically results in large civil penalties. Secondly, the same glass will readily submit to a burglar's attack from an impact item. While the circumstances are different, the result is the same in the form of dollars being drained from the affected business in both situations. Substitute glazing materials that help prevent these occurrences are available. They fall into two categories, safety and security.

Safety and Security Glazing Options

Safety glazing is designed to *reduce* the extent of serious personal injury. **Security** glazing is intended to *reduce* the opportunity of an intrusion. Notice that in both categories the goal is a *reduction* of pertinent incidents. The actual prevention of *all* incidents is an unrealistic goal. Accidents will happen, and given enough time and tools, burglars will find a way past any obstacle.

Also, it is important to appreciate that safety glazing is designed to only work one time. That is, it will perform its function, reducing the extent of injury, with the first impact. Additional impacts (on wired or laminated safety glass) would not offer the same degree of protection. However, because such incidents are accidental, it is unlikely that additional accidental impacts would immediately occur. Security glazing, however, is manufactured with the express purpose of resisting multiple impacts. Burglars are unlikely to stop with just one attempt at breaking a window. Therefore, security glazing is designed to be much stronger and more resistant than safety glazing.

Safety Glazing

Three forms of safety glazing exist. They are: tempered, wired and safety laminated. While they all function as intended they do so with different characteristics.

Tempered Glass

Tempered glass is standard glass that has been heat-treated. That is, standard glass is heated up almost to its melting point and then quickly cooled. This process is called tempering. Tempering creates a molecular structural change in the property of standard glass that creates two unique consequences in the now tempered glass. The first is that the glass is three to five times stronger against impact breakage. (But it is still not designed for security applications). The effect is that a human limb or small child may bounce off the glass instead of breaking it. The second is that when it does break it breaks into very small, lightweight pieces. This precludes large, heavy, sharp shards of glass falling on the person lying in the broken window, thus compounding the injuries.

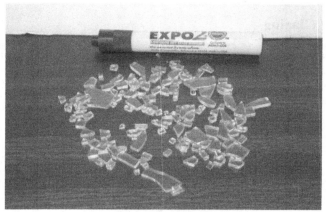

Tempered Glass

Wired Glass

Wired glass is the second form of safety glazing, and this glass looks just as its name implies. It is standard glass with an embedded layer of wire. Its appearance is much like 'chicken wire', one-inch squares of lightweight gauge wire. During the manufacturing process the wire is lowered into the molten glass and is sealed in place as the glass hardens.

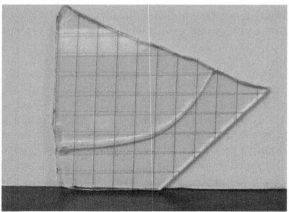

Wired Glass

When broken, the wired glass remains in place around the point of impact. This would normally prevent someone from falling through the glass and suffering greater injury. This glass also holds the broken pieces in place, preventing large pieces from falling onto the person who has fallen into the glass. Because it is made from standard glass, it is no stronger than standard glass and breaks easily. Also, this glass does not stop high velocity items from penetrating and exiting the opposite side of wired glass. As such, it would not be used to protect a worker from a disintegrating high velocity saw blade or similar object.

In the mid 2000's the Federal Government Code and International Building Code eliminated the use of wired glass in areas that require safety glazing due to the risk of human impact. This after a great number of severe injuries and even deaths due to arms being lacerated and amputated when persons fell into wired glass. The wire ended up trapping the hands and arms of the fallen person, creating subsequent cutting injuries.

Laminated Safety Glazing

The final category is laminated safety glazing. This glazing typically bonds two pieces of 1/8th inch thick standard glazing to a center core of plastic, although tempered glass can be used instead of standard glass. An automobile windshield is the most common example of such glazing. Because the entire surface of both pieces of the glass is bonded to the plastic, an impact leaves most of the glass intact, adhering to the plastic core.

Laminated Safety Glazing

The flexible plastic core further resists penetration of the impacting object by absorbing some of the impact energy. Thus, in the case of a windshield, a limb or head is both stopped and cushioned unless the impact is extremely severe.

SAFETY GLAZING SUMMARY

All three forms of safety glazing are designed to resist low impact accidents, such as falling or tripping, and the subsequent human body parts from penetrating the glass and causing serious injury. Within those parameters, these safety glazing forms work well. However, problems arise when people install safety glazing with the intent of securing their property. Safety glazing is designed to work once, breaking away or cushioning the impact. Repeated impacts will quickly allow a burglar access as the material readily gives way. Security glazing applications require their own form of glazing. Safety glazing is covered in this unit only because there will be times when a citizen will query you about their advantages for security. Your response should be a clear negative, and that they should only consider a security glazing for any security applications.

Security Glazing

Security glazing is specifically designed to resist intrusion to the point of possible deterrence of entry. There are two categories of this glazing: glass and plastic.

SECURITY GLAZING – GLASS CATEGORY

There are three types of glass related glazing materials in this category. Burglary Resistant, Bullet Resistant, and Security Film.

Burglary Resistant Glass

Burglary resistant glass, also known as burglary laminated or security glass is formed by bonding two pieces of standard 1/8th inch thick glass to an internal core of plastic. The difference between this and safety laminated glass is the thickness of the plastic core. The burglary resistant plastic core is thicker and better able to resist multiple blows with a blunt instrument. A burglar impacting burglary resistant glass will probably break the glass, depending on the force used. However, the thicker plastic core would normally not allow any initial bodily entry. When, and if, a hole is finally made it may only allow a hand or arm to penetrate, vastly restricting the loss of property. The intent is to delay the entry long enough that the burglar fears discovery and flees before being seen. While the glass will have to be replaced, at most a minimum amount of property is lost. This form of glass typically allows for insurance premium discounts. To make sure that this glass will perform as indicated glazing with a UL designation of UL 972, Forced Entry Rated Glass, should be specified.

Bullet Resistant Glass

The second form of security glass is bullet resistant glass. This glass would ordinarily only be installed in high-crime robbery prone areas. Its application would be to save life rather than prevent property loss. Its usual installation location would be on a counter separating the customer from the clerk. Some form of pass through would allow the transfer of payment and product. Installation on exterior walls would normally only occur on bank drive-up windows or other high-profile VIP, government, or military buildings.

Bullet resistant glass is also laminated. The difference with this category is that bullet resistant glass is composed of multiple layers of glass and plastic. The thicker the overall pane of glass, the greater the bullet stopping power. Notice, however, that the term 'resistant' is used in this classification. If the perpetrator uses a larger caliber weapon or continues to fire at one spot the bullets will quickly penetrate through the glass. A proper assessment on the applicable U.L. rating to be used is critical in choosing this glass. The appropriate UL guide for determining true resistance to bullets would be UL 752, Bullet Resistant Glass.

Bullet Resistant Glass

Besides the actual penetration of a bullet the person on the protected side of the glass must be concerned with another hazard called spalling. Spalling is the result of the frontal impact of a bullet transmitting its energy to the back side of the glass. The shock wave of the impact breaks loose shards of glass from the opposite side of the glass and throws them forcefully back toward the intended victim. A person with exposed flesh could be injured by these flying glass shards.

Underwriter's Laboratory Inc. (UL) standard 752 defines spalling as "no small fragments breaking off the material to the extent that fragments become embedded in or damage a corrugated cardboard indicator approximately 1/8-inch-thick set 18 inches behind the test sample." A careful look at the test procedure, referenced below, should give the consultant information on how to recommend the proper level of glazing.

UL has a commonly used set of standards and conducts testing of bullet resistant glazing. While UL has eight levels of testing only the first five basic levels most commonly purchased and installed in businesses will be addressed here. These levels of protection are:

Level one
This level will stop a 9 mm full copper jacket lead core round.

Level two
This level will stop a .357 magnum lead soft point round.

Level three
This level will stop a .44 magnum lead semi-wad cutter round.

Level four
This level will stop a .30 caliber rifle lead core soft point round.

Level five
This level will stop a 7.62 mm rifle lead core full copper jacket round.

U.L. Testing procedure

The testing for the first three handgun levels consists of firing at a one square foot test sample located 15 feet away. Two sample pieces are used. The first sample must resist three shots 4 inches apart in a triangular pattern in the center of the test piece without spalling. A second sample must resist two shots approximately on center, 1 1/2 inches apart but DOES allow for spalling to occur.

Rifles are tested differently. The sample must stop only one round in the center of the sample.

Test results

The following test results demonstrate the thickness required to prevent the affected bullet from penetrating the glass in each level.

Glass 1 3/16 inches thick passed level one.

Glass 1 1/2 inches thick passed level two.

Glass 1 3/4 inches thick passed level three.

Glass 2 inches thick passed level four.

Glass 3 inches thick passed level five.

These forms of glass are available in sizes up to 84" x 156" (7' x 13'). They are also manufactured in bronze, gray, or green tones to reduce glare or match other glass in the vicinity of the installation.

Due to the weight and installation requirements, special equipment and personnel are required to install this glazing. This dramatically increases the cost of this glazing and, because the building wall was not built for the excessive weight, retrofit applications would not generally be feasible but limited to new construction only.

Note that bullet resistant glazing would not typically be a form of glazing that would be required for most businesses due to the cost and the lack of threat from robbery with a firearm. If the latter is a true threat then a manufacturer representative should be contacted for recommendations.

Security Film

The third form of security glass glazing is called security film.

This glazing consists of a very thin flexible plastic sheet that is used on existing standard glass. It is applied on the inside of the glass with a special adhesive that molecularly bonds the plastic to the glass. Once applied the plastic becomes invisible. When the glass is broken it acts much like laminated security glass with the same characteristics.

The greatest advantage of this glazing is that it does not require the business owner to remove the existing glass to gain immediate additional protection. Security film strengthens the window by 300%, or three times the natural strength of plate glass. The low purchase price of security film makes it the most economical choice for upgrading standard window security. However, it is not as strong as Burglary Resistant Glass and should be carefully evaluated for its resistance if protecting people inside the building. Also, there is no UL rating for Security Film for security or bullet resistance. Manufacturers should present independent testing documents of their product for the end user to examine.

Note that not all glass companies install it. An internet search for the affected zip code location may be necessary to locate a provider.

SECURITY GLAZING – PLASTICS CATEGORY

Two general categories of plastic security glazing exist. They are acrylic and polycarbonate. Neither one of these materials contains any glass. Both materials are 100% plastic with different compositions and characteristics.

Common Characteristics of Acrylic and Polycarbonate

Both plastics will expand and contract in temperature changes. A sample 4' x 4' plastic piece of glazing will shrink in cold temperatures by as much as 1/4 inch in both directions. If an existing glass pane were removed and replaced with plastic without considering this issue there could be problems. At best a potential air draft will have been created and at worst someone leaning on the plastic glazing could literally push the plastic into the building as it comes out of the surrounding molding. As a result, it is important to note that installation requires a thicker replacement window molding that allows for expansion. This should only be supplied and installed by an experienced glazier. In the summer the opposite effect occurs. If the glazing is tightly installed in the frame, the plastic will expand and bow out of the window frame distorting the view through the window. Thus, adequate expansion gaps and related cushioning material must also be installed in the frame. Again, it is recommended that professional installation be done for these glazing materials.

A second characteristic common to both acrylic and polycarbonate glazing is that both plastics are made weaker when holes are drilled into them. For example, a business owner with a rear door containing a standard glass window might want to cover it with acrylic or polycarbonate for improved security. The most efficient method might be to simply cut a piece larger than the window itself and screw the raw plastic sheet into the door around the window. The issue is that the edges of the plastic where the holes have been drilled for the screws are now in danger of breaking off by an impact from the burglar on the outside. Because the hole is next to the plastic edge there is not enough material present to offer the same level of impact resistance. The best method of attaching either sheet of plastic would be to create a picture frame for the plastic sheet and then attach the framing to the door surface.

Both plastics also have surfaces that are susceptible to scratching. This can even occur during routine cleaning. Care must be taken to make sure that the glazing is washed with clean water and a well rinsed out cloth. Scratch resistant coatings are available for both plastics.

Both materials are also flammable. This means that they will support flames while being exposed to fire. They self-extinguish when the flame source is removed. Therefore, applicable fire and building codes should be researched prior to the installation of these plastics. However, most building codes allow the use of plastic glazing.

High temperatures can soften both glazing materials and create a dripping affect. Caution should be exercised in indoor applications. Plastic glazing that is placed too close to a heater or hot incandescent ceiling or wall light may melt. However, this same characteristic allows the plastics to be molded into unique shapes that may serve to better protect an object in a security application.

Finally, both materials can be used indoors or outdoors and both can be drilled, filed, sawed and cemented just as wood might be.

Acrylic Plastic

One of the most common brand name examples of acrylic plastic is Plexiglas. Plexiglas is a trademarked name of the Rohm and Hass Company but is commonly used in generic references.

Acrylic weighs slightly less than half as much as the same sized piece of standard glass. This light weight makes it much easier to handle than glass. It is available in all standard glazing thicknesses and can be specially sized and shaped for unusual applications.

This glazing is 17 times more resistant to breakage than standard window glass of the same size and thickness. When broken it breaks into large, dull edged and relatively lightweight pieces reducing the possibility of injury if the pieces where to fall on someone.

Acrylic is optically as clear as standard glass. Regardless of the thickness it retains its clear, non-distorting view. This makes it ideal for viewing through showroom windows or showcases.

Acrylic is inherently stable and will withstand exposure to hot sun, extreme cold, sudden temperature changes, and salt water spray. It does not deteriorate after many years of service.

Typical applications for acrylic are in the ground transportation industry. Buses and trains frequently have windows made of acrylic. The clear view and resistance to impact makes acrylic the better choice over glass. Indoor display cases are another application, as are front display windows in stores not located in high crime areas. Some business owners will apply glass over the top of acrylic to allow for easier cleaning as well as adding strength due to the plastic.

In security applications the user should consider using a minimum 3/8 inch or thicker acrylic to reduce the chances of a rapid penetration by a strong impact from a sharp weapon.

Polycarbonate Plastic

Polycarbonate is not as well known as acrylic. The most common brand name for this material is Lexan, made by the General Electric Company. Like acrylic, polycarbonate also weighs 50% less than standard glass.

The true appeal of this plastic is its strength. Polycarbonate plastic is 300 times stronger than the equivalent size and thickness of glass, which makes it an excellent burglar resistant material. Sledgehammers will bounce off a 3/8-inch thickness of this material. However, polycarbonate does require a stronger edge engagement than is provided for in traditional glass frames. Without the stronger framing the material could bend and pop out of a traditional glass frame.

One of the issues associated with this glazing is that it has a slight, natural tint. The tint is a very slight blue or gray shade. The thicker the material, the darker the tint. This makes it unattractive in some display windows. The best way to determine acceptability for any specific application is to visit a glazier or glass company and request to view samples of different thicknesses under different lighting conditions, against a white background or the expected application background.

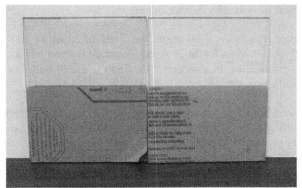

Tint Comparison between 1/4" Polycarbonate and Acrylic

Polycarbonate also suffers from exposure to the sun's ultraviolet light waves. It will discolor in about seven years creating a white, translucent view. The greater the exposure to the sun the more quickly it will cloud after the seven years. However, sunlight protected installations will last much longer.

Given its unique qualities, polycarbonate is best used in high-risk situations. Bank windows, store counter separators in high crime areas, and rear alley windows are some of the typical applications. Some businesses may be able justify polycarbonate as a front display window despite the tinting. However, the tinting tends to discourage its use as an indoor plastic display case.

Plastic Glazing Bullet Resistance

Acrylic is not rated as a bullet resistant material. Polycarbonate glazing can be, and is, very effective when so constructed. As an example, polycarbonate material 1.25 inches thick passed UL's level four bullet resistance test.

Glazing Cost Comparisons

As a general rule, acrylic glazing costs about 1.5 times as much as standard glass of the same size. Polycarbonate will cost about 4 times as much as standard glass. Installation costs for more secure frame edging reinforcement with plastics will add to the overall price. While this may be used as justification not to purchase security plastic glazing, the decision maker must consider additional factors. If a burglar is deterred and thus property is not stolen, it is likely that the value of the property saved far exceeded the cost of the glazing. Additionally, insurance deductibles need not be paid, insurance premiums are not increased, and customers are not inconvenienced and sales lost because of a lack of merchandise. Finally, with installation costs of even standard glass being approximately 3 times the cost of the actual glass, plastic glazing which is still intact after a burglar's attempted entry has already paid for itself. These factors should all be considered when determining the value of plastic security glazing over standard glass.

Bullet Resistant Materials

While this chapter focuses on the use of Glazing materials, including Bullet Resistant glazing, there is a related section that is not addressed in this portion of the chapter. Given the intent to reduce the potential loss of life the author would be remiss not to address any structure that surrounds the protected glazing material. If a bullet passes through a side door, as an example, the danger still exists. Therefore, the following section offers an expanded discourse on bullet resistant materials beyond glazing.

The following information is provided by Silva Consultants.

Bullet-resistant materials are commonly used where the threat of attack by an armed criminal is likely. While the level of security risk at most facilities doesn't warrant the use of such materials, some facilities, due to the nature of their operation or their location, do find the use of bullet-resistant materials to be a necessary security precaution.

Bullet-resistant materials can both protect employees as well as discourage robbery attempts and other types of crimes involving the use of a firearm. Bullet-resistant materials are commonly used at banks, pharmacies, check cashing centers, and other businesses that handle cash or narcotics in high-risk neighborhoods. Bullet-resistant materials are also used at public facilities such as police stations, jails and courthouses.

In recent years, certain types of facilities that didn't previously use bullet-resistant materials are now using them. For example, hospitals in high-crime areas now use bullet-resistant materials on the exterior of their Emergency Departments to protect against gang-related drive-by shootings. Also, some data centers now install bullet-resistant materials in their lobbies to prevent forced takeover of the facility by armed attackers.

Type of Bullet-Resistant Materials

There are four main categories of bullet-resistant materials: bullet-resistant glazing, bullet-resistant panels, bullet-resistant doors, and bullet-resistant accessories.

Bullet-Resistant Glazing

Bullet-resistant glazing is probably the best known type of bullet-resistant material. Bullet-resistant glazing is used when ballistic protection is needed, but direct visual contact is also required between the protected area and the non-protected area. Bullet-resistant glazing is commonly used at bank teller cages and other types of service counters, providing protection between the public area and the area that contains the cash or other valuables. Bullet-resistant glazing is also used on the interior of lobbies, providing separation between the public and non-public side of the lobby. In addition, bullet-resistant glazing is sometimes used on the exterior of the building to protect against stray gunfire or attacks from a sniper.

There are four commonly used types of bullet-resistant glazing, each with their own advantages and disadvantages. The following is an overview of each type of material:

Laminated Glass

Glazing

Consists of multiple layers of glass laminated with protective interlayer, usually polyvinyl butyral (PVB).
Least expensive type of bullet-resistant glazing.
Suitable for both indoor and outdoor use.
Scratch-resistant.
Because it is glass, it can be broken, and does not provide protection against a sustained physical attack.
Heaviest type of bullet-resistant glazing; weight may require special structural considerations.

Acrylic

Available only in lower ballistic ratings.
Offers some degree of protection against physical attack.

Polycarbonate

Best ability to fully capture incoming bullet, prevents ricochets and spalling.
Offers protection against physical attack.
Costs more than laminated glass.

Glass-Clad Polycarbonate

Consists of polycarbonate with a layer of glass added to it.
Suitable for indoor and outdoor use.
Glass side resists scratching and provides weather-resistance.
Weighs less than glass.
Offers protection against physical attack.
Has slight grayish tint; not as clear as glass or acrylic.
Costs more than laminated glass.

Bullet-Resistant Panels

Bullet-resistant panels are most commonly used to protect the walls surrounding the openings where bullet-resistant glazing is used. For example, if bullet-resistant glazing was used at a customer service window in a pharmacy, bullet-resistant panels would be used in the wall on both sides of the window as well as below and above the window itself.

The use of bullet-resistant panels allows walls to be constructed using standard stud-wall construction techniques rather than requiring that a concrete or masonry wall be provided. Bullet-resistant panels are typically fastened to the studs and then covered with regular drywall. When painted, the bullet-resistant wall looks like any other.

There are two popular types of bullet-resistant wall panels: steel, and fiberglass composite. Steel wall panels are the least expensive but weigh more. Steel wall panels are difficult to work with on the job site and usually must be ordered from the factory in the desired size. Fiberglass composite wall panels cost more than steel wall panels but weigh about half as much. Fiberglass composite panels are much easier to work with and can be cut and drilled on the job site.

Bullet-Resistant Doors

Bullet-resistant doors are used when a door is required in a wall that forms part of a bullet-resistant barrier. Bullet-resistant doors are specifically designed to provide ballistic protection and usually come as a complete unit consisting of both door and door frame. Bullet-resistant doors come in both wood and metal versions and are available with or without windows.

Bullet-Resistant Accessories

Bullet-resistant accessories are used when it is necessary to pass objects through a bullet-resistant barrier. Bullet-resistant accessories are also used to allow direct audio communications between both sides of the barrier. Bullet-resistant accessories include speak-through devices, money trays, gun ports, and package receivers that allow packages of various sizes to be passed through the barrier.

Suggestions for Using Bullet-Resistant Materials

The decision to use or not use bullet-resistant materials should only be made after a comprehensive security assessment has been conducted. The security assessment should provide guidance as to where bullet-resistant materials should be used, and establish the minimum UL rating level required based upon the level of risk at the specific facility.

A systems approach must be taken when designing a bullet-resistant barrier; the wall, glazing, and any accessories must all be rated to provide the minimum desired UL rating level. It doesn't make sense to provide a Level 3 rated window when the wall surrounding the window is unprotected. Also consider the possibility of ricochet and the potential for a bullet to penetrate the adjacent walls, ceilings, and floors. Always use materials that are UL listed and labeled. Some manufacturers can be deceptive and use terms such as "tested to UL standards", "meets requirements of UL Level 3", etc. even though their products haven't actually been tested by UL.

The thickness and weight of bullet-resistant materials can have an impact on building construction and may affect everything from the size of the structural beams to the type of window coverings used. Be sure to involve your architect or other design professional in the planning of your bullet-resistant system. Employee security awareness training must be provided in conjunction with the installation of a bullet-resistant barrier. Employees need to know how to react when a weapon is presented, even if they are behind a protective barrier. Employees may also be at increased risk when entering or leaving the protected area, and need to be given guidelines on how this can be accomplished safely.

Summary

The law enforcement officer who makes a recommendation, the security professional or consultant who must analyze options and the business owner or security director who will make the decision must weigh a host of options in considering what type of glazing is most appropriate to the situation. Besides the cost, the person must consider the business location and goods being sold, the crime rates in the area, the intent of the glazing, the degree of optical clarity needed and the level of threat toward the merchandise or property. Only when all these variables are factored in can a final decision be made. A proper evaluation will lead to a proper decision.

Glazing

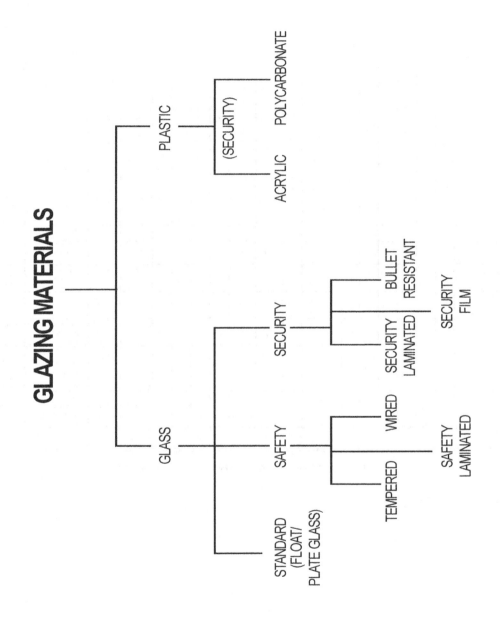

19

GLAZING TYPE	BASEBALL BAT 1-5	SLEDGE HAMMER 1-5	THROWN OBJECTS 1-5	BOMB BLAST WAVE 1-5	BOMB SHRAPNEL 1-5	BALLISTIC LEVEL 1-V	THICKNESS INCHES	ANTI-SPALL CHARACTERISTICS 1-5	SUPPORTS FLAME Y/N	TOXIC FUMES Y/N	INTEGRITY 1-5	AGAINST PROFESSIONAL 1-5	AGAINST NON-PROFESSIONAL 1-5	SERVICE LIFE RATING 1-5	APPROX. COST RANGE (square foot) $ per sq. ft.	SAMPLE COST (4' BY 5') $	MAJOR ADVANTAGES	MAJOR DISADVANTAGE
STANDARD PLATE, GLASS	1	1	1	1	1	-	-	1	NO	NO	1	1	1	5	$1.50 --$20	$80 (1/4")	Low Cost	Easily broken
SECURITY FILM ON PLATE GLASS	3	2	3	4	4	-	-	5	NO	NO	4	2	3	3	$6.00 + glass	"	Much better "Smash & Grab" deterrent	"
BURGLAR RESISTANT GLASS	4	3	4	4	4	-	-	2	NO	NO	3	3	4	5	$10-- $18	$202 (5/16')	"	Cost
ACRYLICS	2	1	3	2	2	-	-	1	YES	YES	1	1	2	3	$6-$8	$140 ½" to 3/8"	Lightweight. Excellent clarity.	Easily gouged. Supports fire. Scratchable.
POLYCARBONATES	5	5	5	5	4	-	-	5	NO	YES	1	1	4	3	$15-- $20	$340 ½" to 3/8"	"Unbreakable" Lightweight.	Not fire-resistant, toxic fumes. Easily scratched gouged. Clouds with age.
BULLET RESISTANT GLASS	5	4	5	5	5	1-V	1-3/16 - 3"	4	NO	NO	4	3	5	5	$60-- $125	$1260 (I)	Bullet resistance at a relatively low cost.	Very heavy. Increased thickness.

THE CHART ABOVE LISTS THE RELATIVE PERFORMANCE CHARACTERISTICS OF GLAZING MATERIALS BASED ON THE FOLLOWING SCALE

1-POOR   2-FAIR   3-GOOD   4-VERY GOOD   5-EXCELLENT

Courtesy: Security Glass Co.

References

US Glass Magazine, March, 2017

ARCHITECT July 2010; RESEARCH: Shock and Awe

Functionalized security glazing; Patent 8102585 Issued on January 24, 2012. Estimated Expiration Date: July 15, 2024.

US Glass Magazine; Which is Which? Choosing the Right Bullet-Resistant Glazing Materials for the Job by Fred Gebauer

Building Operating Management; Window Replacement: 7 Mistakes To Avoid; By Pat Toner - Sept. 2002

Double Glazing Security; By Sarah Clark

Perspectives On Testing Security Glazing: Failure Limits; Mr. Jeffrey D. Granato and Mr. Ray V. Foss

http://www.rimbach.com/scripts/Article/IHN/Number.idc?Number=58

http://www.security-glazing.com/attack_resistant.html

http://www.shattergard.com/home.html

http://www.pinnaclearmor.com/pdf/security-glazing.pdf

http://www.hpwhite.com/services/security-glazing/

http://www.standardbent.com/bullet_glazing.php

http://www.wbdg.org/resources/glazingmitigation.php

http://www.saflex.com/en/ArchiSecurity.aspx

http://www.acrylite.net/product/acrylite/en/application-areas/security-glazing/pages/default.aspx

http://www.protectiveglazing.org/resources/Security%20Glazing%20Specification.pdf

http://www.lexgardlaminates.com/products/amor_gard_bullet_res.php

http://www.sabicpolymershapes.com/polyshapes/en/Products/SecProductLineType3/glazingmaterial.html

http://www.defenshield.com/pdf/ASTMglazing.pdf

http://www.armorglassinternational.com/

http://www.wisegeek.com/what-is-bullet-proof-glass.htm

Chapter Three

Safes and Vaults

Security and Record Containers Performance Objectives:

- Differentiate between fire and security safes
- Identify the appropriate applications of fire and security safes
- Cite the three forms of fire safes
- Cite the ratings for each form of fire safe
- Explain the meaning of the numbers in fire safe ratings
- Describe what differentiates money safes needing anchoring or not anchored
- Explain what the letters mean in a money safe rating
- Explain what the numbers mean in a money safe rating

Introduction

In commercial and retail establishments, cash kept on hand during business hours and overnight must be protected in some fashion. Incorrect or inadequate security measures in this area may be as ineffective as keeping the cash in a shoebox. This chapter describes the various types of safes that can be used in the protection of cash.

This chapter also addresses the adequate protection of important business paper documents. Such documents, if lost in a fire, would likely prevent a business from reopening. Vital records that are needed to get a business back into operation after a fire should be protected inside a different kind of safe.

Finally, this chapter will allow the reader to identify when an existing safe is inappropriate for the application. Many business owners make a purchase decision on a safe strictly based on price. Then, after a fire or burglary, they are dismayed to discover that their decision has cost them their money or even their business. Even after a burglary an owner may continue to make the wrong safe replacement decision because of a lack of proper information. After a burglary, law enforcement officers will now be able to properly guide business owners in replacing the burglarized safe. Security professionals will have the knowledge to make recommendations or decisions for their employers or clients regarding the purchase and storage of valuable papers, products or cash.

Safes and vaults do provide the final line of physical security protection for both vital record documents and high-value items. However, many people have the impression that because a safe is called a 'safe', that it will protect the contents from all threats, both fire and burglary. Most people are surprised to learn that safes actually have limitations and can be compromised. The proper type and classification of safe is important to adequately protect against different threats. This means that we must learn the capabilities and vulnerabilities of all safes in order to correctly recommend and utilize them.

The ratings of the safes discussed in this chapter follow the most common rating system for safes in America; that of Underwriters Laboratories. Their ubiquitous label is as follows:

UL Rating Label

A note of clarification is needed at this point. The reader will find the use of the word 'container' both in this textbook and in industry related literature. The word container and safe should be considered synonymous in this reading.

Misconceptions

There are two typical misconceptions related to safes. The first is that a safe or vault provides both fire and burglar protection. As we will see, most safes are designed for a single purpose, resistance to *either* fire or burglar attacks. There are dual-purpose safes on the market, called composite safes, but the cost of these safes makes them difficult to justify in all but the smallest size container.

The second misconception is that a safe or vault will provide absolute protection against the threat they are designed to resist. Resistance is the key word. Both types are rated for *resistance*, not absolute prevention against forced opening or records destruction. A determined burglar with the right tools and enough time will probably make entry into any money safe. Likewise, a fire that is hotter than anticipated may destroy the paper records of a fire safe that was under-classified for its location and purpose.

Types of Safes

There are two types of safes available to end users. The first is called a *Record Storage Safe*, also known as a *Fire Safe*. This safe protects the contents by resisting the effects of heat generated during a business or house fire. The second safe is called a *Money Safe*. It is designed to resist the efforts of burglars in gaining access to valuables within the money safe. It is also known as a *Burglary Safe*.

Fire Safes (Record Storage Safes)

Record storage safes are designed to keep business documents safe from destruction by fire. It is imperative for a business owner to visualize a disaster scenario to properly appreciate the importance of this type of safe. The business owner needs to envision a total loss of building and contents to a major fire and then envision rebuilding their business. Of course, to rebuild the business, many records would have to be utilized. It is these very records that may be lost in a fire. According to the U.S. Chamber of Commerce, 43% of businesses struck by fire fail to reopen. When surveyed as to the reason, the primary reason cited was the destruction of vital records.

The rule of thumb in keeping the proper records is this: if it can be replaced or duplicated by an outside agency, it can safely remain in a regular file cabinet. If it cannot be replicated outside of your business, then it should be stored in a fire container. Asking a business owner this simple question will likely identify the most valuable asset he or she has in their business: "What is the most valuable item or record in this building that would cause you to go out of business." It may be a document or it may be some tangible item that must also be secured.

A sampling of suggested records to be kept in a fire container follows:

- o   Employee Personnel Records
- o   Payroll Documentation

- o Accounts Payable
- o Accounts Receivable
- o Inventory Records
- o Insurance Records
- o Vendors
- o Customers
- o Business Reciprocity Documents

To better understand why these records are important after a fire, the need for each type of record should be examined.

Employee personnel records will be useful for help in cleaning and salvaging company property. Employees who learn of the fire may assume that their employment is no longer needed. Having these records means those employees can be called in as needed.

The Internal Revenue Service and a business' employees may be sympathetic to a fire at a business. However, when taxes are due, both parties will be expecting the proper paperwork to be filed with them. Payroll documentation records must be kept safe from a fire.

While one can expect that vendors will continue to send bills for products shipped to a business, duplicate bills occur in any business. However, following the crisis of a fire a business may not have the documentation to prove previous payment. Paying a bill twice is simply not good business practice.

Accounts receivable is important because many customers pay their bills based on a billing notice. If the billing documentation (accounts receivable) is lost in a fire, the business is likely to lose most of the money it is owed.

Inventory records will be needed for the insurance adjuster. Unfortunately, the business owner's word on just having received a double shipment of raw materials will not appease the insurance company. Up-to-date intact records are imperative for proper settlement.

An alternative service does exist that might supplant the need for this level of documentation. It is called 'off-site storage'. Basically, you would send a copy of all your electronic records to a business some distance away from your physical location. That way if there were a tornado, fire, etc. at your facility the off-site storage company could simply send you a copy of everything you lost. The downside is that the storage facility will charge you a monthly fee that varies depending on the amount of computer space your documents will consume. Thus, a fire safe at your own business might be less expensive and is necessary for any actual paper records. Today, a business might take advantage of 'cloud' storage. However, that form of storage is just another brick and mortar building with many electronic memory storage units.

Other issues regarding insurance settlements must be considered. Without proper documentation a business may not know what deductible it has after a fire. Payout limits may be identified by the insurance company that cannot be disproved by the business. Rental equipment and insurance riders may have been part of an updated premium payment that the insurance company does not yet have on file. If the business insurance policy is destroyed in the fire it may be awhile before your insurance company is able to provide a complete replacement.

If a business has properly planned for this type of disaster then it will be able to quickly re-open operations. However, contacting vendors for replacement materials is critical at this point. A business cannot wait until after a fire to learn that the vendor account manager is unavailable due to a vacation or unplanned event.

After a fire, customers may also wonder about businesses status. They may have heard about the fire, assume the worst and are looking for another supplier. Other customers may be wondering about the delay in delivery of finished goods. Contacting customers quickly and with an honest explanation and plan of action may mean the difference between a successful re-opening and bankruptcy.

Finally, the wise business owner will have made a disaster reciprocity agreement with a local competitor, if possible. The agreement would allow use of each other's business machinery until the other party can re-open their plant. Such an agreement should be kept in a fire safe and periodically reviewed for current relevance.

To facilitate the contacting of all the various parties involved it is suggested that business owners contact temporary employment agencies for temporary help staffing telephones. Calls to employees, customers, vendors, etc. should begin as soon as the contents of the safe become available. Contacting the phone company to re-route business calls to a temporary office should be done immediately as well.

SAFE CONSTRUCTION

The basic construction of a fire safe is a steel box within a steel box. The space between the two steel box walls is filled with a wet, heat resistant insulation. As it dries, some moisture is captured. This same moisture assists in dissipating the heat developed during a fire. This is done in the form of escaping steam. The steam and the insulating material keep the safe interior temperature below 350 degrees F. While this is well below the actual spontaneous combustion point of paper, it assures a margin of safety. It also prevents the charring of paper, which is a part of the standard maintained by Underwriter's Laboratory (UL) for record storage containers.

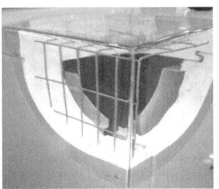

Fire Safe Construction

One final point on the construction of fire safes. They are normally constructed with wheels on the base. This allows the safe, constructed as a fire-resistant file cabinet, to be easily moved between offices. While this does make it easier for burglars to move a safe out of a building, it must be remembered that fire safes were never intended as storage for high value items of any kind or to be used as burglar resistant safes. Any such use is contradictory to their intent and testing.

As Fire Safes are designed for protection only during a fire they are not built for protection of money or valuables. The use of fire safes for storage of valuables is documented in many safe burglaries as evidenced below.

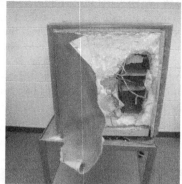

Fire Safe Burglaries

CERTIFYING AND TESTING

Underwriter's Laboratories (UL) does the certification and testing of each class of fire safe. The safes are subjected to heat, explosion, as well as impact testing. The explosion testing is done to determine if explosive gases are released during the fire and the impact testing is done to simulate the falling of a safe through a burned floor.

To receive a UL fire safe certification, label the safe manufacturer must submit actual safe samples to UL for thorough testing. Depending on the class of fire safe, each safe is inserted into a furnace and tested to an exterior temperature of up to 2000 degrees F. The specific safe rating will dictate how long the safe has been heated and to what exact exterior temperature. Additional testing occurs for explosion resistance (cooled and quickly reheated) and for impact. The impact test is done by dropping the red-hot safe from a height of 30 feet onto a pile of rubble standing 3 feet high. This simulates falling through three floors into a debris-filled basement.

The current numerical ratings that are identified in this book were instituted in 1972. Prior to 1972 UL safe ratings were given letter designations. These older letter designations will be identified to assist in the dating and classification of older model fire safes that are still in use. However, it should be noted that old fire safes may no longer effectively resist heat penetration due to deteriorating inner insulation. You would also never recommend any fire safe today by its, now defunct, letter designation.

CLASSES OF RECORD-STORAGE SAFES

There are three classes of record storage containers. They are, Insulated Record Safe, Insulated Filing Safe, and Computer Media Storage Safe. The first two are specifically designed to protect paper documents and the last to protect computer disks and tapes, videotapes, audiotapes, CDs, DVDs, USB thumb drives, and photographs.

Insulated Record Safe/Fire Safe

This class of fire safe offers the highest protection level for paper records. These safes are subjected to exterior fire and heat exposure at 2000 degrees F., explosion, and impact testing. U.L.'s test results require 100% legibility of the paper contents without any evidence of charring. UL classifies three individual ratings for this class of safe. They are:

350-4 – with a former rating of 'A' (prior to 1972)
350-2 – with a former rating of 'B'
350-1 – with a former rating of 'C'

The ratings require some interpretation. The first three numbers reflect the maximum interior temperature that cannot be exceeded in a fire. This is measured in Fahrenheit degrees. The fourth digit, after the dash, is an indication of the number of hours that the safe will protect the contents at 350 degrees F. This also reflects the number of hours in which the safe was put into a furnace for testing.

UL is thus certifying that, for example, a 350-2 insulated record container will protect the internal paper documents from damage by fire and charring for a period of two hours during which time the internal temperature will not exceed 350 degrees F.

Manufacturer Self Rating Record Safe Label

Insulated Filing Container

These forms of safes offer considerably less protection for paper documents than do insulated record safes. They have been furnace tested at a lower exterior temperature of 1,700 degrees F. and have not been impact or explosion tested. However, the interior temperature of these safes continues to offer protection against fire and charring by maintaining a maximum of 350 degrees F.

These safes/containers can come in a variety of shapes and sizes including a common locking file cabinet. The only sure method of determining which safe you are looking at is to carefully read the UL label. It will clearly state 'Insulated Filing Safe'. It may also read 'Insulated Filing Device' or 'Insulated Filing Container'.

There are two ratings for this safe:

350-1 – with a former rating of 'D'
350-1/2 – with a former rating of 'E'

The former would be rated for 60 minutes at 350 degrees F. while the latter for only 30 minutes at 350 degrees F.

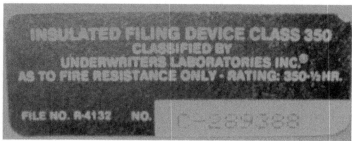

File Safe Label

Computer Media Safe

Also known as *Computer Data* safes, these containers are specifically designed to protect electronic data processing (EDP) media such as computer magnetic tapes and discs as well as photographic and digital images. Also, memory cards, thumb drives, DVD and Blu Ray discs. EDP format records must be stored and protected differently than paper records. These electronic records are affected by and begin to lose data at much lower temperatures than paper records. Besides the heat threat they are also susceptible to loss of information from excess humidity. Additionally, these safes require 'heavy magnet' protection from environmental and sabotage threats. Standard paper record-keeping fire safes will not protect against these additional threats. Attempts to protect such media in paper document safes will result in the same loses as would have occurred with no safe at all.

In addition to the standard temperature, impact and explosion testing, UL certification for these safes involves more aggressive and additional testing methods. Interestingly, because computer storage floppy *disks* lose data at a lower temperature than do computer storage *tapes*, two rating levels have been developed for EDP (computer data) safes.

Data safes for tapes are rated for 150 degrees F. and 85% humidity. Data safes for disks and electronic hardware storage devices are rated for 125 degrees F. and 80% humidity.

There are five ratings for each of the two classes:

Computer Tapes

150-4 - former rating of 'A'
150-3 - former rating of 'B'
150-2 - former rating of 'C'
150-1 - former rating of 'D'
150-1/2 - former rating of 'E'

Computer Disks

125-4
125-3
125-2
125-1
125-1/2

Because the '125' classification was created after 1972 there are no former letter ratings for this class.

Like the fire safes, the '150' or '125' is the maximum temperature measured in Fahrenheit degrees that the interior of the safe will reach given the stated number of hours after the dash indicator.

These safes should also be used for storage of photos to prevent the deterioration of the photo face due to chemical reaction to the atmosphere. Treasured or valuable older videotapes should likewise be kept in EDP safes.

Most businesses that utilize electronic storage today would probably use USB thumb drives or CD/DVDs. *Therefore, you would no longer recommend the 150 category of computer safes for any business today.* If conducting a security survey, it would be wise to examine, with permission, the current labels of any computer data safes in existence to make sure that, unless they are protecting exclusively computer tapes (unlikely) they are not of the old, 150, classification.

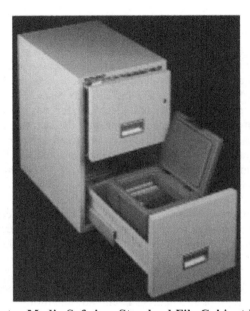

Computer Media Safe in a Standard File Cabinet Drawer

RECORDS STORAGE SAFES CAUTIONS

Two cautions must be addressed regarding record storage safes. The first regards the purchasing of a second hand safe. While a safe may look almost new from the outside, purchasing a used safe from an unknown party is not recommended. A used safe may have been involved in a fire and been painted over. The concern is that a fire safe is only effective once. Once the safe and its insulation have been exposed to fire or the heat of fire the certification is void. The insulation will have absorbed the heat and in the process, much of its protective qualities will have been compromised as it was intended to do.

The second concern relates to older record storage safes. Newer safes can take advantage of new technology in insulation materials. Older safes have last generation type insulation. In some cases, this may be as good as today's technology. The problem is that there is no way of knowing. Older insulation can dry out, crumble and lose its heat absorbing ability. Old insulation can also dry out and settle within the walls of the safe. This will effectively leave an upper portion of the safe without protection. The simplest way to determine the age of UL fire safes is to look at the UL label. If it is rated with a letter, it was made prior to 1972. This will give you a starting point on how old it is today. Safes that are not rated by UL will not have this reference point. If it is older than 1972 and the contents of the safe are irreplaceable it would be wise to replace the entire safe. Fire safes made after 1972 may not have a date stamp anywhere on the safe. Of course, there is no way of knowing, either, what the insulating material is on any of today's fire safes. Knowing any serial number and then checking with the safe manufacturer would be a place to start for replacement advice.

RATINGS LABEL LOCATION

UL labels on older fire safes can be located anywhere on the safe. The label is frequently located on the outside frame below the door. It was soon discovered however, that this allowed burglars to view the label and know the type of safe prior to an attack. Newer safes rated by UL now have the label located on the interior side of the safe door. Non-UL certified safes might continue to place their labels wherever they choose. Caution should be exercised in purchasing a non-UL certified safe, as insurance companies may not recognize it as meeting their minimum specifications.

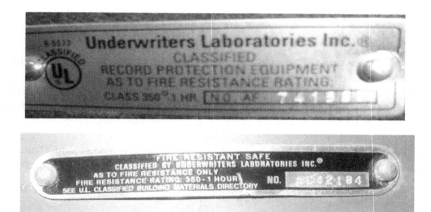

Current UL Fire Labels

CHOOSING A RECORD SAFE

With such a variety of safes to choose from, it can be difficult to know which safe is best for any specific business or application. While there are no hard rules to follow there are guidelines to assist with making a decision.

The first decision is what *class* of safe to purchase. For paper records there are two choices and the insulated record safe is the better of the two. It is tested to a higher standard. It is also more expensive because of the higher standard. The insulated file container may be appropriate if you have a specially designed fire-resistant room on the first level of a business. If not, the container may not survive a very hot, extended fire or a drop through a burned floor. Media safes, of course, are designed to protect computer or other forms of electronic documents and the only choice is a 150 or 125. If a mixture of electronic storage mediums were being stored together then a 125 would be the best choice. Putting computer disks or tape into a desk drawer or even a paper record storage container constitutes a grave risk in the event of a fire.

The next decision to make is what *rating* to choose. This decision is more complicated because it requires some judgment and analysis. The items to evaluate include the type of building construction, the contents of the building, and the distance and type of fire department servicing the building.

The building construction makes a difference in how hot and long the building might burn. Wood construction will burn hotter and faster than will concrete block construction. A business that sells petroleum or paper based products is more likely to suffer a fire in many areas of the building than will a ceramic tile shop. A full-time fire department is usually better trained, better equipped and has a faster response time than a volunteer fire department located in a remote area. In the worst-case scenario, it may be easy to justify a 350-4 insulated record container. The best-case scenario would get by with a 350-1/2 insulated file container. Most businesses will probably fall somewhere in the middle of this spectrum. Only the individual in charge of each business can make the final judgment based on your advice.

Money Safes (Burglary Safes)

The obvious purpose of money safes is to protect financial instruments, cash, or items of high value from burglary. It is important to remember that these safes do not protect the contents from fire. Money safes are rated for resistance against burglary only. It is an interesting point to note that money is a potential threat on both fronts. Currency, although actually made of cotton, is subject to both theft as well as fire. Options for dual protection from theft and fire will be discussed later in this chapter.

MONEY SAFE CONSTRUCTION

Money safes are made of layers of steel and other materials bonded together. Copper, aluminum, chromium, ceramic, and even reinforced concrete have all been used in lieu of steel. The different layers of materials are just one of the security features built into money safes. Any power drills being used on the safe would rapidly dull as they contact the various resistive qualities of different materials. This would require the burglar to make frequent drill bit changes, increasing the delay time.

There are no fire-resistant materials contained in the construction of a money safe. The primarily metal sides of a safe would rapidly conduct heat to the interior of the safe and potentially destroy any paper documents.

MONEY SAFE RATINGS

These safes are all rated for resistance to physical attack. They are divided into two categories. The first category lists safes that are rated for attack against the door and front face of the safe *only*. The second category lists safes that are rated for attack against both the door *and* the entire body (all six sides). There are ten ratings of money safes as certified by UL. They are as follows.

Door and front face only:

TL-15
Deposit Safe
TL-30
TRTL-30

Door and entire body:

TL-15X6
TL-30X6
TRTL-15X6
TRTL-30X6
TRTL-60X6
TXTL-60X6

In all the money safe ratings (except the Deposit Safe) the beginning set of letters indicates the type of tools against which the safe is rated for resistance from forced attack. After the letters the first two numbers specifies the time, in minutes, the safe can withstand entry by the specified tools. Finally, the 'X6', when present, identifies those safes that are certified to withstand an attack against all six sides, again with the specified tools. The specific details of each safe are listed below. They are described in order of complexity of the attack tools.

TL-15

The 'TL' indicates that the safe is 'tool resistant'. The rated tools for this safe are common hand tools as well as portable mechanical and electrical tools including 1/2-inch carbide drill bits.

TL 15 Burglary Safe Label

The safe door and front face are the only parts of this safe that were tested and thus rated. The door and face must resist intrusion for a period of 15 minutes against these tools. The safe is deemed to pass the standard if the two-person UL test team fails to either open the door or create a hole in the door or front face of the safe larger than 6 square inches.

This rating requires that the safe weigh a minimum of 750 pounds *or* be equipped with structural anchors to secure it to the floor. Either option is acceptable.

While the body of a TL-15 safe is not tested for attack entry it is required to meet a UL 'construction standard'. That construction standard requires that the body of this safe be at least 1-inch thick steel or the equivalent material. It should be emphasized that only the door and front face of this safe are tested. The body, of one-inch steel, may be more vulnerable to attack. This rating allows for some certification of attack resistance (front face only) while keeping the manufacturing and testing costs lower which results in a lower retail price as well.

Deposit Safe

This safe is tool resistant against the tools listed in the TL-15 rating, also against only the door and front face. However, because this safe contains an opening for envelope or money bag deposits, it is also tested for devices that burglars might use to remove the bags via the top or front opening. These tools are called fishing and trapping devices. They are frequently made with fish line and hooks or by securing a hidden bag inside the safe to catch and trap deposit bags. The certification attack by UL using forced entry is for 15 minutes. Fishing and trapping attacks are also attempted for an additional 15 minutes.

The safe is deemed to have met the standard if the door is not opened, if the test cannot create a hole larger than six square inches in the door and front face, and if one money bag cannot be removed or more than three envelopes removed through the deposit slot. The later loss may seem significant but reflects the reality of using Deposit Safes for the storage of money deposits.

This safe must weigh at least 750 pounds or, as an option, it can weigh less but must then be anchored to the floor or wall.

Again, the body of a Deposit Safe must be one-inch thick steel or an equivalent material.

Deposit Safe

TL-30

This safe is also tool resistant. It is tested with the same tools listed in TL-15 but adds two additional tools: abrasive cutting wheels and power saws. The UL test attack is, again, only against the door and front face. The attack time is increased to 30 minutes. For certification purposes the safe must meet the same result as the TL-15 safe.

The weight of this safe must be at least 750 pounds or, as an option, it can weigh less but then must be anchored.

Like the previous two safes, the safe body must be one-inch steel or the equivalent. This again leaves the body untested and more vulnerable. Note that the body on this higher rated safe is the same thickness as the TL-15 and Deposit Safe. The extra cost for this safe is reflected in the increased resistance to forced entry to the door and front face.

TL-15X6

This safe is rated for the same tools as identified in the TL-30 safe. The total time of attack, however, is again 15 minutes. Note that this safe includes the 'X6' as part of its designation. That means that all six sides of the safe are now subject to attack as part of the certification process.

This safe is deemed certified if the two-person UL attack team fails to open the door or create a hole anywhere in the safe at least 6 square inches in size.

The weight of this safe remains at 750 pounds as a minimum or, if weighing less, it must be anchored.

Because this safe is rated for all six sides there is no applicable body thickness construction standard.

TL-30X6

This safe is rated for the exact same tools as listed for the TL-15X6. The only change is that it must resist attack entry for a total of 30 minutes. The safe again meets certification if the attack fails to open the door or create a hole anywhere in the safe at least 6 square inches in size.
This safe has the same two weight options. Either it must weigh at least 750 pounds or be anchored.

Construction is not specified as this safe is rated on all six sides.

TRTL-30

This classification of safe is both torch and tool resistant. The 'TR' in this case indicates it is torch resistance. The entry test tools are the same as in a TL-30X6 with the addition of an oxygen and fuel cutting torch. The safe is deemed to have passed certification if the attack fails to open the door or make a hole larger than 2 square inches in the *door or front face*. Notice the absence of the 'X' factor. Therefore, body construction is again a consideration. Also note that the size of the potential entry hole has changed and is now much smaller than the previous ratings.

There is another difference with this safe. That is the fact that there is no longer an anchoring option with this classification. This safe *must* weigh at least 750 pounds. This is intended to discourage burglars from carrying away the safe from the site of the burglary.

The body of this safe, again, must be one-inch steel or an equivalent material. One additional, and unique, difference with this safe is that the metal body must be encased in three inches of reinforced concrete or its equivalent. This is the last safe that is rated for door and front face entry only.

TRTL-15X6

The TRTL-15X6 safe is rated for both torch and tool resistance. The door and entire body must resist attack with the tools and torches listed for the TRTL-30 (previous) plus electric impact hammers for a total of fifteen minutes. The safe passes the UL certification test if the attack fails to open the safe door or fails to penetrate any part of the safe with a two-square inch or greater size hole.

This safe must weigh a minimum of 750 pounds. Because of the certification on all six sides it does not have a construction standard.

TRTL-30X6

This safe has the same characteristics and requirements as the TRTL-15X6. The only difference with this safe is that it must withstand attack for a period of 30 minutes.

TRTL 30x6 UL Safe Label

TRTL-60X6

This safe has all the same characteristics as the TRTL-15X6 and 30X6. However, note that the attack time has increased substantially. The UL attack team had considerable opportunity to open this safe under controlled conditions and the rating passed the test.

TXTL-60X6

This safe is torch, tool and explosive resistant. The addition of the 'X' in the letter designator identifies this safe as being explosive resistant. The stand-alone 'T' now means 'torch resistant'. The TL remains as a classification for tools. In this rating the entire safe body, including the door and front face, must resist attack with all the tools and torches previously described plus a total explosive charge of eight ounces of nitroglycerin or its equivalent. However, the sixty-minute attack rating is for the torch and tools only. The explosives are a separate rating of eight ounces of nitroglycerin spread over two attacks. The UL certification specifies that the eight ounces be tested in two four-ounce explosive charges. However, the charges can be placed on the same spot for testing purposes. However, even with the two explosive charges the safe must remain closed and secure.

The other change in this safe rating is that the weight of this safe is a unique, *minimum* of 1000 pounds. There is no anchoring option for this classification.

Because of the six sided 'X' factor there is no construction standard for this safe.

Non-U.L. Construction Ratings

All the safes that have just been examined are certified and rated by Underwriter's Laboratories. This means that each of the listed safes has been tested for resistance against attack. One of the indirect results of this testing, is the high cost of these safes. The testing procedure is expensive and these costs must be passed on in the retail price of the safe. However, not everyone wants or needs, a UL rated safe.

In response to this issue there is a separate *insurance classification* that also rates safes. (This should not be confused with the insurance *rating*s that go along with the UL rated safes and are found in the supplemental material at the end of the chapter). There are three classifications assigned to non-U.L. tested safes. These safes are frequently called Money Chests, but may also be called burglary safes and deposit safes. However, they are not labeled with a UL rating label. The safe rating label must be carefully examined to determine what rating and level of safe you are obtaining. Only UL tested safes are allowed to be labeled with the black and white or black and silver UL rating label.

The three (non-U.L.) Insurance Classifications are as follows:

> ➤ Class B
> ➤ Class C
> ➤ Class E

These safes are classified for *construction only*. They are not tested for resistance in any form. Details of the construction criteria are as follows:

CLASS B RATING

This safe must be constructed of steel, with a safe body 1/4-inch-thick and a door 1/2 inch thick.

CLASS C RATING

This safe must be constructed of steel, with a safe body 1/2-inch-thick and a door 1 inch thick.

CLASS E RATING

This safe must be constructed of steel, with a safe body 1 inch thick and a door 1 1/2 inches thick. Class E rated safes meet the same criteria for construction as a UL TL-15 safe without the UL label.

It is worth noting that any modification to any UL rated safe that is not factory authorized and tested by UL voids the original UL rating. For insurance purposes, the modified safe would also convert to one of the above applicable non-U.L. insurance classifications.

Recommendation Consideration

The choice of safe to recommend to a business should not be measured based on the strongest or most secure safe. Any time you increase the rating of any safe you increase the cost. At some point the business cannot afford and would not need a more secure safe. This goes back to the 10% rule. The choice of safe should be evaluated by the owner and/or police or security consultant working with the business owner. As an example, the TXTL 60X6 safe sounds like the overall solution to everyone's needs. However, this safe would cost well over $100,000. Then it also needs to be shipped and installed. As these safes are normally shipped from overseas manufacturers, and weighing in at1,000 pounds, the shipping and handling could cost half as much as the price of the safe. Thus, this safe would probably never be recommended for typical businesses. A business needs-analysis will allow for the best specification or recommendation. The safe just below that, the TRTL 60X6, has the same type of limitations. It is also not likely to be recommended for 99% of small businesses. Keeping in mind that most small business owners would have less than $15,000 overnight in their safe, referencing the money storage value chart in the supplemental materials at the end of this chapter is a wise decision for the professional advisor.

Another consideration on fire safes relates to the paper safes versus the computer data safes. While businesses will always have a need for paper records the increasing use of computers means that some or many small businesses will have some records on a form of digital storage medium. Obviously, a paper record safe would not suffice for the safe storage of digital data. With this in mind it might be prudent to discuss the purchase of both a larger paper fire safe with the storage of a smaller computer data safe inside of it.

Safe or Vault

A safe is really designed as a portable means of protection for smaller quantities of property. A vault is designed for permanent placement and larger storage capacities. The choice is based on the physical volume of the item being stored.

VAULTS

Vaults have the same two divisions as safes do: fire resistive and burglar resistive. Vaults are a permanent fixture with walk-in capabilities and are designed for the large storage of records while a safe remains a portable means of protection.

The one major difference between the two is that a vault is constructed on site with the door of vault being the only component supplied by the manufacturer. The other five sides must be designed and built to individual specifications. With U.S. banks and some other federal institutions these specifications are set forth by federal administrative code.

In building a vault, the occupant must choose which form of vault is required. This decision is needed so that the proper door (fire or burglary) can be ordered and installed. Ratings for fire doors can go as high as 6 hours. Of course, given the thickness of a burglar resistant vault, there would be some natural fire resistance built into the vault.

For those prevention professionals that might be charged with K-12 school security, vaults should be a focus, particularly in high schools where student records are kept. Vaults in schools are typically built to fire standards. In essence the walls of the vault may be constructed with hollow concrete blocks. A burglar can easily punch a hole into the side of the vault and gain entry. As high schools can amass a large amount of money due to fundraisers, sports activities, etc. they become attractive targets for high school burglars. Options such as expanded steel mesh, and alarm sensors, described elsewhere in this text, address these entry solutions.

Even Burglary vaults can be burglarized if the surrounding walls are not properly designed and built. In the photo below, the wall to the left of the open vault door is part of the interior of the vault. Burglars drilled their way through the concrete wall to gain entry.

Burglarized Vault

In Ground Safes

These types of safes are designed to be directly installed into the ground and encased in concrete. UL does not rate in-ground safes because there is no effective means of determining the quality of the installation. They can have either a manufacturer burglary or fire rated top cover/door or no rating. The locks in the covers may be UL rated. Also, C/B/E construction ratings on the body may be available. Because of their location in the ground they are effective at deterring both fire and forced attack. However, they are best installed during new or remodeled building construction as later excavation and installation would be difficult. While not true of all in ground safes, generally round doors are money safes and square doors are fire safes. The round doors make prying with standard pry tools difficult. Both types of safes have doors that lift off when unlocked.

In Ground Fire Safe

In Ground Money Safe

Concrete Encased Fire Safe on Concrete Floor
An Attempt to Make It Burglary Resistant

Residential Safes

A rating that typically would not be used by commercial businesses would be the *Residential Security Container* (RSC). This is a UL designation for residential security safes. It means that the safe is rated to withstand five minutes of attack with common mechanical hand and electrical tools. UL describes the process as "The Ability to withstand 5 full minutes of rigorous prying, drilling, punching, chiseling, and tampering attacks by UL technicians". The RSC safe is rated for all six sides. Such testing is conducted under UL Standard 1037. This rating might be found on Gun Safes when a 'Security' rating is attached to the safe. A look inside the safe door, typically on the door edge, would quickly determine this rating. Note that it may also have a UL fire rating label on the door edge.

RSC Rating

Combination Safe with RSC and Fire Record Labels

Wall Safes

These safes are designed to provide hidden protection for both documents and valuables. They are manufactured for easy installation between 16" on center standard construction wall studs. Wall safes come predrilled for anchor holes into the studs and with a flange to finish off the cut plasterboard. Manufacturer fire ratings are available with pry resistant doors. As with any safe they are available with mechanical or electronic combination or key locks.

Wall Safe

Wall safes, like floor safes, have the unique advantage of being hidden. This is one of their advantages. However, their location makes them susceptible to theft. A simple reciprocating saw will cut through the top and bottom of each of the two studs allowing easy removal of the safe from the wall. The thief can then carry the safe to another location to finish the actual attack. There is only one way to positively know that this will not occur, and that is to never give away the presence or location of a wall safe.

Gun Safes

Gun safes are normally rated for fire, not burglary. However, those that *are* 'security' rated are typically rated RSC (previously referenced). Some generic safes are not rated by any outside agency and may not have any labels attached to them while others may have a non- UL rated label. The buyer must be cautious with these safes and non-UL ratings. Non-locksmith businesses selling gun safes may think they understand what their gun safes will protect but a check with the manufacturer by phone or via the Internet before purchasing the safe would be a wise investment of time. U.L. and non U.L. labels attached to the safe must be carefully studied to denote the true rating.

Burglarized Gun Safe

Miscellaneous Considerations

IMPORTED SAFES

As imports enter the U.S. other certifications also come into effect. One of the most common imported certifications is the J.I.S. label. This is a label from Japan and is an acronym for Japanese Industrial Standards. This may be a completely acceptable safe but the business insurance carrier should be consulted for applicable premiums before purchasing such a safe.

JIS Label

RELOCKING LABELS

Some safe doors have an additional UL label on them called a 'Relocking Label'. This indicates that if a burglar were to attempt to punch the combination dial through the door that this action would automatically lock the door bolts in place. If this occurs only a locksmith will be able to open the safe door, typically by having to drill into the safe door.

Safe Relocking Label

INSURANCE CONSIDERATIONS

Many people will also make their purchasing decision based on price. While this is certainly valid, other factors must be considered. For example, a TL-30 safe is less expensive than a TRTL-30X6 safe. However, when annual insurance discounts for the more expensive safe are included in the calculations, it may prove to be as economical as the less expensive safe. A check with the business insurance carrier may prove to be a wise economic decision. A sample insurance savings appendix is located at the end of this chapter.

DISCONTINUED MONEY SAFE RATINGS

Safe manufacturers change the construction of their safes, at times, and therefore the UL ratings will also change. That means that there may be a rating on a UL label that has not been identified in this chapter. Research will have to be done to determine exactly what the attack rating means.

Discontinued UL Rating

COMPOSITE SAFES

More manufacturers are now designing 'composite' safes. Composite safes are both fire and burglar resistant. They obviously will cost more, but do offer fire and theft protection in one container. This would be a good safe for the storage of currency where the threat of both fire and theft exists. However, similar protection can be obtained by installing a small fire safe into a larger money safe. Another option is to weld a money safe into a fire safe. However, caution must be used in making sure the fire safe is large enough that burglars cannot easily remove the safe out of the area it is contained in.

GSA SAFES

GSA is an acronym for General Services Administration, the U.S. entity that oversees purchases of all U.S. government property. GSA has its own standard for safes to be used by most government agencies. Their rating system is completely different from U.L., or any other private certification agency. GSA safes concentrate on forced entry ratings of 10 or less minutes, surreptitious entry ratings of minutes or hours, and only two of the six primary ratings related to one hour of fire. It would be unusual for the private sector to see or want to purchase a GSA safe, except in a government surplus sale. Should the reader need more information on GSA safes he or she is encouraged to contact GSA directly or consult with their local locksmith or safe manufacturer.

GSA Safe Generic Exterior Safe Label

OLD VAULT DOORS

If, when closing an older fire vault door, white powder is seen spewing out of the seams it may be asbestos. While the exact amounts that may be harmful are in dispute, the fact that asbestos is harmful is not in dispute. Appropriate tests should be done to determine the exact form of insulation that is contained in the door. Even if it is not asbestos, the powder residue is an indication that the insulating material has dried out and may not be as effective as the rating indicates.

SAFE PLACEMENT

Businesses also frequently ask what the best location for their safe is. The answer for most retail businesses is to put it in a location that is clearly visible from the outside front of the store. This normally means in the front windows toward one of the ends. The logic is that a burglar who cannot work unobserved will be deterred from attacking the store safe. On the other hand, a safe tucked in the back of a closed office provides excellent concealment while the burglar attacks it.

Another possibility is the use of floor safes. These offer better protection than their above ground counterparts because of the difficulty in attacking them. Even then the floor safe should not be hidden in a back room where former employees would know of its location and take advantage of the concealment to attack the safe. The author is aware of one unique installation that bears mentioning. A gas station owner, reasoning that visibility was a deterrent, had his safe installed in the center of a gas pump island. While he certainly deterred burglary, the author observed him late one evening turn off all the lights, lock up his store and then carry the day's receipts across the parking lot to the pump island and unlock his in-ground safe. He was commended for his creativity in the placement of his safe but strongly counseled on the danger of robbery in getting the money to the safe!

ELECTRONIC SAFE LOCKS

Traditional safe locks are commonly the dial type. These locks work well but in the event of an internal loss all personnel with knowledge of the combination are suspect. Today's locks offer a digital keypad option. This allows each person authorized to open the safe to have their own PIN combination. The lock will keep track of who has opened the safe and when. This information, stored in memory, can be accessed by a manager with a laptop computer or mobile device. It helps to both deter internal theft and narrow down a list of suspects who were in the safe during a given time.

Electronic Combination Safe Lock

POSTING OF FIRE SAFE COMBINATIONS

Fire safes are used, of course, for the storage of important paper and computer media documents. They would not normally have valuables stored inside. However, a burglar may not understand the type of safe he is looking at. He may also think that money is stored inside regardless of the type of safe. Therefore, he may attack the safe on the chance of finding valuables. There is one controversial solution to this issue.

If the business owner truly has only paper documents inside the safe that are only of personal benefit after a fire than the sole purpose of the safe is to prevent loss during a fire. Burglars would not have any interest in the contents, unless the threat was from a competitor, in which case the contents need more security than a simple safe. The controversial solution is to actually post the safe combination on the top of the safe. During a burglary the burglar would discover the combination and unlock and open the safe. However, not finding any valuables inside he is likely to explore other areas of the business or leave for another business. The intent is to prevent replacement cost and to prevent the insulation dust from penetrating and ruining every electronic piece of equipment in the surrounding area. It is a concept that a business should be aware of to make an informed decision.

Summary

Understanding the different types, classifications and ratings for each type of safe or vault is the most important component in deciding about which one to purchase. Determining the cost of any particular safe can be done via the internet. However, not all safes are sold by all dealers. Additionally, shipping and delivery inside a building can greatly alter the price. For the most accurate pricing it is recommended that you contact a local locksmith/safe supplier for availability and pricing.

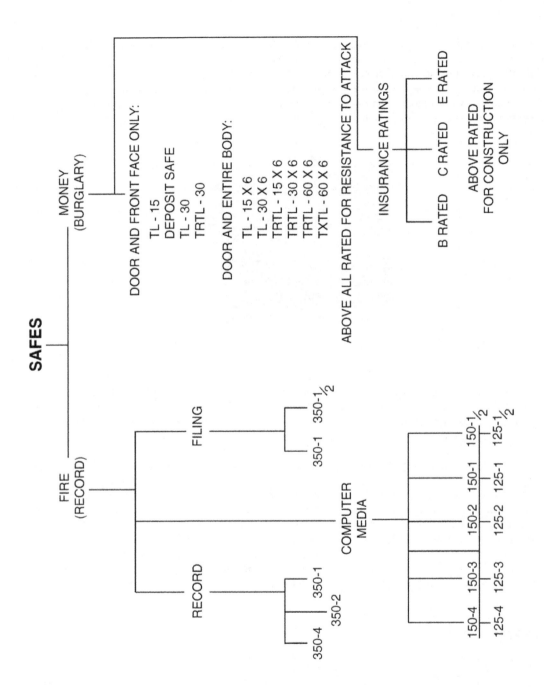

Safes and Vaults
Storage Values

Maximum Values to be Stored in UL-Listed Safes		
UL Classification	Risk Classification	Maximum Classification
TL-15	Low	$150,000
TL-30	Low	$200,000
TL-15x6	Moderate	$300,000
TL-30x6	Moderate	$400,000
TRTL-30*	Moderate	$500,000
TRTL-15x6	Moderate to High	$750,000
TRTL-30x6	High	$1,000,000
TRTL-60x6	High	$2,000,000
TXTL-60x6	High	$2,000,000
*When the body of the safe is encased in reinforced concrete or constructed of a material equivalent to steel and reinforced concrete.		

Maximum Values to be Stored in UL-Listed Vaults	
UL Classification	Maximum Values
Class M	$1,000,000
Class 1	$2,500,000
Class 2	$5,000,000
Class 3	$10,000,000

Courtesy of the Central Alarm Association

Fire Safes

Underwriter's Laboratories
Testing Methods

Fire Test

Insert safe into a furnace
Turn on furnace
Start timer (4/3/2 hours, etc.)
Furnace turned off
Safe remains inside until cooled
(Six temperature probes and paper are placed inside the safe for test purposes)
Furnace Temperatures:
350-4: 2000 degrees F
       350-2: 1850 degrees F
       350-1: 1700 degrees F
Results: no charring/burning or temperatures above 350 degrees F.

Explosion Test

A new safe sample is used
Furnace preheated to 2000 degrees F
Safe is inserted into furnace
Timer is set for 30 minutes
If no explosion after 30 minutes, reset furnace to 1550 degrees F
Then gradually raise temperature again to 1700 degrees F over an additional 30 minutes

Impact Test

Using the safe sample from the explosion test:
Remove safe from furnace
Hoist and drop 30 feet onto pile of rubble three feet deep
Return safe to furnace
Reheat for one hour at 1700 degrees F
Allow to cool and remove from furnace
Results: no charring/burning and papers must be legible

Note: explosion and impact tests are conducted at slightly less time and temperature for 350-2 and 350-1.

Loss Probability and Security

Loss probability is based on the demand for an item and can be assigned a risk factor of high, moderate, or low. Demand refers to the desirability of goods from the standpoint of theft. It takes into consideration, among other things:

➤ The value of the goods;
➤ The marketability of the goods, which is the potential market for the goods, with consumer goods having the largest market; and
➤ The desirability of the goods, which is the ease with which goods can be resold (or fenced).

The table on the next page lists various target items based on a perceived demand for them. This list was developed by considering burglary loss data reported by alarm companies, insurance companies, and government agencies, such as the Federal Bureau of Investigation.

A high demand item is one that is readily marketable, such as clothing; has a high unit value, such as jewelry; or is considered a luxury item, such as furs. This category also includes items of relatively low value, such as children's toys, but which have a large consumer market.

A moderate demand item, on the other hand, is one that may have a high unit value, such as main frame computers, but which appeals only to a limited market. It also includes consumer items which are very marketable, such as household furniture, but are not desirable to the burglar because of the difficulty in re-selling them (assuming that most legitimate businesses will not accept stolen property for resale).

A low demand item is generally one which is of low value, such as salt; or which appeals to a very small segment of the population, such as dry-cleaning equipment; or which is bulky and heavy, such as building construction materials. Also included in this category are items that are readily perishable.

The demand for an item may vary due to factors such as supply and price. Therefore, caution must be exercised in assigning risk factors to commodities. These are items in general, not just those that would be placed into a safe. The categories follow.

High Demand	Moderate Demand	Low Demand
Ammunition and explosives	Boating supplies	Air conditioning equipment
Antiques	Business computers	Adhesives
Automobile parts and accessories	Carpets and rugs	Books, magazines, and stationery
Bicycles	Contractors' equipment	Building materials
Coins and stamps	Curtains and draperies	Chemicals
Cosmetics	Dishwashers	Coffee, tea, and spices
Cameras	Duplicating machines	Containers/drums
Cigarettes and tobacco products	Electrical equipment	Cotton bales
Clothing and accessories	Fabrics and cloth	Cordage, rope, and Twine
Computer accessories (printers, modems,	Frozen foods (wholesale) Groceries (non-perishable)	Dental equipment and supplies Dry cleaning

etc.)	Hotel equipment and supplies	equipment
Computer parts (chips, memory devices, etc.)	Household furnishings	Frozen foods (retail)
Computer software	Household furniture	Fruits and vegetables
Copper	Industrial pumps	Heavy fabrics
Currency, notes, securities, etc.	Jewelry (imitation and novelty)	Heavy industrial machinery
Drugs, including narcotics	Lumber	Hospital supplies and equipment
Exotic and rare metals	Metalworking machines	Industrial carpeting
Fine arts	Musical instruments and supplies	Main frame computers
Furs and pelts	Office machines and supplies	Newspapers
Gold	Office furniture and fixtures	Plumbing supplies
Household appliances	Personal hygiene items	Rolled paper
Industrial diamonds	Pet foods and supplies	Salt
Jewelry	Photographers' supplies	Sandpaper
Liquor, wine, beer	Refrigerators	Scrap metal
Luggage and leather goods	Shoes and boots	Sugar
Perfumery	Sound recording equipment	Textbooks
Personal computers	Television and radio equipment	
Precious or rare metals	Tires and tubes	
Precious stones	Upholstery fabric	
Silver	Washing machines and dryers	
Sporting goods		
Stereo equipment		
Tapes and CDs		
Televisions		
Tools		
Toys and electronic games		
Watches		

Courtesy of the Central Alarm Association

Underwriter's Laboratories (UL)
Money Safe Ratings
Synopsis

Safe Rating: **TL-15**

Weight: 750 lbs minimum or anchored.

Body: 1" thick steel or equal.

Tools: Common hand and electric tools and pressure applying devices.

Time: 15 minutes.

Part of safe rated: Door and front face.

Safe Rating: **Deposit Safe**

Weight: 750 lbs minimum or anchored.

Body: 1" thick steel or equal.

Tools: Common hand and electric tools and pressure applying devices. Fishing and trapping devices through deposit opening.

Time: 15 minutes.

Part of safe rated: Door and front face only. Fishing and trapping attacks for an additional 15 minutes.

Certification: Door not opened. No hole larger than six square inches. No money bags removed. No more than three envelopes removed through slot.

Safe Rating: **TL-30**

Weight: 750 lbs minimum or anchored.

Body: 1" thick steel or equal.

Tools: Common hand and electric tools, pressure applying devices, abrasive cutting wheels and power saws.

Time: 30 minutes.

Part of safe rated: Door and front face.

Safe Rating: **TRTL-30**

Weight: 750 lbs minimum. No anchoring option.

Body: 1" thick steel or equal, encased in reinforced concrete.

Tools: Common hand and electric tools, pressure applying devices, abrasive cutting wheels, power saws and a cutting torch.

Time: 30 minutes.

Part of safe rated: Door and front face.

Safe Rating: **TL-15 x 6**

Weight: 750 lbs minimum or anchored.

Body: Material to resist attack.

Tools: Common hand and electric tools, pressure applying devices, abrasive cutting wheels and power saws.

Time: 15 minutes.

Part of safe rated: All six sides.

Safe Rating: **TL-30 x 6**

Weight: 750 lbs minimum or anchored.

Body: Material to resist attack.

Tools: Common hand and electric tools, pressure applying devices, abrasive cutting wheels and power saws.

Time: 30 minutes.

Part of safe rated: All six sides.

Safe Rating: **TRTL-15 x 6**

Weight: 750 lbs minimum. No anchoring option.

Body: Material to resist attack.

Tools: Common hand and electric tools, pressure applying devices, abrasive cutting wheels, power saws, impact tools and a cutting torch.

Time: 15 minutes.

Part of safe rated: All six sides.

Safe Rating: **TRTL-30 x 6**

Weight: 750 lbs minimum. No anchoring option.

Body: Material to resist attack.

Tools: Common hand and electric tools, pressure applying devices, abrasive cutting wheels, power saws, impact tools and a cutting torch.

Time: 30 minutes.

Part of safe rated: All six sides.

Safe Rating: **TRTL-60 x 6**

Weight: 750 lbs minimum. No anchoring option.

Body: Material to resist attack.

Tools: Common hand and electric tools, pressure applying devices, abrasive cutting wheels, power saws, impact tools and a cutting torch.

Time: 60 minutes.

Part of safe rated: All six sides.

Safe Rating: **TXTL-60 x 6**

Weight: 1000 lbs minimum. No anchoring option.

Body: Material to resist attack.

Tools: Common hand and electric tools, pressure applying devices, abrasive cutting wheels, power saws, impact tools and a cutting torch. Additional 8 ounces of nitroglycerine (2 tests at 4 oz. per test maximum.)

Time: 60 minutes.

G.S.A. Approved
Class 1•2•3•4•5•6 Security Containers
for the U.S. Government

This appendix is added only to purchasers or users of GSA (General Services Administration) safes. GSA safes comply with U.S. Federal guidelines and have no relationship to U.L. or U.L. labels. Explanations and GSA ratings follow.

Federal Specifications (AA-F-358F) for filing cabinet, steel, legal and letter size, insulated and non-insulated, security. (Government security containers)

Conforms to standards for security equipment as set forth in "National Security Council Directive Governing the Classification, Downgrading, Declassification and Safeguarding of National Security Information."

General:

Specifications are always reviewed and notes made where improvements may be added.

Face hardware (excluding combination locks) shall be satin finished anodized aluminum or type 430 corrosion resistant steel or satin finished chromium or steel or die-cast zinc, brass, or bronze.

Paint color to be gray No. 26134 of Federal Standard 595.

Non-insulated containers must satisfactorily pass a 36' and a 30' drop test.

If insulated, unit must be UL "C" rated fire resistive (Class 350-1 hour) or be certified by the manufacturer to be at least that level.

Overall dimensions and weight of safe and drawers are specifically stated, as are the drawer components, suspension, latch, pull handle, label holder and stops.

The containers and their locks must pass a radiological test (to determine lock combinations), forced entry test, and general material inspection tests; the rack, suspension, drawer pull, follower block, and moving tests are all carried out.

Containers are to be specifically packaged for delivery as per sections 5.0-5.32.

All containers will be marked on the outside of the front face of the container "General Services Administration Approved Security Container" along with the name of the manufacturer.

All containers will have a certification label affixed to the external side of the locking drawer stating: This is a U.S. Government Class (number specified here) Cabinet which has been approved by GSA under Federal Spec. AA-F-357F, and it affords the following protection:

SAMPLE:
30 Man-minutes against surreptitious entry
10 Man-minutes against forced entry
20 Man-hours against lock manipulation
20 Man-hours against radiological techniques

All GSA units must be equipped with a combination lock capable of resisting manipulation and radiological attack for 20 man-hours.

In addition, the following requirements apply:

CLASS I	Insulated (1 hour) 10 minutes forced 30 minutes surreptitious
CLASS II	Insulated (1 hour) 5 minutes forced 20 minutes surreptitious
CLASS III	Not insulated No forced entry test requirement 20 minutes surreptitious
CLASS IV	Not insulated 5 minutes forced 20 minutes surreptitious
CLASS V	Not insulated 10 minutes forced 30 minutes surreptitious
CLASS VI	Not insulated No forced entry test requirement 30 minutes surreptitious

Class VI equipment is approved for storage of classified information including top secret. Insulation and forced entry features are not required.

All containers will also bear an identification label on the side of the locking drawer showing the cabinet model and serial number, year of manufacture, and government contract number.

All containers must have a UL rated Group 1 or 1R combination lock installed and be equipped with a top reading (spy-proof) dial ring and snap-on dust cover.

Insurance Codes for Safes

B rated locker construction   ¼" steel body, ½" steel door

C rated construction   ½" steel body, 1" steel door

E rated construction   1" steel body, 1½" steel door

ER, R rated construction 1" steel body, 1½" steel door or equivalent, with hard plate, UL combination lock, burglary attempt bolt relockers, as well as UL label TL15 or TL30

TL   tool resistant

TR   torch resistant

TX   torch and explosive resistant

TRTL   torch and tool resistant

TXTL   torch, explosive and tool resistant

T-20   UL label used on record safes attesting to use of a combination lock relocker

TL15/TL30   UL labels attesting to a safe door that is resistant to attack by specific tools for 15 minutes (TL15) or 30 minutes (TL30)

TRTL30   UL label attesting to a safe that is resistant to torch and tool attack upon the door by specific torches and tools for 30 minutes

TRTL15x6, TRTL30x6, TRTL60, TXTL60   UL labels attesting to a safe that is resistant to attack by specific torches, tools, or explosives (TXTL60) over all six sides of the safe

The time factors allocated in these UL labels does not mean that the safe can be opened in 15, 30, or 60 minutes, only that it cannot be opened in that time or even penetrated with a hole of specific size.

Mercantile Safe, Chest, and Cabinet Insurance Classifications
Per the Insurance Services Office Manual of Burglary Insurance Information available from: Insurance Services Office, 160 Water Street, New York, NY 10038

Each safe, chest, or cabinet must be equipped with at least one combination lock except a safe or chest equipped with a key lock and bearing the label, "Underwriters' Laboratories, Inc. Inspected Keylocked safe KL Burglary."

Mercantile Classifications Safe, Chest, or Cabinet	Construction	
	Doors	Walls
B (fire-resistive)	Steel less than 1" thick, or iron	Body of steel less than ½" thick, or iron
	Any iron or steel safe or chest having a slot through which money can be deposited.	
C (burglar-resistive)	Steel at least 1" thick	Body of steel at least ½" thick
	Safe or chest bearing the following label: "Underwriters' Laboratories, Inc. Inspected Keylocked Safe KL Burglary"	
E (burglar-resistive)	Steel at least 1½" thick	Body of steel at least 1" thick
ER (burglar-resistive)	Safe or chest bearing the following label: "Underwriters' Laboratories, Inc. Inspected Tool Resisting Safe TL-15 Burglary"	
F (burglar-resistive)	Safe or chest bearing one of the following labels: "Underwriters' Laboratories, Inc. Inspected Tool Resisting Safe TL-30 Burglary" "Underwriters' Laboratories, Inc. Inspected Torch Resisting Safe TL-30 Burglary" "Underwriters' Laboratories, Inc. Inspected Explosive Resisting Safe with Relocking Device X-60 Burglary"	
G (burglar-resistive)	One or more steel doors (one in front of the other) each at least 1½" thick and aggregating at least 3" thickness	Not applicable
H (burglar-resistive)	Safe or chest bearing one of the following labels: "Underwriters' Laboratories, Inc. Inspected Tool and Explosive Resisting Safe TX-60 Burglary" "Underwriters' Laboratories, Inc. Inspected Torch Resisting Safe TR-60 Burglary" "Underwriters' Laboratories, Inc. Inspected Torch and Tool Resisting Safe TRTL-30 Burglary"	
I (burglar-resistive)	Safe or chest bearing the following label: "Underwriters' Laboratories, Inc. Inspected Torch and Tool Resisting Safe TRTL-15x6 Burglary"	
J (burglar resistive)	Safe or chest bearing the following label: "Underwriters' Laboratories, Inc. Inspected Torch and Tool Resisting Safe TRTL-30x6 Burglary"	
K (burglar-resistive)	Safe or chest bearing one of the following labels: "Underwriters' Laboratories, Inc. Inspected Torch and Tool Resisting Safe TRTL-60 Burglary" "Underwriters' Laboratories, Inc. Inspected Torch, Explosive, and Tool Resisting Safe TXTL-60 Burglary"	

Money Safes and Insurance

Insurance premium savings also play a part in the selection of the type of safe selected. Basically, purchasing a more expensive safe may pay for itself in reduced annual insurance premium savings. For example, in a typical retail operation, annual premium payments for $5,000 (broad form and mercantile) safe coverage would be as follows:

Safe Rating	Premium	Cost/$1000 block of insurance
B Rate	$650	$130/1000
C Rate	555	111/1000
ER Rate	390	78/1000

Based on the cost of an ER rated safe versus a B rated safe, one could not justify buying an ER rated safe or replacing a B rated safe with the savings of $260 per year.

If, however, the coverage required is $25,000, the premium payments would now be:

	Premium
B Rate	$3250
C Rate	2775
ER Rate	1950
G, H, I Rate	1475

With annual savings of $1300 by converting from a B rated to an ER rated safe, the purchase of a better safe can now be justified. An ER rated safe could be purchased and in two or three years have a premium savings of $1300 per year. A torch and tool resistant safe could be purchased with the savings in premiums over a four to six year period.

References

http://www.schwabfiles.com/customer-service/fireproof-buying-guide/ul-standards-and-certifications/index.html; 8/20/15

http://www.safeandvaultstore.com; What Kind of Safe Do You Need?; By Wendy Moyer; Submit Your Article.com; 10.

http://www.thekeypedaler.com/safedoc.html; Filing Cabinets and Safes for Protection of Paper Records, Computer Media, and Photographic Records from Fire damage; John E. Hunter; CRM Volume 16, No. 5, 1993

http://www.usgs.gov/usgs-manual/handbook/hb/440-2-h/440-2-h-ch7.html

Kenneth Durkin Blog 12/3/10; Safes That are Fireproof or Fire Resistant

Peter W Stronge; Understanding UL Classifications for Fireproof Safes; Home Improvement: Security • Published: April 3, 2012; EzineArticles

K.L. Security Enterprises, UL 72 Fire Resistance Testing Standards; Choosing The Right Safe

http://www.yoursecurityexperts.com/frequently-asked-questions.html; Electronic Fire Safes Information

http://www.vaultandsafe.com/electronic_fire_safe_information.shtml

The Best Ratings for Fire Safes; By Alan Sembera, eHow Contributor

Read more: The Best Ratings for Fire Safes | eHow.com http://www.ehow.com/info_8068773_ratings-fire-safes.html#ixzz1tH5IgGpq

Which Safe is Best for You?; http://www.factory-express.com/buyers_guide/which_safe.html

Safety Deposit Boxes and Fireproof Safes – Store and Protect Valuables; by RYAN GUINA

http://cashmoneylife.com/safety-deposit-boxes-fireproof-safes/; Massachusetts Archives
William F. Galvin, Secretary of the Commonwealth; Technical Bulletin 1
Performance Standards of Safes and Vaults; Issued by the Supervisor of Public Records; May 18, 1995

Which Gun Safe For You?; http://www.internetarmory.com/safes.htm

Choosing and using a home safe; Consumer's Reports, January, 2011

Developing and Maintaining a Vital Records Program; EPA 220-F-00-003; March 2005
Environmental Protection Agency

Introduction to Security; Chapter 11, The Inner Defenses: Intrusion and Access Control
By Robert J. Fischer, Gion Green; Safe Classification;
http://www.safessanjose.info/safe%20classification.html

Product Spotlight: Safes & Safe Locks; Safes and safe locks.; ARTICLE • February 1st, 2006
Locksmith Ledger Magazine

Floor Safe Video with Dye the Safe Guy; You Tube

Hidden Safes; http://www.private-investigator-info.org/hidden-safe.html

UL Ratings Guide; http://www.alliedsafe.com/ul_ratings.php

Which Safe is Best For You?; http://www.factory-express.com/buyers_guide/which_safe.html

How Safes Are Made; http://www.tech-faq.com/how-are-safes-made.html

Types of Safes; http://www.ehow.com/info_7754992_types-safes.html

Electronic vs. Combination Safes; http://ezinearticles.com/?Electronic-Vs-Combination-Safes&id=5435073

http://www.bonafidesafe.com:
Burglary safes include in-floor safes, depository safe, money safes, wall safes, gun safes and vaults.
In-floor safes are designed to be installed below grade in a concrete floor. They offer excellent burglary protection and are ideal for homes and small businesses.
Depository safes allow money to be deposited into a locked compartment either from outside the safe or from inside the safe, where the deposited money is accessible only be designated personnel.
Money safes provide excellent temporary protection of valuables or large amounts of cash. They are highly resistant to attacks using tools. These safes are commonly used by retail stores, jewelers, gas stations and financial institutions. For greater protection, money safes that are torch-resistant as well as tool-resistant are available.
Wall safes are designed to fit between wall studs and are the depth of 2x4 framing; thus they are commonly only 3-1/2 inch in depth. Because these safes are in the walls, they can be hidden. But they do not provide a high degree of security.
Gun safes are designed to secure weapons but offer a limited amount of burglary and fire protection
Vaults are generally built with concrete block walls and security vault doors. Vault doors are designed to offer either fire protection or security protection.
Fire safes, sometimes called record safes, are designed to protect paper from heat from fires. The internal temperature of these safes cannot exceed 350 degrees, which is the temperature paper begins to char. Fire safes are further rated on how long they can resist furnace-level fires, and on their resistance to flash fires and to being dropped.
Fire safes also are used to protect computer and film media but should not be used to protect other valuables, because fire safes are designed to protect documents from fire rather than being designed to thwart burglaries.

Chapter Four

Security Lighting

Security Lighting Performance Objectives:

- Define a lamp
- Define color rendition
- Cite the three main types of lamps
- Cite the characteristics of the following light sources:
    - Incandescent
    - Fluorescent
    - High pressure sodium
    - Metal halide
    - Mercury vapor
    - Low pressure sodium
    - LED
- Cite the four types of light fixture designs
- Define light pollution
- Explain the issue of lamp depreciation
- Explain the issue of light pollution
- Explain the issue of light trespass
- Explain the issue of motion sensor lights

Introduction

Law enforcement officers take advantage of lighting every night they are on patrol, many times without any conscious thought. Traffic stops are made under streetlamps whenever possible. Squad car spotlights light up the interior of stopped cars, building doors, and inside of buildings on patrol. Interior store lights allow officers to view the presence of an intruder after hours. Exterior lights on buildings illuminate open doors or suspects prying on locks. Evening surveillance using video cameras would be difficult and expensive without lighting. Yet, in most cases the typical police officer or security professional cannot tell you anything about the light that they are using to their advantage. In their defense no one has ever pointed out to them why they would need to know. This unit of instruction is designed to not only point out the applications where that knowledge might be important but to also teach the reader the basics of security lighting so that they might become more comfortable in recommending appropriate security lighting to their clients and constituents.

Law Enforcement Applications

These short scenarios will assist the law enforcement officer in applying security lighting techniques to his/her crime prevention advice or investigations.

You respond to an assault in progress on the street. When you arrive six minutes later the street is devoid of pedestrian traffic. You get out looking around but observe no obvious evidence of an assault. You see a large black oil spot on the sidewalk next to the curb but nothing to indicate any assault. You call in an 'all clear' and leave. What you did not observe in this example is that the streetlights in this area of the city cast a strong yellow light that is devoid of color. The black oil spot on the sidewalk is actually a bright red blood spot that, had you known what kind of lighting was in the area, would have caused you to investigate further.

On daytime patrol you observe a retail business installing a dual flood lamp fixture in the rear of the store facing out to the alley. You smile and wave at the owner pleased that he is doing something about the dark area that you have complained about in your previous third shift tour. Four weeks later, when you have rotated back to the third shift, you drive down this same alley and when you drive past the rear of the same store you find yourself blinded by the light shining back at you and unable to see anything along the rear side of the store. Too late you realize that while you asked him to put in a 'security light' you failed to tell the owner what kind of light fixture would be the best type to use in this situation.

Another business has a low level of light in their parking lot. You are continually taking investigative reports about thefts from vehicles. You finally locate the building owner and advise him of the frequency of these reports and ask him to consider putting in some additional lighting in the parking lot. You drive away satisfied that you have accomplished something in crime prevention. What you don't know is anything about the store's profit margin or the cost of the lighting you just advised him to put in. Most people and officers have no clue of the cost of a single commercial light fixture. Those same people might be surprised to learn that the cost of the pole to mount the light can run twice as much as the light fixture itself. The installation cost of the pole adds to that and running electricity to the pole may require trenching up an asphalt parking lot and quadruple the cost of the project. The owner, living on an already tight profit margin passes on the installation. When the extra lighting is not installed the police officer silently or vocally criticizes the building owner for ignoring the advice and vows never to assist the store with anything in the future. The relationship between the building owner and the law enforcement agency/officer sours and the crimes in the area continue unabated.

You take an evening prowler report from a homeowner. When you leave you feel compelled to advise her that she should have a motion sensor light installed in the back yard to deter such activity. You feel good about this standard crime prevention advice for a homeowner. She contacts an electrician who installs such a light at a considerable cost but she feels relief at having this extra security measure on her home. Two weeks later she is assaulted in her home by an intruder who entered through an unlocked rear window. When you respond to the crime she recognizes you as the officer who told her she would be safer with a motion detector light. She wants to know why the security light you recommended did not illuminate, scaring off the intruder or at least giving her warning. What you did not know is that there is a serious application flaw in many motion detector lights.

Another homeowner is advised to install security lighting in his backyard. The homeowner tells you he cannot afford the electric bill required to light up his backyard for security. You acknowledge that it might be expensive but tell him that is just the cost of security. But what is the real cost? Do you really know or are both of you assuming that because a light bulb is illuminated that it will cost a lot of money? With the right choice of light fixture the reality is quite the opposite which should please the homeowner and make your suggestion much more acceptable.

The jurisdiction you work in has just instituted a new minimum-security lighting ordinance mandating a certain lux or foot-candle, a measurement of light. You willingly visit all the businesses in your area and inform them of this new law and their requirement to comply with it. You tell them what the minimum lighting standard is and then drive off knowing that crime will certainly taper off in these areas. 24 months later there is a brutal attack and robbery in a parking lot of one of these businesses. The store owner shows you documentation indicating that the lighting had been upgraded to the specifics of the law as you had outlined. However, a security consultant representing the victim has determined that the actual light output is below the required minimum. The victim is suing the store. Only later, under cross examination of the security consultant in civil court, do you learn about a concept called 'light depreciation' that reduces the light output of installed security and streetlights. Had you known about it you could have better advised your city law makers and spared the victim a traumatic experience as well as saving the store owner hundreds of thousands of dollars in settlement fees.

The Economics of Security Lighting

Security lighting is important to crime prevention and security professionals because of its deterrence value. While important to business owners also the more immediate impact they see is the cost of the electricity. When a business spends money, they want to know what their return is going to be. Therefore, we will also be looking at the economics of various lighting options by comparing the efficiency of different light sources. Thus, along with the pros and cons of light sources and fixtures the reader will be able to offer advice on the relative costs of these lights compared to each other.

Lighting is measured in lumens per watt (LPW), not a particularly helpful measurement to the lay person. However, this same measurement could roughly be compared to miles per gallon (MPG). Like in gas mileage, the more lumens per watt the greater the efficiency and, of course, the less expensive to operate any given lamp. Therefore, wherever lumens per watt is cited in a light source the reader might consider translating those same numbers into miles per gallon of gasoline and thus a more understandable comparison can be made. Note that this formula is a based on the author's own opinion and is not backed by any scientific research.

The Color of Lighting

When we look at something under the light of the sun we see pure color under pure light. The sun gives us the best ability to see colors exactly as they are. The ability of artificial light to replicate these colors is called color rendition. Color rendition in light sources is measured by a system called a Color Rendering Index (CRI). The scale goes from 100 to 1. For practical purposes the incandescent light source (referenced later in this chapter) would be a 100. All other light sources are then compared to incandescent light (the light bulb that is now extinct from retail store shelves). For our purposes we will use subjective terms to describe the color rendition of light sources.

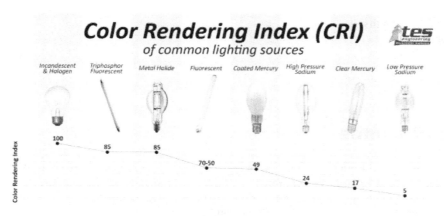

Color Rendering Index

Terminology

There are several terms in lighting that can be confusing. To better understand those terms in this chapter please refer to the following definitions.

Lamp: a consumer replaceable component that produces light. Most people understand this to be a light bulb in a typical living room lamp.

Light Fixture: a device used to create light. It includes at a minimum the lamp, perhaps a reflector to direct the light and a lens to focus the light. The porch light on your house is an entire light fixture. Outdoor security lights are a bit more complicated but are also complete light fixtures.

Light Source: the specific type of light being emitted from the lamp. The various types of light have different strengths and applications as described below.

Lumen: a measurement of brightness.
      Examples: 40 watt incandescent emits 450 lumens
                60 watt incandescent emits 800 lumens
                75 watt incandescent emits 1100 lumens
                100 watt incandescent emits 1600 lumens

Watts: a measurement of energy use.

Note, there are additional terms at the end of this chapter.

Lamp Life

All light source lamps are rated in hours. However, a rating figure of 20,000 hours requires most of us to reach for a calculator or take a guess at how long a time period that is. To take the guess work out of it and to make sure you have accurate information a list of the most common ratings for the light sources discussed in this chapter are listed below. The following assumptions have been made on these calculations: lamp will be illuminated for an average 12-hour day and for 30 days a month.

1,000 hours = 2.5 months
12,000 hours = 2.7 years
20,000 hours = 4.6 years
24,000 hours = 5.5 years
50,000 hours = 11 years

Types of Lamps

Artificial light is created from a combination of mechanical and electronic components all enclosed in one housing called the light fixture. The culmination of these components creates and directs light from the lamp (bulb). These lamps will each deliver a different type of light depending on the manufacturing process. The final light that a lamp gives off is considered a light source.

Artificial lighting lamps come in three different formats: 1) *Filament*, 2) *Discharge* and 3) *Solid State* best characterized as LED (Light Emitting Diode) lamps. Filament light sources might best be used for spot illumination while Discharge and LED sources are best for area lighting.

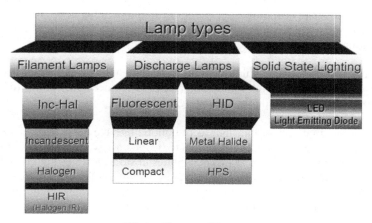

Three Types of Lamps

Filament Lamps and Light Sources

Filament lamps operate with a very thin metal filament inside the glass housing that glows when electricity is passed through the filament. The thin filament glows with resistance to the power of the electricity, which is viewed by the naked eye as light. Filament lighting fixtures can accommodate light bulbs (lamps) with different wattages having the same lamp base size and style. Lamps that work in these types of fixtures come in two forms: *incandescent* and *halogen*.

Filament Light Sources

INCANDESCENT LIGHT SOURCE

The incandescent lamp (bulb) is most commonly found in homes as indoor and outdoor fixtures. The light fixtures are inexpensive as are the bulbs for the fixtures which make them popular and prevalent. Incandescent lamps come with a screw base and a variety of wattages which are interchangeable among all fixtures. The fixture cost for incandescent lights is the lowest of all light fixtures. The color rendition is considered excellent, in the 98 to 100 range.

Incandescent Bulb

Incandescent lamps have a relatively short life span of between 500 and 1000 hours with some 'rough use' lamps claiming a life of 10,000 hours accommodated by a heavier filament and thus lower efficiency. The frequency of illumination and vibration to the filament dictates much of the life span.

This lamp is also the most costly lamp to operate. Only 10% of the electrical consumption is used for actual light with the rest being lost in the form of heat. As a result, the consumer is only getting 10 cents on the dollar for light with incandescent lamps. The lumens per watt are in the 10-15 LPW range. When compared to the equivalent in gas mileage of 10-15 MPG the poor efficiency of this lamp becomes obvious. From a business and economic standpoint, the high operating costs of this lamp and the labor required for constant lamp replacement makes incandescent a poor choice for a security lamp as a primary source of illumination.

Standard, back yard type floodlight fixtures contain incandescent lights and suffer the same energy costs that the traditional light bulbs do. Both fluorescent and LED replacement options (discussed below), which are more efficient, exist for common flood light fixtures.

Readers should be aware that standard incandescent light bulbs have been discontinued from manufacture and sale in the U.S. by an act of Congress. Deemed to be too energy inefficient the final production phase out went into effect on January 1, 2014. Current supplies in storage can be sold until the stock is gone. Specialty bulbs for appliances, decorative devices, and rough use bulbs will continue to be produced. Replacements in the form of CFL (Compact Fluorescent Light) and LED (Light Emitting Diode) are now being sold instead. These replacement lamps are designed to insert into the same fixture as an incandescent lamp.

HALOGEN LIGHT SOURCE

Halogen lights, the other form of incandescent light, also exist in many places. Because of their intense, bright light they are used as heat lamps, car headlights, outdoor entertainment areas, decorator lighting, chandeliers, stage plays, concerts, photography, and sporting events.

Halogen lamps use the same inefficient metal filament as a source of light. However, the filament in a halogen lamp is encased in a stronger glass bulb. Inside this stronger bulb is halogen gas that is under high pressure to make the lamp more efficient to operate. Also inside the bulb is a coating that serves to reflect and create more light, remain hotter, and recycle the heat. The gas inside the sealed bulb allows the halogen bulb to last three times longer than the standard incandescent bulb and operate at between 25% and 35% better efficiency. Their fixture attachment is also different from incandescent lamps. Halogen lamps have a two-prong arrangement that requires the lamp to be pushed into place. All halogen lamps are sensitive to any debris on the exterior of the glass. Even handling these lamps with bare fingers will leave an oil residue that will result in premature failure and the potential of exploding lamps.

The cost of halogen lamps is about three times greater than incandescent lamps. They are, however, still far less efficient than their replacements, fluorescent and LED. Because of their varied uses they are not subject to the same manufacturing restrictions placed on incandescent lamps. Note, however, that their extremely high operating temperatures have caused burns and ignited numerous fires when used in residential applications.

Discharge Lamps and Light Sources

Discharge lamps come in two forms, *standard pressure* and *high pressure*. Named because of the internal gases that are under pressure, these lights operate utilizing an arc of controlled electricity to ignite the gas contained within their glass housing. The igniting of the internal gas illuminates the interior of the glass globe giving off the visual light.

The most common of the standard pressure is the Fluorescent lamp. The other category of discharge lamps, high pressure, is so extensive and involved that it will be covered as a separate topic after fluorescent lamps.

Standard Pressure Lamps

Standard Pressure Light Source

FLUORESCENT

Fluorescent lamps are typically tube shaped. The interior of the tube is filled with inert argon gas. Inside the tube is also a small amount of mercury. Finally, the interior of the tube is coated with phosphors powder. When the lamp is illuminated an electrical arc extends from one end of the tube to the other. The arc of electricity causes the mercury to vaporize and, in turn, activate the phosphors inside the tube which creates the light.

The fixture cost of fluorescents is low to moderate. Color rendition would be classified as fair to good at 60 CRI. Fluorescent lamps sold as 'warm' are coated on the inside to make them more 'color balanced' which enhances the color rendition and makes them more pleasing to the human eye.

The life span of fluorescent lamps is a respectable 12,000 to 20,000 hours. These lamps have an efficiency rating of 67-83 LPW, comparable to the same MPG for cars, making it a very good light for efficiency. The operating costs for this fixture are lower than incandescent. However, they are still higher than the next category of HID fixtures. This is because more fluorescent fixtures are required for the same amount of HID light output.

One consideration to the outdoor security use of fluorescent lights is the effect of cold temperatures. The colder the outdoor temperature the lower the light output. In areas where the temperature can reach 15 degrees F the light output will only be 20% of the potential maximum, effectively minimizing the security affect. Note, however, that there are some screw-in base fluorescent lamps and some temperature adjusted lamps that do not dim quite as much and are designed for outdoor use. Their packaging would state this.

The replacement fluorescent bulb for incandescent bulbs is a CFL or Compact Fluorescent Lamp. Again, cold weather will affect their ability to come up to full lighting ability.

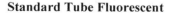

Standard Tube Fluorescent　　**Compact Fluorescent Bulb (CFL)**

High Intensity Discharge (HID) Light Lamps

All HID lamps are classified as High Pressure. However, they are commonly called *High Intensity Discharge* lamps. HID lamps produce light by striking an electrical arc across tungsten electrodes housed inside a specially designed, high pressure, inner glass tube. This tube is filled with both gas and metals. The gas aids in the starting of the lamps and the metals produce the light once they are heated to a point of evaporation. Some lamps will have an additional protective glass housing around the inner tube.

HID fixtures operate differently than filament light fixtures. All HID fixtures contain a magnetic ballast that regulates the incoming electrical current and matches it to the lamp wattage. That simply means that you cannot switch out a 100-watt lamp for a larger wattage if you want a brighter lamp (or smaller for less light.) Another unique aspect of HID fixtures is that you are stuck with the light source you specified. If you don't happen to like the yellow light of an HPS light source after it is installed you cannot, for example, change out the lamp for a metal halide light source.

HID Lamp

One of the unique operating considerations of HID lamps is that none of them give instant light when they are turned on. Upon being switched on their design characteristics create a delay of 30 seconds to 5 minutes before they are at full illumination. Therefore, they would not be effective when used with motion sensor switches. This is also true in the event of a power outage. Once power is interrupted to the lamp it must cool down before it can again be, automatically, illuminated. The most common example of the latter is during lightning storms. Dusk to dawn light sensors, built into the fixture, will detect the lightning, think it is daylight, and shut off the light fixture. Of course, the sensor will immediately detect the darkness again and restore electricity to the fixture, but the cool down period will prevent the immediate re-illumination of the lamp. The security consideration is that there would be a short period of darkness during which an intruder can gain undetected access. High security application clients would want to talk to the major distributors of HID lamps for their 'hot-strike' option HID lamps which restarts immediately with the help of built in high voltage capacitors.

Note, as color is not an option in this book the reader is encouraged to view color images of each of the light sources by going to Google Images and inputting the specific light source to be seen.

High Pressure Light Sources

MERCURY VAPOR LIGHT SOURCE

This HID fixture cost is low to moderate. The light that is projected by this lamp is characterized as bluish-white. Because of this color output the color rendition is classified as fair to good at 45 CRI. Mercury vapor light does a better job of highlighting green and blue in the light spectrum but does not do as well with red objects.

The lumens per watt for mercury vapor lights are 45-63. This reflects well when compared to miles per gallon for efficiency. The rated life of this light source is 20,000 hours. However, the practical life is much less. Mercury vapor lights suffer from a sharp drop in the burning curve between years two and three. Simply put this means that while the lamp continues to consume the same amount of electricity there is a considerable drop in the light output. Users of this light source indicate that the lamp seems 'to burn forever'. What they don't see is the gradual drop in light output and therefore the loss of area or perimeter security protection.

The same Energy Policy Act that stopped production of incandescent lamps also addresses Mercury Vapor lamps. Because of the health hazard associated with mercury the Act prohibited the manufacture of Mercury Vapor ballasts, but not the lamps themselves. So, as the lamps fail they can be replaced with new lamps which can still be manufactured. However, the Act further states that as the *ballasts* fail the entire fixture must be replaced with a different light source.

Note that there are 100s of thousands of these fixtures in existence in the U.S. They will continue to function for decades longer and will be seen in many older business sections and even street lighting. However, with the Energy Act in mind the recommendation for installation of new Mercury Vapor lighting systems would not be prudent.

METAL HALIDE LIGHT SOURCE

These fixtures are classified as moderate to high for their cost. Increasing sales are lowering their cost. The light output of these lamps is a very distinctive white. As a result, they offer excellent color rendition. Most outdoor sports facilities built since the turn of the century are illuminated by metal halide light fixtures as the visual results are pleasant to the eye and for the television camera. Many auto sales lots install metal halide fixtures to better illuminate the colors of their automobiles. These lamps are rapidly replacing mercury vapor in popularity. Also, the white light and excellent color rendition of 65-90 CRI makes it the best light source for those properties that are being monitored by security cameras. It re-creates the best image on the viewing monitor and for recording purposes.

The 90-100 lumens per watt rating is another reason for the growing popularity of metal halide. When compared to miles per gallon this lamp is almost miserly in electrical consumption and may pay for itself in replacement of older forms of light fixtures. Metal halide lamps also have an excellent average life span of 24,000 hours.

Metal halide lamps are designed for a specific burning position; these may be base up, base down, or horizontal burn only. Placing them in a different position will cause an early lamp failure (burned out.) Therefore, while it is up to you to determine what kind of light source you want in your parking lot it would be prudent to hire an electrician or lighting expert to design the system once they understand what you want.

One of the interesting side effects of installing metal halide lamps is the affect it has on neighboring businesses. While the surrounding businesses may have adequate illumination, when the entity with metal halide fixtures fires up their lights the brilliant white light makes adjacent businesses with lower light levels of illumination appear darker than they actually are. This can discourage customers from patronizing these businesses as they now appear too dark to safely park and enter at night. The use of white paint on the walls of adjacent businesses is a mitigating factor. Parking garages should also paint their walls white to overcome the perception of dark corners and perimeter walkways when metal halide light fixtures are used.

Even though it does not have the highest efficiency rating of HID lamps, metal halide fixtures are quickly becoming the most popular HID exterior light for security and general lighting applications.

HIGH PRESSURE SODIUM VAPOR LIGHT SOURCE

High pressure sodium vapor lamps (HPS) are also known simply as 'sodium' lights. The fixture cost is moderate to high. The light emitted by HPS lamps is a distinctive light golden yellow color. The color rendition of HPS lamps is considered fair at 24 CRI.

At 100-140 lumens per watt this HID light source is the most efficient, practical light for many outdoor areas in need of illumination. There is very little drop in the illumination level prior to the end of its life cycle. Compared to mercury vapor or metal halide the high-pressure sodium lamp imparts a warm feeling to those who transverse its light. It also has a service life of 24,000 hours. For non-camera monitored security applications this light source is an excellent choice.

Recent research has uncovered one detractor for HPS light, however. HPS may not be the most effective or safe light for areas that are populated by people over the age of 50. This is because the light gathering cones of the aging human eye are not as efficient at gathering yellow light as they are with white light. This would affect the ability of a person to clearly see safety or security issues at night. Obviously, if the area that is being surveyed for artificial light primarily serves the more mature adult this must be taken into consideration.

While this recent research may alter the future use of HPS lighting, one of the most common applications for it has been in street lighting. Countless miles of roadways are illuminated with high pressure sodium lighting for all the previously cited attributes. This is similarly true of thousands of private and public parking lots and walking spaces. As the cost of maintaining these fixtures is the simple replacement of expired lamps it is likely that they will remain intact for decades to come.

LOW PRESSURE SODIUM VAPOR LIGHT SOURCE

The final HID light source is the low-pressure sodium vapor (LPS). These fixtures are also moderate to high in purchase cost. They are the least common light source and replacement lamps are more difficult to locate and purchase. These factors will cause LPS fixtures to lean toward the higher pricing end.

These lamps emit a very distinctive yellow light. The best visual descriptor might be the light of a yellow 'bug' light. The result is that the color rendition of low pressure sodium lights is characterized as poor. The characterization is accurate. LPS light actually creates a monochromatic view. All colors visible to the human eye become shades of gray under low pressure sodium light. Witnesses to a street crime may describe a gray car fleeing the scene when it actually was blue or even red in color. Officers investigating a street crime may overlook critical evidence because it appears to be an oil stain or dirt. At times HPS fixtures are mistaken for LPS due to the visible pale, yellow illumination. However, a quick glance around for the presence or absence of color will identify the correct light source.

The life of low sodium lamps is a very respectable 22,000 hours. However, LPS excels in the efficiency department with 130-190 LPW. Equating that to the same level of miles per gallon and the efficiency of the LPS becomes clear. Nevertheless, the color rendition issues will prevent this light source from ever becoming popular in the U.S. at a -44 CRI (a negative number.)

Applications for this light fixture are extremely limited. Unmonitored outdoor storage areas are the most common and probably the best application. They should not be used in parking lots as people would have difficulty identifying their monochromatic cars. An interesting side note to the application of LPS is the energy crisis and oil embargo of the 1970s. For the first time in the history of the United States communities across America were hit with oil and gasoline shortages. In looking for ways to reduce energy consumption many communities studied their biggest user of electricity – public streetlights. They found that the efficiency of using LPS over the then popular mercury vapor lamps would quickly pay for the replacement of the entire light fixture. While it did accomplish the goal of efficiency many communities failed to consider the color rendition issues and the subsequent public backlash. Residents walking down their own streets at night had facial skin tones that resembled something out of a horror movie. Their parked cars all had the same color tones. Residents in these areas let their community leaders know of their dislike for these new lights. Shortly after the energy crisis ended the more affluent communities again switched out their streetlamps for the more people-friendly HPS. Most communities followed suit as they could afford to do so or as the fixtures were damaged or worn out. However, there are still pockets of neighborhoods in older sections of larger U.S. cities that continue to have their streets illuminated by LPS. Note that these light sources are difficult to even purchase today. A search of You Tube will give excellent examples of LPS lighting.

Solid State Lighting

Solid state lighting (SSL), in the form of LED s (Light Emitting Diodes) has been in existence since the early 1960's but only as on/off types of indicator lights in electronic devices. Solid state lighting consists of electronic semiconductors that convert electricity into light. Early technological developments allowed LEDs to evolve into signal devices, like traffic lights and exit signs. That led to the current applications of residential and commercial lighting systems. LEDs are the only form of solid state lighting therefore the next section will solely focus on this form of SSL lighting.

LEDs themselves are not hot to the touch, unlike most other forms of lighting lamps. However, the process of creating the light does create heat in its base. For the LED to work this heat must be removed. The solution for this problem has been to design a 'heat sink' on all LED fixtures. Heat sinks remove heat by absorbing and dissipating the heat to the outside. This can be seen in many LED residential lamps in the form of 'fin's. These same fins, or substitute heat exchangers, exist on commercial lamps as well.

LED Fixture and Light Source

LEDs are 'directional' light sources. Their natural light radiation pattern is pretty narrow at only 20 degrees from center. That means that they emit light in a specific direction, unlike HID, incandescent, and CFL bulbs. For directional lighting this allows the light to be used more efficiently in illuminating a specific area. However, it also means that there is some technical engineering needed to produce an LED light bulb that shines all around when light is needed the way it is on the familiar teardrop shape of an incandescent bulb. Thus, multiple LEDs are produced in an array and installed in a fixture with curved reflectors to overcome this directional issue for area lighting.

A Small LED Light Array

LED lamps have a much longer life span than their HID cousins. When HID lamps are rated for life they are measured based on how long the average lamp reaches its failure point of burning out. LEDs, and by default, their entire 'lamp' array, or base of LEDs, simply do not wear out. When properly designed and installed in their fixture LEDs can function for decades. Thus, their lifetime is measured differently, in terms of Light Depreciation. Later in this chapter we will specifically discuss in detail exactly what comprises lamp depreciation. Basically, it is a measurement of how long a lamp will produce enough lumens to give off the same amount of light upon its initial installation.

As LEDs do not burn out 'light depreciation' is that measurement for when an LED lamp array should be replaced. The industry accepted figure is set at 70%. Simply put, when the LED array light output begins to fade out and decreases to a level of 70% of its original light output it is determined to have reached its 'end of life' and should be replaced. Studies have also determined that it takes about 50,000 hours to reach that point with some manufacturers claiming their LEDs will last longer than 100,000 hours. Other companies have developed LED lamps that will remain at up to 85% of their original lighting for that same number of hours. Continuing research and development will probably increase these numbers over time. Company web sites are an excellent resource for determining these specifications.

Area Security Fixture with Visible LED Array   Fixture with Multiple LED Arrays

While fluorescent and HID lamps are affected by cold temperatures, warm up times, and re-lamping issues, LEDs are not affected by any of these issues to reach instant, full brightness. They also are not affected by frequent on/off cycles and can be dimmed if manufactured for this function and used with special dimmer switches.

LEDs have a very good CRI of between 80-85. However, even LED lamps can be cheaply made with a reduction in CRI to as much as 50. Various manufacturers utilize different quality components in making their LED arrays. Checking with the manufacturer or their web site should reveal the necessary specifications for your CRI security application.

LEDs do not conform to typical efficiency measurements of Lumens per Watt. This is because all other forms of lighting are measured based on their lamps alone, not as part of the entire light fixture. LEDs do not stand alone as light lamps. They only work when built into a complete fixture unit. This changes the ability to simply measure watts and lumens and rate them equally for efficiency. True measurements of LED lighting efficiency in a fixture housing are still being developed by the manufacturers. The better comparison for all lamps would be how much light is being delivered to the area being illuminated. In this regard the 'footcandle' or 'lux' measurement should be used. However, for efficiency rating at this point, the best LED lighting, in a fixture, is measured at about 50 LPW. Readers might hear of 200 and even 300 LPW for LED lamps. Note that those lamps are lamps that can replace incandescent and fluorescent lamps in homes and offices.

A major down side of LED fixtures is their cost. From the retail store to major commercial and industrial applications, LED light fixtures cost about 4 times the price of HID fixtures. For budgeting purposes this is a big issue. The purchaser must be able to justify, and afford, the huge up-front costs for these lights. However, the much lower cost of maintaining these lights, the low-cost efficiency of LEDs, as well as the very long lamp life of LED lights usually justifies the decision to go with LED lighting.

Security Light Fixture Types

The security light fixture serves only to direct the angle and control the amount of light that falls onto the ground below or the area to be served. Almost all the security light fixture types can be manufactured to use any of the previously discussed forms of security light sources. It only requires an engineer to design either the lamp (bulb) or the LED array to fit within the fixture hood. An examination of lighting manufacturer and distributer websites will reveal a variety of fixture types that will meet both functional as well as decorative security applications.

Cobra Style

The *cobra styles* are what you would typically see on many public roadways. The fixture is attached to the end of a horizontal arm which is further attached to the top of a, usually, roadside installed pole. The intent of this fixture style is simply to illuminate a roadway directly below the fixture. The longer the horizontal arm, the further out the light can reach over a multi-lane road. Cobra head fixtures can also be found in commercial parking lots. The fixture head resembles the hood of a cobra snake, hence the name. The fixture directs light straight down, and with a protruding lamp type lens will further direct light out to the sides as well. It will accommodate all forms of lamp source technology.

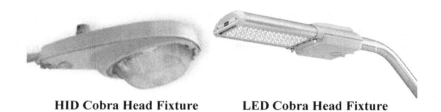

HID Cobra Head Fixture   **LED Cobra Head Fixture**

Box Style

The *box style* directed light fixture looks like a box flood lamp. The difference is that this light fixture is mounted horizontal to the ground. Most or all the light from these box fixtures is directed downward, although an optional protruding lens will further direct some of the light out to the sides of the fixture. Box lights (they are sometimes circular shaped) can be mounted singularly, in pairs, or even in sets of four on the top of each pole.

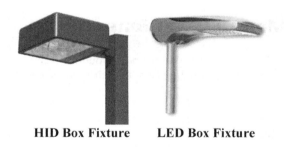

HID Box Fixture   **LED Box Fixture**

Hurricane Style

The *hurricane* light can be found on paved residential streets or as a rural yard light. Hurricane luminaries are also installed from a hanging wire supported between two poles mounted above a country road intersection, or above someone's garage. Note that there is no standard terminology for this style light fixture. It has been commercially described as: farm light, barn light, dusk to dawn light, bucket light, roadway light, street light, non-directional light. Regardless of its name, when used with an HID lamp it functions to put out light at a 360-degree circle in a wide arc. While they can be fitted with LED lighting the light focus would be much more contained in a downward direction.

HID Hurricane Fixture   **LED Hurricane Fixture**

Flood Style

Flood style lamps, as the name implies, simply floods a large area with a lot of light, aiming it straight ahead with some light spreading to the sides. They would usually be used over a broad expanse of ground without concern for bothering neighbors or lighting up a specific area, such as a door, or piece of fixed equipment. The intent is to discourage trespassing and quickly spot a person walking within the lighted area.

HID Flood Fixtures   **LED Flood Fixtures**

Light Fixture Mounting Options

Security light fixtures typically come in three forms; pole mounted, wall mounted, and ground mounted. They are almost exclusively HID or LED fixtures due to their more efficient operating characteristics.

POLE MOUNTED

Pole mounted light fixtures are commonly seen in parking lots and storage lots. The fixture on the top of the pole will either be a flood lamp or directed light. The flood lamp, usually a square box shaped fixture, is typically angled slightly downward toward the area to be protected. It broadcasts light outward in a wide, general area in front of it. If the fixture has a 'knuckle', allowing up and down pivoting, it is a flood lamp. The hurricane fixture would be attached to an extension over a road or parking lot. The decorative Post Top light fixture is commonly found in downtown areas to evoke a quaint feeling for pedestrian traffic.

**Flood, Post Top, Hurricane
Pole Mounted Fixtures**

WALL MOUNTED

Wall mounted lights are used to illuminate the area directly surrounding a building. They are normally a rectangular shaped HID fixture. These fixtures offer security and safety to persons approaching or leaving a building. They also illuminate, and thus discourage intruders who attempt to make forced entry into the perimeter of a building. A variation on this style is used in parking garage ramps. Here they would be ceiling mounted with a wrap-around lens providing light in a 360-degree circumference.

Wall Mounted Fixtures

GROUND MOUNTED

Ground mounted fixtures are usually used for landscaping purposes and direct the light in a way to illuminate a specific object, or area. In a security application they shine upward, typically lighting the exterior perimeter of a building that may contain a window or doorway. Their ability to be angled and rotated makes them ideal for ornamental light applications. While they do illuminate the exterior walls in the same fashion as wall fixtures their ground level installation creates a vandalism and intruder attack situation. Therefore, absent unusual situations they would not normally be recommended or used for security applications.

Ground Mounted Fixtures

Lighting Issues

While few people would disagree with the need for security lighting (some studies would debate this) there are some issues and potential problems associated with it. The following concerns are applicable to all forms of light fixtures and light sources.

GLARE

Glare is simply an intense and blinding light that causes discomfort and a reduction in one's ability to see. Glare is technically a result of excessive contrast between bright and dark areas in the field of view. Many rural road drivers have experienced this when an oncoming car fails to dim its bright lights. Glare can occur with security lighting, especially with flood lights. When mounted on a pole and directed toward a parking lot the installer or system designer may fail to notice that the light is also pointed toward on oncoming city street. Drivers on that street may be blinded as they approach this business. Complaints from drivers or an accident will rapidly cause the property owner to reconfigure the light source or location. Both solutions come with a significant price tag. Preplanning would have prevented this. The same issue occurs when well-meaning store owners attempt to install security lighting at the rear of their stores that border an alley. Without proper guidance some of these owners will choose the least expensive light fixture, an incandescent dual unit flood lamp. However, once operating, the glare from the floodlight directed toward the alley will blind anyone who looks in that direction. It is conceivable that a burglar could be standing at the door located directly under the floodlight fixture and a patrolling officer would not be able to see him. The solution in this case would be the use of a downward light directing fixture.

Glare Issues for Drivers and Pedestrians

LIGHT TRESPASS

Another issue with security lighting is light trespass. Just as the name implies it is stray light from a fixture illuminating a neighbor's property. Adjoining residential neighbors normally do not mind having their neighbor's light spill over onto their property, providing it is not glare. However, the problem arises when a commercial business builds or adds security lighting to their property which borders a residential area. In that case the amount of light spilling over into a neighbor's yard can be so bright as to interfere with the resident's ability to sleep. If a business fails to respond to a neighbor's complaint communities may create light trespass laws that simply forbid any light from leaving the property owning the lights. While after-market light fixture shields can be installed it would be less expensive to use lighting design software to properly plot out the light pattern prior to purchasing and installing a light fixture.

Light Trespass to Adjacent Homes
Down Lighting on Left and Up Lighting on Right

LIGHT POLLUTION

Light pollution is yet a different issue. Light pollution can be defined as light that intrudes on an otherwise natural or low light setting. Most people would not notice light pollution outdoors. However, those who appreciate viewing the stars in the sky or looking out at a dark landscape or horizon have a strong aversion to it. Light pollution occurs when light fixtures are aimed straight out (like floodlights) and much of the illumination is lost into the sky instead of being directed toward the ground where it was intended to go. Likewise, cobra fixtures and pole mounted box light fixtures with lenses that bow out of the bottom of their fixture cast light sideways as well as down to reach further across the protected property. The problem is that this same light is now visible for quite a distance at a horizontal plane, irritating those from afar, described in the previous 'glare' section.

Fixture Design that Contributes to Light Pollution

Examples of Light Pollution

Bright White Spots Highlight Light Pollution from Space

Light pollution solutions are available in the form of flat lenses on fixtures and flat bottom light box fixtures that only direct the light straight down. These fixtures are classified based on the amount of light that escapes the lens and is not directed downward. The classifications are: *No Cutoff*, *Semi-Cutoff*, *Cutoff*, and *Full Cutoff*. The full cutoff is the only fixture design that prevents any light from escaping, or viewed above, a 180-degree flat, horizontal plane, thus limiting upward light pollution and directing the light downward.

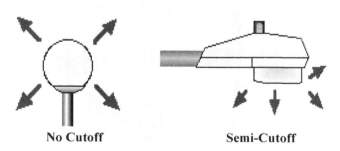

No Cutoff   **Semi-Cutoff**

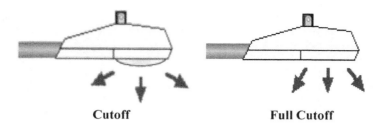

Cutoff   **Full Cutoff**

Arrows Indicating the Direction of Light Distribution

Some communities have passed 'Dark Sky' ordinances to combat light pollution. The state of Arizona is a leader in this area. You will want to check with your city or county planner to see if these ordinances affect you or your client. For more information on this topic readers are referred to www.darksky.org.

LAMP DEPRECIATION

Some communities have created minimum standards of illumination for business parking lots and outdoor security lighting in the form of foot-candle or lux measurements. This is done for the sake of safety and security for pedestrians and patrons. Some police departments train and equip their police officers with light meters to check on the compliance of businesses before or after a crime. However, even compliant businesses can fall into non-compliance in as little as a year's time. The problem is known as lamp depreciation. From the moment a lamp is illuminated it begins to deteriorate, lowering its level of illumination. Even more critical is the fixture housing the lamp. The lens can become less transparent because of UV rays. Dust accumulating on the interior of the lens will block the light. Insects, attracted to the light, will find their way into the interior of the fixture and eventually perish, falling onto the lens further blocking the light.

Manufacturers are aware of these issues and have a formula to account for the loss of illumination over time. It is called a lamp loss or lamp depreciation number. Every fixture has such a number assigned to it. Thus, if you know that you will need 6 footcandles of light in an area you can specify a fixture with a loss number that will, at first, exceed the minimum standard but will remain in compliance in the future as the light levels fall off due to lamp depreciation.

RESIDENTIAL MOTION SENSOR LIGHTS

Motion lights are a very popular security light with homeowners. Incandescent types are inexpensive to purchase, and take no electricity until activated by movement, turning off by themselves a few minutes later. Police officers almost universally recommend them. But they have a negative side to them. Most motion sensors have a detection unit that is fixed to pick up motion starting at approximately 6-10 feet in front of it and then fan out from there. This is the issue for motion lights. A prowler, home invader, or rapist does not walk through the middle of backyards to approach a house, window, or door. These criminals slide along the wall of a house, trying doors and looking into windows as they move along. Intentionally or not, these attackers move under the motion sensor and do not trip the light to come on. The tragedy of the situation is that the person inside of the home feels completely safe because the motion sensor light protecting them has not activated and alerted them to the presence of the intruder. Thus, curtains are left open, windows may be left unlocked and the occupant takes no precautions for defense. Essentially, the motion sensor light has inadvertently assisted the very attacker it was installed to detect. Even more sophisticated motion lights with special 'look down' sensors to detect someone under it won't work if the intruder approaches and enters the home from the opposite side of the house, prior to passing by the sensor light.

Residential Motion Sensor Light Fixture

HPS Residential Lighting Solution

An easy solution to this very serious problem is available. It comes in the form of a residential model HPS light fixture. Available in 35 and 50 watt versions they are designed to replace any currently installed porch or security light fixture. They will attach directly to the existing flush or surface mount electrical box on the house and use the existing wiring. These fixtures come equipped with a dusk to dawn light sensor so that they will automatically come on when it gets dark and shut off when it gets light outside, alleviating the need to remember to turn the light off in the morning. Intruders and window peepers do not want to enter a lighted rear yard, and if they do so, they cast shadows as they move and are easily spotted, making these lights a great criminal deterrent.

Homeowners concerned about the operating cost of these lights should know that they share the efficiency of their commercial brothers. A 35 watt light consumes only about $1.50 per month of electricity while operating 12 hours a day, 12 months a year, based on national estimates. It illuminates a large rear yard with enough light to see a person but not to project into your neighbor's windows. The lens is very well designed to prevent glare and directs the light to the sides of the house and into the yard. The 50 watt version is designed for larger rural properties. If you can make recommendations on residential security lighting, this is the light you should be educating the homeowner about. LED lighting could also be used for residential applications. In that case you would want to compare lumens for the appropriate level of brightness. Note that if your hardware store does not carry the wattage you are looking for you should ask them to special order what you want.

Summary

Security lighting is more than just a physical security device. It is a concept that quells fear of the dark and offers safety and even enjoyment to those who seek entertainment in the evening. The proper selection, application, and maintenance of these systems that calm fears, offer security, and provides safety is now no longer an abstract thing. Make it work for you and for those you serve.

SECURITY LIGHTING TERMS

Average Life
Expected useful life of the bulb.

Average Lumens
Average output over the life of the bulb.

Footcandle
The amount of illumination at a given point. Use a horizontal plane light meter to measure. Footcandles are being phased out as a measure of illumination in favor of the Lux measurement. Ten lux equals one footcandle.

Glare

Horizontal illumination that hinders vision that can be greatly reduce by keeping mounting heights at least 12 feet above walkways and driveways and avoiding directional lighting where drivers or pedestrians would have to go towards the fixture.

Group Relamping
Changing all the bulbs at the average life and not waiting for each bulb to burn out. This is especially cost effective when considering labor cost and the need for special equipment to reach the fixtures.

Lumen
The brightness output of the bulb.

Lumens per Watt
Measurement of how efficient a lighting source is.

Lux
The amount of illumination at a given point. Use a horizontal plane light meter to measure. Lux is a metric unit of measurement; ten lux equals one footcandle.

Uniformity
How even the illumination is in each area – avoid pools of light with darkness between.
- 6:1 ratio from the brightest to the darkest point (usually no greater for security and safety)
- 3:1 ratio (required for older population)

Visibility
Size, brightness, contrast, and time.

Watt
The amount of electricity used.

Lighting Cost Calculation

The following example will show you how to figure out a lighting cost calculation. Note, however, that this calculation will not be accurate for LED lighting.

Givens:

w = watts (of the lamp)
h = hours (per day)
$ = cost of electricity per kilowatt hour (You must get this figure from your local power company. It would look something like .045 or 1.32 KHW)
# = your answer in cents per hour (You must multiply this times 365 (days) to get a year)

Equation:

(w x h) ÷ 1000 = kilowatts per hour (KWH) of electricity being used by that lamp

KWH x $ = #

x 365 = Annual Cost

Example:

- 150 watt light bulb
- illuminated 12 hours a day
- .0876 cents per kilowatt hour

Calculation:

150 x 12 = 1800

1800 ÷ 1000 = 1.8 KWH

1.8 x .0876 = .15768 cents

.15768 x 365 days = $57.55 annual cost

Security Lighting
Miscellaneous Considerations

Area Lighting

- Photometrics on cut sheet will show the distribution pattern. Order from manufacturer or request from vendor.
- You can specify beam distribution pattern to fit needs. (Types 1-5)
- Design your lighting system to avoid spill lighting and glare on adjacent properties. Sharp cutoff type fixtures have a flat lens with all of the distribution occurring inside of the fixture and the light focused down.
- Rule of thumb – pole mounted fixtures should be spaced apart no more than four times the pole mounting height (each fixture usually capable of covering two times the mounting height). Wall mounted fixtures should not be spaced more than six times the mounting height.
- For design specifications, the desired level of illumination should be expressed as the 'average minimum maintained level of illumination' to allow for lumen and dirt depreciation and the related loss of light.

Directional Lighting

Flood or spot lights usually produce much glare unless mounted high and aimed downward rather than horizontally.

Landscape and Up-lighting

These are lighting fixtures usually placed on the ground and aimed up to highlight landscaping and/or buildings

- Can aid security around windows and doors if done properly.
- Must use care to avoid glare around corners where driveways may be present.

Controlling Operation of Lighting Systems

Timers

Need to adjust timers for seasonal changes and HID cooling time after power outages. There are timers available that automatically adjust for seasons and have a battery backup in case of a power outage.

Photocells

Photocells turn lights on at dusk and off at dawn. Need to properly aim them so other light fixtures do not cause the photocell to turn off the lights it controls. Photocells may turn on circuits on overcast days. Can use with a timer so lights come on at dusk and go off at a predetermined time instead of dawn.

Motion Sensors

Motion sensor is good for demand use situations and even for detection when two units are used facing each other; can only be used with incandescent type light fixtures (instant on). Motion sensors should not be used in residential applications as a trespasser can easily walk beneath the fixture and not trip the light. Higher end units have corrected this deficiency by including a 'look down' sensor that detects motion beneath it. However, the light will still not illuminate if the trespasser never actually passes the light and instead stops at a window prior to the mounted fixture.

Energy Management Systems

Energy management systems use a computer to control heating and cooling systems and may also control interior and exterior lighting. Need to consider photocells to signal overcast conditions and prevent exterior lighting from turning on during the daytime.

References

Security lighting: What we know and what we don't . Lighting Magazine; December 1991. Boyce, Peter

Security With a Light Touch. Security Management Online; March 1997. Russell Leslie

Parking Lot and Area Luminaires. NLPIP, 2004. Michele McColgan, John Van Derlofske

Outdoor Entry Lighting. Snapshots, Issue 11.

Understanding Parking Lot Fixtures. Lighting Management and Maintenance, December 1993. Robert G. Davis

Exterior Security Lighting. Smart Building Index, Building Product Information. David D. Owen.

Light Up The Night! Quick Facts about Outdoor Lighting. Home Lighting Articles. Debbie Rodgers.

Amber Property Management. Not All Lighting is Security Lighting: 6 Points for Added Safety, May 11, 2011 by Kim Weiss

Article Niche Project. Industrial Lighting Fixtures for Better Output in Manufacturing Units, May 4, 2011 by Scott Mathews.

Wise Geek. What are the Different Types of Security Lighting? By S.E. Smith

Article/.com. Importance of Outdoor Security Lighting, March 23, 2012 by Alex Sanders.

http://www.securitylighting.com/

http://www.smsiinc.com/pdfs/security-lighting-guide.pdf

http://www.residential-landscape-lighting-design.com/outdoor-wall-mount-lights.htm

http://www.lighting.philips.com/main/lightcommunity/trends/white_light/security.wpd

http://www.reedconstructiondata.com/smartbuildingindex/articles/exterior-security-lighting/

http://www.networx.com/article/the-nuances-of-automatic-securityhttp://www.consumersdigest.com/home/bright-ideas/outdoor-lighting-lights

http://amberpm.wordpress.com/2011/05/11/%EF%BB%BFnot-all-lighting-is-security-lighting-6-points-for-added-safety-article-by-kim-weiss/

http://www.facilitiesnet.com/lighting/article/Changes-in-Technology-Legislation-and-Codes-Improve-Safety-and-Security-Lighting--9395#

http://www.facilitiesnet.com/lighting/article/Outdoor-Lighting-Strategy-Can-Balance-Safety-Security-and-Environmental-Stewardship--12857

http://www.rlldesign.com/outdoor-security-lighing-t-25_36.html

http://www.johnsoncitytn.org/uploads/Documents/Planning/Zoning%20Code/ART%2013,%20Lighting.pdf

http://ecmweb.com/content/security-lighting-primer
http://www.ehow.com/facts_5787631_halogen-lights-used-for_.html

http://lifx.co/lighting101/light-types/halogen/

http://www.edisontechcenter.org/halogen.html

http://www.consumerenergycenter.org/lighting/bulbs.html

http://www.edisontechcenter.org/Fluorescent.html

http://info.eyelighting.com/blog/bid/345200/Are-Mercury-Lamps-Still-Legal

http://www.lighting.philips.com/main/prof/lamps/high-intensity-discharge-lamps/hpl-high-pressure-mercury/mercury-vapor-standard

http://www.energystar.gov/index.cfm?c=lighting.pr_what_are

http://whatis.techtarget.com/definition/light-emitting-diode-LED

http://hyperphysics.phy-astr.gsu.edu/hbase/electronic/leds.html

http://www.mge.com/saving-energy/home/lighting/led.htm

http://www.britannica.com/EBchecked/topic/340594/LED

http://www.lrc.rpi.edu/programs/nlpip/lightinganswers/led/lightProduced.asp

Chapter Five

Burglary Prevention

Locking Devices Performance Objectives:

- Explain where most burglaries occur on a building
- Define a hollow core door
- Define a solid core door
- Define a metal clad door
- Cite and explain the grades of door locks
- Explain the operation of a lock cylinder
- Explain the purpose of locking devices
- Explain the differences between latch bolts and dead bolts
- Describe two common door lock attacks
- Explain the operating characteristics of the three forms of deadbolt locks
- Explain the purpose of key in the knob locksets
- Cite the methods of preventing door lock attacks
- Explain what an exit device is
- Describe a rim lock
- Describe a mortise lock
- Explain the purpose of a security hinge
- Explain the concern with common wall businesses
- Cite miscellaneous security applications and solutions
- Explain how to determine a relevant building threat level
- Apply a residential security survey to a residence
- Apply a business security survey to a business

Introduction

Burglary is frequently mis-identified as robbery in the media and conversation. Even police officers will mis-state this crime at times. Therefore, a clear understanding is needed. Burglary is defined as the entering of a building or structure without the owner's consent and with the intent to commit a crime.

The primary difference between the two is that a *burglary* involves the theft of property from a building while *robbery* typically involves the use of or threat of force against a person while demanding and taking their personal property.

In this unit of instruction, we will examine the typical construction of a building. We will concentrate on commercial buildings. However, as commercial business owners also own homes and have related security questions there is a separate section covering residential security as well.

Recalling the three hats, a burglar will approach a potential building target with the first hat in mind. He will examine all the standard points of entry into a building for any weakness that he can take advantage of. If the normal points of entry have been upgraded with security some burglars will bring tools with them with the very intent of entering the building through non-traditional entry points. The purpose of this unit is to help the reader more clearly see that same building through the eyes of a burglar. Without some standard building construction knowledge most police officers or security professionals would not see what the burglar sees. Let's look at a building, then, as the burglar would.

Methods of Entry

WINDOWS

Most burglaries are committed by gaining entry through either windows or doors. Commercial establishments are often victimized by both, either by breaking out a window or by breaking a window in a door and unlocking it to gain access. Prevention methods for window burglaries are discussed in a separate unit on glazing materials.

DOORS

Doors are manufactured in a variety of configurations, depending on their application. The differences are of construction and application. The wrong door for any building application can be an open invitation to burglars.

Door Types

HOLLOW CORE

This form of door is truly hollow in its core. It is framed with solid wood strips and then cardboard stock is placed between two sheets of wood veneer faces. The thin veneer wood looks attractive but offers no actual security. These doors are designed for interior residential use on bathrooms, closets and bedrooms. These categories of interior doors are called privacy doors. The problem arises when they are used on exterior entrances. Kicking or even punching through the door easily compromises them. This allows access to the interior side of the lock, which the burglar can easily open. These doors are sometimes used on residential entrances by building contractors attempting to cut costs. They are also routinely used on apartment doors, as these doors are not true exterior doors. However, they are still the first line of physical defense to the residents and as such should be of a solid core.

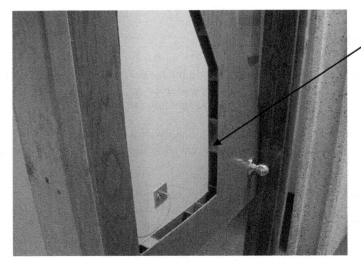

Hollow Core

Hollow Core Door

SOLID CORE

This door is, as the name implies, a solid door. It is initially constructed the same way that a hollow core door is except that the cardboard center is replaced with a solid core of scrap wood. This type of door is virtually impossible to break through by kicking or punching at the door. Note that this is not the same as kicking *in* the door. That involves kicking and breaking the doorframe and is discussed elsewhere in this unit.

Solid wood doors are designed primarily for residences and commercial office doors. When these doors are used with appropriate locking devices they become a good security barrier against brute force. However, as battery operated power tools become more common it can be expected that these types of tools will become a typical tool for burglars who will simply cut through the door and bypass the lock. If the burglary threat is this great, the most effective prevention method would be the installation of an intrusion alarm system. This does not prevent entry, but does signal a notification of entry. In these higher threat situations, the economics of the alarm system must be weighed against the potential cost of the burglary.

METAL CLAD DOORS

These doors come in two types: aluminum clad and steel clad. Aluminum clad doors have an insulating foam core and are installed on houses as an alternative to solid wood doors. Because of the flexible aluminum and compressing nature of foam, these doors are not likely to be kicked or punched through. Steel clad doors may have either an insulating foam core or a cardboard core. They most often are installed on industrial buildings. The steel cladding is the best security against kicking and punching. However, just as with the wooden doors, both types of doors can be sawed through. High-risk burglary sites may require an intrusion alarm system.

GLASS ALUMINUM FRAMED

Retail stores are the primary user of this form of door. It is customer friendly with its large glass pane, but obviously is a security threat. The soft aluminum frame is easily pried back, the glass can be broken, and the standard mortise lock cylinder can be too easily removed. While all of these issues can be addressed with upgraded security hardware and security glazing, these doors typically do not include any extra security considerations from the manufacturer. Without security upgrades there is very little to stop a burglar from attacking these doors. An alternative measure is an intrusion alarm system. Any intrusion alarm system is, however, only as good as its security/law enforcement reporting and response system. A smashed door that allows the burglar to enter, commit the theft and exit within two minutes is not effective if the response time is five minutes or greater.

Door Lock Considerations

DOOR LOCK GRADES

All door locks come in one of three grades. Grade 1 is considered industrial quality, and is the highest grade. It is tested to withstand rough handling for many years. Grade 2 is a commercial quality lock. It is commonly used in office settings where users are not as abusive in their surroundings. The final grade, grade 3, is considered a residential lock. It is the most lightweight and lowest quality. This allows it to be sold inexpensively to homeowners and builders. However, it wears out more quickly than the other two grades leading to early failure on heavily used doors. Any of the locks can be installed on any building application unless building codes require otherwise. Early failure and easy burglaries occur when a grade 3 lock is installed on commercial or industrial doors. Check the packaging or speak to a licensed locksmith about grades of locks.

Commercial door locks come in a variety of formats. Some are designed to accommodate a particular door frame, while others can be installed on a variety of different style doors. Specific formats will be discussed later in this chapter.

DOOR LOCK CYLINDERS

Lock cylinders are a component of any key operated mechanical lock. It is the face of most locks. Door lock keys are inserted into the cylinder's key plug and control the locking and unlocking of the physical lock. Thus, it is considered the security of the lock itself.

The operation of a lock cylinder is not complex. A row of five or six small key (bottom) pins has a matching set of smaller driver (upper) pins resting on top. Without the key inserted the top driver pins block the turning of the key plug which is attached to the lock bolt that extends into the door frame. (Photos below). Inserting the correct key lifts the pins and creates a straight shear line between the top and bottom pins which will allow the plug to turn and the lock bolt to be retracted, unlocking the door.

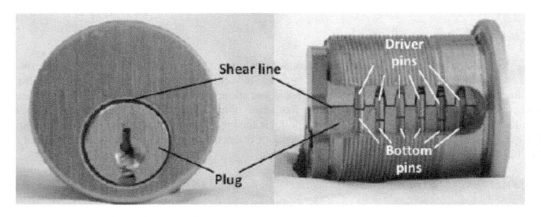

Lock Cylinder Face with Key Plug   **Cutaway Showing Internal Pins**

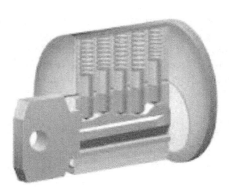
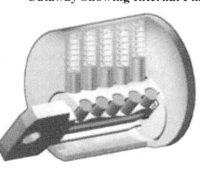

Correct Key Creates Shear Line - Allows Key Plug to Turn

Standard door locks are subject to manipulation allowing a knowledgeable person to pick or bump open a lock. Doing so allows the key plug to turn without a key which also turns the lock bolt. Neither attack method leaves any obvious entry. Any retailer selling goods that would attract a professional burglar would be wise to install a high security lock. Pick, bump, and attack resistant locks are available in a variety of configurations. However, they are much more expensive because of the added security features built into both the cylinder and lock housing itself. Determining which high security lock is best for a business should be done in consultation with a qualified locksmith, security, or crime prevention professional. Purchasing a UL (Underwriter's Laboratory) approved lock will certify that the lock is attack resistant from most threats.

Door Lock Bolts

It is obvious that door locks are used to lock doors. Not so obvious is the component of the lock that actually secures the door into the door frame. This component is called the *lock bolt*. Door lock bolts are of two standard types. The first is a **latch bolt**, the second a **dead bolt**.

LATCH BOLTS

A latch bolt is characterized by a bolt throw of between 3/8" and ¾", with an average of 1/2". It also has a beveled or slanted shape edge and is always spring loaded even when the lock to which it is attached is in the locked mode. Key-in-the-knob locks (the type on virtually every residential door in America) almost always have this kind of bolt. The danger with latch bolts is their design. Their typical ½" throw means that the bolt only extends out of the door by that length. However, for business doors that have a 1/4" gap between the door and the door frame only ¼" of the bolt is actually inside the adjacent door frame and strikeplate. Inserting a pry bar would allow a burglar to only have to pry and separate the door frame by ¼" to pop open the door.

Another issue is the beveled edge, which allows the bolt to retract when the door is closed. This means that the latch bolt is spring loaded. The burglar who can see the bolt through the frame and door gap can access that bolt. This is true of any door which swings outward, usually business doors. With any variety of tools, usually a pocket knife or ice pick, the burglar can simply push the spring loaded bolt back into the lock, easily opening the door. With doors that swing inward, such as residential doors, a thin but flexible piece of plastic inserted between the door and doorframe can frequently force the latch bolt back into the lock, unlocking the door.

Dead latch pin

Plain Latch Bolt   **Dead Latch Bolt**

A modification to the latch bolt has created the 'Dead Latch' latch bolt. Essentially, a small extra bolt (dead latch pin) is overlaid on top of the spring bolt. When the door is closed this dead latch pin remains *inside* the lock, held back by the strike plate. With the dead latch pin held in this retraction mode the latch bolt is actually blocked from being pushed back, acting like a deadbolt. This helps to defeat the attack with the knife or ice pick. Locating such a lock and practicing this action on the lock (typically a residential front door key-in-the-knob lock) will demonstrate the concept. Simply hold open the door and then push back the dead latch pin with your finger. Now push the latch bolt back and you will see how it does not retract, locking the bolt in place. (If it does retract it is defective.) However, the almost ¼" latch bolt movement prior to locking up might still be enough to force open some business doors with a large gap between the frame and door. Note that this dead latching feature does nothing to prevent the actual knob and lock itself from being attacked.

91

Latch bolts are not a very secure form of lock bolt. However, they offer a great level of convenience by allowing occupants to simply close a door behind them and have it 'lock' by itself. As you can see, the concept of security and a locked door are misplaced with a latch bolt. The only real solution to this security vulnerability is a supplemental dead bolt lock installed above the latch bolt lock. Before doing this check with your local fire department or locksmith for code requirements.

DEAD BOLTS

Dead bolts are characterized by the following: minimum 1" bolt throw, a flat bolt face (no beveled edge), and a 'dead' throw, meaning it is not spring loaded and cannot be pushed back into the lock when fully extended.

The 1" throw should be a minimum on any dead bolt lock. Any dead bolt lock that has a shorter throw should not be used in a security application. A 1" throw makes it very difficult to pry back a door frame to disengage the bolt from the door frame strikeplate. A flat bolt face indicates that it is not spring loaded. The dead throw means that once the bolt is thrown, or locked, it cannot be pushed back into the lock. To retract the bolt, you must turn the thumb piece or key on the lock itself. This makes deadbolts the typical choice for locks that are installed in holes bored through the door, typically called tubular deadbolts for their shape.

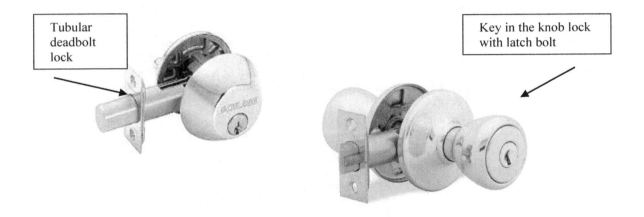

Tubular deadbolt lock

Key in the knob lock with latch bolt

Lock Bolt Attack

Some burglars will still attempt to attack a lock bolt by using a short piece of hacksaw blade to cut through the bolt. This can be prevented in one of two methods. The first is to buy a 'high security' deadbolt lock. The bolt on these locks has either a ceramic insert which is impervious to cutting by metal blades or a spinning metal dowel in the center of the bolt that a cutting tool would simply spin without cutting through. The other solution is to purchase what is commonly called a 'latch guard' plate. This plate is bolted onto the door next to the lock and covers the gap between the door and the door jamb effectively denying access to the bolt.

Latch Guard Plate

Door Lock Types

KEY IN THE KNOB/LEVER LOCK

This type of lock is very common and found in some form on virtually every home in North America. Many small businesses will have it on their front doors and larger businesses frequently have them on their standard side and rear entry/exit doors. The difference between the knob lock and lever lock is the handle design. As the name implies the 'knob' is shaped just like that. It has been the standard door handle for the last 100 years. Subsequent ADA (Americans with Disabilities Act) laws mandated changes in the knob style because it is difficult to grasp and turn for some disabled persons. By law new or remodeled commercial buildings are required to have lever handles rather than knob handles. Lever handles do not require any grasping action and can be turned by either lifting or pushing down on the handle. Other than the handle design they function the same.

Key in the Knob Lock

Key in the Lever Lock

KEY IN HANDLE ATTACKS

The 'key in the knob' name comes from the fact that you insert the key into the outside lever/knob of the lock to unlock or lock it. However, when you consider that the knob/lever is the actual locking part of the lock then all the security of the lock is protruding out of the door. This leaves it vulnerable to attack and most burglars are very aware of this.

The most common, and always successful, attack method is to use a pipe wrench, locking pliers, or slip lock pliers and place the jaws of the tool around the knob/lever. Even though the lock is in the locked mode a forced turn on the knob with any of these tools will force back the spring bolt and allow entry in less than two seconds. Furthermore, it is done noiselessly. The favored tool for commercial lever locks is a 2"-3" diameter pipe that easily slips over the lever. The length of the pipe quickly overcomes the locking resistance of these higher quality locks. A solution for businesses is to replace the lock with a twist resistant model called a 'clutch lever' lock. These locks have a friction clutch that breaks free when excessive resistance is applied and allows the lever handle to harmlessly turn without engaging the bolt. Any Internet search for 'clutch lever locks' would bring up manufacturers. Any locksmith would have them or could order them. They do not look any different than the lock they replace.

Forced knob turning is a favorite burglary method on residential doors when the homeowner is gone during the daytime. However, it becomes particularly dangerous when the burglary takes place after the occupants have retired for the evening. The best that can be said for these locks is that they keep the door from blowing open in the wind. The security solution to these types of locks is to install some form of deadbolt lock, particularly for homeowners.

Commercial building codes and fire codes will also forbid the installation of certain locks on business doors. The reason is two-fold. During an emergency evacuation, business customers may have to evacuate through a rear non-public exit. These exit doors must have locks that require no special knowledge to operate and open. Additionally, firefighters who must escape a burning building will need to open these doors after hours. Doors that fall under fire codes or life safety codes will be identified with an 'EXIT' sign above or to the side of the door. Unless otherwise prohibited by local fire codes doors that do not have an exit sign associated with them can be secured by any form of locking device.

SINGLE CYLINDER DEADBOLT

These types of deadbolts are commonly recommended for homes by law enforcement personnel. This form of deadbolt has a keyway on the exterior of the door and a thumb latch on the inside. (The portion of the lock in which the key is inserted is called a cylinder. Therefore, one keyway equals a single cylinder). When used in conjunction with a high security strike plate in the door frame containing four screw holes and three-inch screws it is very effective against a kick-in type of forced entry. It is likely that a burglar will injure a part of his leg before the doorframe would break apart with such a lock and strike plate combination.

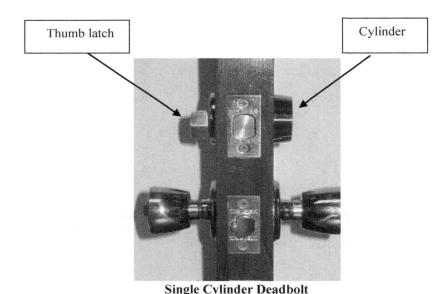

Single Cylinder Deadbolt

Single cylinder deadbolt locks are designed to be installed in doors where there is no glass or window within 40 inches of the lock. This precludes a burglar from breaking a window, reaching around inside the house and unlocking the door. This lock should have a minimum one-inch throw deadbolt (cannot be pushed back into the lock when extended). It also should have a spinning cylinder guard around the perimeter of the lock. This prevents the burglar from placing a pipe wrench or locking pliers on the cylinder (keyway portion) and twisting open the lock.

DOUBLE CYLINDER DEADBOLT

This deadbolt has the same characteristics as the single cylinder deadbolt. The only difference is that it has a keyway on both sides of the lock (two cylinders). It was specifically designed to be used on doors in which there is glass or a window within 40 inches of the lock. This prevents the burglar from breaking the adjacent window and unlocking it while reaching through the broken glass.

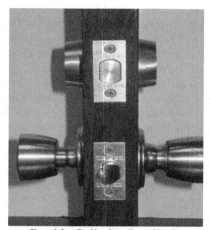

Double Cylinder Deadbolt

While it is an effective means of deterring a burglar, who does not wish to attract further attention with more sounds of breaking glass, it is not safe in the event of a fire. Because this lock can be locked from the interior of a home and then the key removed the residents can be locked inside the home in the event of a fire. Some communities in varying U.S. states have passed city ordinances forbidding their installation for this very reason.

Door Glass Burglary (laminated glass)
Lack of Double Cylinder Deadbolt

The author agrees with the life safety dangers of double cylinder locks and supports their non-use on residential doors. However, human nature being what it is, residents have and will continue to install this lock on doors in which glass is nearby. Should the homeowner or renter accept this risk the following advice is offered to mitigate the potential for death or serious injury in the event of a fire.

For doors in which a curtain is present over the adjacent windows it is recommended that a spare key be attached to a thread and pushpin. The pushpin should be pushed into the window frame behind the curtain that is at least 40 inches from the lock or potential broken window. In the event of a fire all residents, guests, and child sitters in the home should be made aware of its presence and purpose. While precious seconds will be lost in the retrieval of the key it is better than the alternative. The key should be suspended approximately six inches above the surface of the floor. All potential users, but especially young children, should be drilled on its location and use. Children should be required to pull on the string and insert and turn the key while blindfolded so that they will know how to do so in a smoke-filled environment. Being blindfolded assures that they will feel the cuts on key and insert it correctly. Turning and actually unlocking and opening the door means that they will not turn it the wrong way in an emergency possibly preventing their exit.

CAPTURE KEY DOUBLE CYLINDER DEADBOLT

This double cylinder deadbolt lock is actually a fire code approved residential lock. It looks exactly like a standard double cylinder deadbolt. The difference is that when the door is locked from the inside with the key the lock captures the key. The key cannot be removed from the inside without withdrawing the bolt, which, of course, unlocks the door. Because the lock captures the key when locked it will always be there in case of emergency. In essence, the double cylinder lock has reverted to a single cylinder lock whenever the home or business is occupied.

The typical reaction to this lock is that the resident has gained nothing in the way of security. This is not true. First, the majority of home burglaries take place during daytime hours. The presumption of the burglar is that people are working or away during the daytime. During these hours the capture key double cylinder deadbolt lock does not have a key on the interior of the house (it is removed when the homeowner exits this door). A burglar who breaks a pane of glass and reaches around will find only the empty keyway. Secondly, if a burglar does attempt entry during the evening hours (when the key is present in the locked position) it will require the breaking of glass. This means a noisy entry and the possibility of awakening the residents or pets. No burglar wants to encounter a potentially armed and prepared homeowner in the middle of the night on his/her own turf or risk the chance that the police have been called. Also, contrary to many Hollywood movies, burglars do not usually cut glass or tape the window to gain entry. Burglars who do use this type of entry are highly skilled and will be working against high priced homes containing high priced valuables. Such residences will need much more security than any simple survey or recommendation can provide.

Readers should be aware that capture key deadbolts do not command a large market because most people are not aware of their existence or their operation. Therefore, most manufacturers do not make them. One manufacturer of this lock is Medeco High Security Locks. Medeco only sells high security locks and their capture key lock is constructed in the same manner. Thus, it will cost considerably more than the equivalent non-high security lock. Medeco locks are only sold through locksmith shops.

RIM LOCKS

Rim locks are mounted on the interior of doors on the 'rim' of the door which is the door lock edge of the door, the area in which a lock is mounted. They are usually rectangular shaped and can ordered with either a key or thumb turn on the inside.

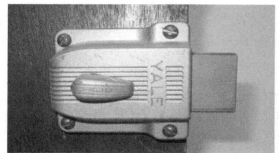

Dead Bolt Rim Lock

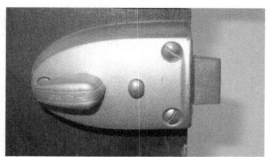

Latch Bolt Rim Lock

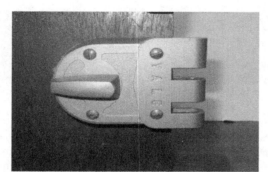

Vertical Throw/Interlocking Dead Bolt Rim Lock

Rim locks are classified as supplemental locks. The door would still need a knob or lever lock to open and close the door. Rim locks are designed for simple installation and offer varying levels of security. They come in both latch bolt and dead bolt styles. For best security, of course, it should be purchased with a deadbolt. Rim lock strikeplates must be securely mounted into the door frame to offer resistance against door kicks and forced entry. Better rim locks (vertical throw types) have an interlocking dead bolt and latch plate for superior strength and resistance against prying and kicking.

MORTISE LOCKS

Mortise locks are those locks that are inserted into the cut out (mortised) edge of a door. The only part visible to the exterior is the key cylinder and handle, if applicable. The actual lock is contained in the door and only the bolt is visible and protrudes from the door edge. Note that these locks, like all locks, can be equipped with either a latch or dead bolt. These locks are most commonly found today on department store aluminum framed glass doors. They are also found on higher end solid wood business office doors

Office Door Mortise Lock

Commercial Door Mortise Lock

Latch Bolt Mortise Lock with Deadlatch Pin Below Bolt

The latch bolt on both types of locks operates like any other latch bolt. The only design difference is that the deadlatch pin is a separate pin located below the latch bolt. On aluminum framed glass doors with a deadbolt, the deadbolt pivots up from the edge of the door instead of traveling in a horizontal fashion as most deadbolt locks do. (See photo) The pivot function allows these bolts to be as long as 1.5" and still fold into a narrow door edge. Business office doors have a traditional horizontal throw deadbolt.

Mortise locks were also very common on older house doors that still use skeleton keys (a very insecure lock).

EXIT DEVICES

This door lock is also commonly referred to as a 'panic bar', after the older style door lock release hardware that had a tubular bar running across the face of the door that you pushed to open the door. Today's exit hardware has a larger rectangular bar that is mounted flush with the interior face of the door. (See photo). The terminology has also changed and this locking device is now called an exit device or panic hardware. The primary function of a panic exit device is to provide a single motion egress for anyone inside a secured, locked area. Basically, that means someone only has to push one thing on a door that offers minimal resistance to get out of a room or corridor that might be locked from the outside. The challenge is to build in a level of security that also keeps unauthorized people from forcing open the door from the outside and entering the area protected by the panic exit device.

Older Style Exit Device

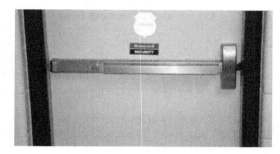

Newer Style Exit Device

An exit device normally has a beveled latch bolt that automatically closes behind a fixed, protruding latch plate mounted to the surface of the surrounding door frame. The flat portion of the latch bolt locks behind the latch plate making a secure fit for the bolt and the door. The latch is not visible to the exterior and thus cannot be pushed or pried back. This design makes for a secure locking device while meeting the requirements of life safety codes for emergency exiting. Panic hardware can also be fitted with an automatic deadbolt that would be thrown into a mortised strike plate cavity upon closing. Pushing the bar would retract both the latch bolt and the deadbolt. This lock can be installed on most doors and would be an acceptable, although more expensive, alternative to standard deadbolt locks. Note, however, that only an exit device would be allowed on any door classified as a fire exit. These doors would be identified with the 'EXIT' sign above or next to the applicable door. When in doubt a call to or visit by the local fire department inspector or certified locksmith would be appropriate.

In some cases, double doors do not use a center door frame piece (mullion) leaving no place to mount the latch plate (strikeplate). In those situations, the bolt runs vertically and extends up and into the door header (top of the door frame) and, normally, a secondary bolt enters the floor for a more secure latching function. However, this arrangement can create a security vulnerability. A simple coat hanger can be inserted into the gap between the doors and when pulled back would hook and unlock the exit rim bar or push bar, unlocking the doors.

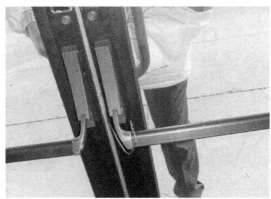

Coat Hanger Opening Door

To prevent this, an auxiliary plate the length of the door is typically affixed to the exterior of one of the doors, thus necessitating the addition of a 'door controller'. The door controller ensures that the doors close in the proper order to allow the door with the plate to close last.

Another option for older style bar exit devices is to insert a block between the bar and the interior of the door. This prevents the bar from being depressed. However, the local fire inspector must be consulted to make sure that this does not violate local fire codes.

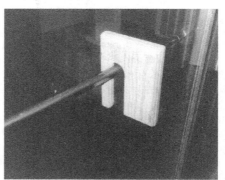

Push Bar Block Solution

Yet another option is to install a removable mullion that is placed behind the center of the doors from top to bottom and blocks the insertion of a coat hanger or other opening device. Locksmiths are best suited for this retrofit operation.

Removable Mullion

Doorframes

Many burglary prevention methods focus on the lock on a door. However, the lock is only as effective as the doorframe into which the lock bolt secures. In wood framed doors (most residences) the frame is the weakest component. Because it is hidden behind the doorframe molding few people see it. If they could they would observe that it is typically made of pine and is only 1/2 inch thick. When the door is locked, the lock bolt that protrudes from the door lock is entering a 'strike plate' secured with two very short screws. In addition, there is a gap between the door frame and the house frame. The bolt passes through the hole in the weak door frame and extends into the empty space between the door frame and the house frame. This makes for a very weak and vulnerable door lock. (See photos following.) Metal door frames commonly found on office and some business doors do not have this vulnerability.

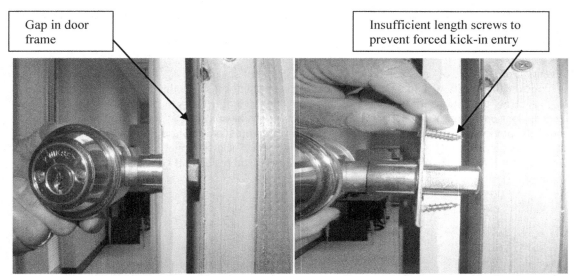

Gap in door frame

Insufficient length screws to prevent forced kick-in entry

Typical ½" Thick Door Frame   **Typical 3/4" Screws in Strikeplate**

If a burglar were to kick at the center of the door, next to the lock, all the force is being concentrated right at the lock bolt and strike plate. This amount of force will almost always split the doorframe at the bolt allowing the door to swing open. This deficiency can be reduced dramatically by the installation of a high security (four hole) strike plate. Standard strikeplates have only 3/4-inch screws. These fail to even reach the wood studs surrounding the doorframe. These screws should be removed and, along with the high-security strike plate, replaced with 3-inch screws.

Kick-in Solution Using 3" Screws in Strikeplate
Entering Frame of Building

Commercial grade solid steel doorframes do not have the same vulnerability as wood frames. In fact, steel door frames are very good security by themselves and do not need additional reinforcement against kicking threats.

Door Hinges

Fire codes require most perimeter commercial doors to open outward. In emergencies, this allows people to exit a business by simply pushing on a door rather than pulling against a potential crowd of people behind them. The problem with security is that many of these doors have their hinges located on the exterior of the door. This means that the door hinges are exposed to the exterior. Burglars will take advantage of this access by simply pushing up and removing each of the hinge pins and prying open the door from the hinge side. This can be done with a screwdriver and a hammer.

Prevention of this type of entry can be accomplished in one of several ways. The best method is to replace the hinges with security type hinges. These hinges have a small set screw that tightens down the hinge pin, preventing the removal of the pin while still allowing the hinge wings to swivel around the pin for standard door operation. Commercial and industrial versions have a shallow mortise (groove) cut into and around the pin into which the screw would set which would prevent the pin from being manually forced out. The set screw is only accessible when the door is open. Security hinges are designed to replace all standard door hinges. These hinges come in both industrial and residential versions.

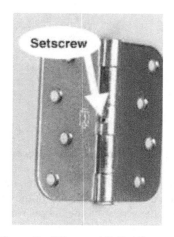

Security Hinge with Set Screw

Residential security hinges have an additional security feature called a hinge stud. When the door is closed a protruding stud on the hinge inserts into a hole in the opposite wing of the hinge. When closed the stud would seat itself into the hole preventing the hinge from separating if the pin were removed. This works because the door would have to be slid out of the doorway to gain entry. The hinge, with the stud embedded in the opposite wing, prevents the two hinge wings from sliding past each other as the door is being forced out of the doorframe. This is a very effective security measure on any out-swinging residential door.

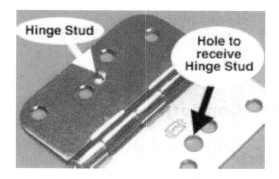

Security Hinge with Security Stud

A second method is to open the door and access the screws holding the hinge in place. Remove, and discard, the center screws on both sides of the top and bottom hinges. Obtain a 1 to 1 1/2 inch metal pin. A finishing nail with a narrow head works well. Insert the pin into the frame side screw hole left by the screw, or hammer in the nail until about 3/4" is exposed. Do this on both the top and bottom hinges. Now, slowly close the door and observe that the pin/nail protruding from the frame will fit into the opposing empty screw hole. If it extends too far out simply hammer the pin or nail further into the frame. In effect you have created two deadbolts on the hinge side.
Note that this works best with solid core doors, but will have a deterring effect on hollow core steel doors as well.

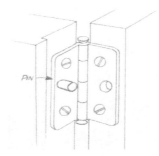

Pin or Nail Inserted into Screw Hole

Another form of security hinge is the crimped hinge. During the manufacturing process the hinge pin is crimped directly to the body of the top and bottom portions of the hinge preventing the removal of the pin. To remove the door with these hinges, the screws in the hinges would have to be removed.

Crimped End Hinge Pins

A final method of securing an exterior hinge is to weld the pin in place. This is a quick method of securing industrial type hinges. This will, of course, necessitate the removal and discarding of the hinge if it ever needs servicing.

Alternative Entry Concerns

While burglars will usually choose to burglarize a building through the simplest points, if those points have been adequately protected burglars are forced to seek alternative methods of entering a building. These alternative entry points must be examined and potentially addressed to completely secure a building.

WALLS

When burglars are deterred from doors and windows, the walls of a building are the next favorite entry points. In a retail setting, strip malls, shopping center malls and downtown buildings are the most vulnerable because of their shared walls. While one retailer may have expensive and easily fenced items that a burglar covets, the neighboring business may stock discount, paper or food items that are not normally attractive to a burglar. The first retailer, recognizing the value of its merchandise, takes appropriate precautions: installing high quality locks, lighting, glazing, even a perimeter alarm system on all doors and windows. The adjacent retailer has minimal security precautions to fit the perceived threat to his/her business. A burglar who surveys this arrangement may quickly recognize the differences. A burglar might also recognize that if he burglarizes the lesser protected business he has only a common wall separating him from the more valuable business. In many cases the common wall is nothing more than a standard wood/metal studded wall with a sheet of drywall on each side. The burglar could simply kick his/her way through the thin drywall and gain entry to the adjacent business. In the process he/she has bypassed all the security hardware on the target business, including the alarm system on the doors and windows. The burglar steals what he/she came for and exits back through the hole in the wall and out the adjacent business.

Common Wall Interior Business Burglaries

A similar situation exists for those businesses or industrial manufacturers that are in industrial parks or remote, stand-alone buildings. Burglars can simply sledgehammer their way through a concrete block wall, bypassing the secured and alarmed doors and windows. A hole large enough for a man to pass through can be punched through a hollow concrete block wall in less than ten minutes. By parking a panel van in front of the attack point documented entry has even been accomplished in a business district next door to an attached 24-hour restaurant without attracting any attention.

Commercial Building Exterior Wall Burglaries

Pole buildings made with aluminum or steel panels are also subject to attack. These wall panels are attached to the wall studs with either nails or screws. In either situation the burglar may simply pry the nails out or, using a cordless drill, back out the screws and pull a single panel away from the building. Behind the panel will likely either be empty space, or insulation and drywall. The burglar may either walk in or kick away the drywall and gain entry.

Two options exist for prevention. The first is the use of expanded metal mesh or screen. This heavy gauge steel mesh would be installed over the wall studs and then covered by the standard wall covering material (sheetrock, etc.) It cannot be kicked in. It is very difficult to cut even one strand, and will not bend once installed on walls. It is an excellent physical barrier. It can be ordered in large sheets from fencing companies.

Expanded Steel Mesh

The second option is a room based motion sensor alarm to detect entry into the room from any direction. Except in the case of very high threat level businesses (jewelers, banks, furriers, gun shops, etc.) this form of burglar alarm sensor is the best defense against wall entry burglars. Higher threat businesses should consider wall mounted alarm sensors, as well as redundant alarm systems with cut phone line supervision and cellular phone notification backup.

ROOFS AND CEILINGS

Another favorite entry point is through a roof. This entry takes a little more planning but is very successful for one important reason: the attack and entry point are not usually visible from outside at ground level. A burglar must first, of course, gain entry to the roof. This may be done via an adjacent business roof (burglarize and use the internal maintenance roof ladder), climbing an overhanging tree, adjacent fence, garbage receptacle or other available object. Suspects have also been known to park a truck next to the business and either pulls a ladder up behind them or has an accomplice drive away and pick up the burglar and stolen goods after a cell-phone call.

On the roof the burglar may use an ax to chop a hole through the roof or may easily pry off a ventilation fan unit. Most roofs are only composed of ½ or ¾ inch plywood and covered with tar. Roofs were never designed to prevent this type of forced entry and burglars take advantage of this. The burglar might tie off a rope to a roof pipe and lower him/herself into the business. If a vent was pried off to gain entry the burglar could lower him/herself into the ductwork and kick it apart at a seam. While this may seem rather involved the work effort is like any other forced entry to a building. In either situation, even if there is an alarm system, the police will not detect the burglary. This happens because the responding police will usually check all around the building, but finding no sign of a forced entry will write off the "false alarm" and the burglar can continue his/her work. The only method of detection would be to request a business key holder to respond to the alarm and have the interior searched by the police or responding security officers. Unfortunately, jurisdictions that have implemented false alarm penalty fees are forcing business owners to receive the initial call and respond themselves without police assistance, saving themselves the penalty fee. The danger has been documented in murders of business owners who have surprised burglars.

Business Roof Burglaries

Roof entries are much more of a concern for malls and businesses with a shared roof. A burglar who gains entry to any portion of the common roof has access into the ceiling area of all the businesses. In some cases, he/she can crawl around the entire complex through the ceiling without hindrance. In other cases, fire break walls will block his/her progress only momentarily. These firewalls are made of drywall and are easily compromised by punching through them. Once above the true target business the burglar could lift out the drop ceiling tile or break the drywall ceiling and drop into the chosen business. While this is more work than some other forms of burglary, the rewards are great for the burglar. High threat businesses are routinely burglarized in this manner. Preventative measures are the same as for wall entry prevention: expanded steel mesh or the use of interior motion alarm sensors.

VENTILATION/AIR CONDITIONING UNITS

Any building that has side mounted ventilation grates is also subject to burglary. Vent covers are screwed in place and a cordless drill can readily take out the screws. Using security screws or welding the grate in place are two solutions.

Ventilation Burglary

Small businesses that use window mounted room air conditioners are very vulnerable. These units are usually installed from the inside using short screws into the window frame. Because of this installation method they are easily pushed back into the building, leaving a large hole for the burglar. These window units should have a machine or metal screw eyebolt attached to the undercarriage of the A/C unit with a heavy steel cable attached to another screw eyebolt deeply imbedded into a wall stud below the exterior of the window. Pulling the cable tight will prevent the burglar from unscrewing either of the attachments. Other, more structurally sound, options are displayed below.

Window Air Conditioner Security

FLOORS

This method of burglary is the least common and is normally restricted to very high threat level businesses such as large financial institutions, art museums, and jewelry and furrier wholesalers. Burglars either use existing utility or drainage tunnels or dig their own tunnels to gain access to the floor of a target business. Burglars will rent and occupy an adjacent business or dwelling and tunnel from that point. Existing underground utility tunnels are the favorite method of attack. These tunnels run under most major metropolitan businesses and roadways without public knowledge. A check with the city engineering office should verify the presence of such tunnels under or around a business.

Business Floor Burglary

Other areas of concern are drainage and sewage tunnels. As businesses grow and expand downtown, what used to be an exterior manhole cover may now be found inside the business lobby or under the carpet of an office. A close inspection of what is in a building is in order if the business is in an older downtown district. Again, a check with the local county or city engineering department would be a good start.

When a vulnerable opening in a building is discovered it should be evaluated for potential entry. The security industry has a standard relative to evaluating such openings in any portion of a building. The standard states that any opening that is 96 square inches in size or has any one measurement that is greater than 6 inches should be secured against entry. The normal solution is welding iron bars or attaching expanded steel mesh across the opening. Local law enforcement or even a security consultant may be needed to assist the building owner in determining all the risks and potential solutions.

Determining the size of any opening is done by simply multiplying the two sides. Thus, a 10" by 10" opening equates to 100 square inches and would qualify for a security barrier. Likewise, a 5" by 15" is only 75 square inches, but the 15" opening exceeds the 6" minimum and should also be barricaded.

Miscellaneous Burglary and Theft Prevention Points

Business owners must do more than just attend to the building perimeter to secure their business from theft. The following items allow the business owner to view a more complete prevention picture for their building.

EMPLOYEE PARKING

Any business can suffer losses from a thief. Unfortunately, the company's employees are no exception. When employees are allowed to park in the rear of a business and are then provided unrestricted access to the rear door, theft prone employees have just been enabled. Company policy should require all employees to enter and exit the main entrance as any customer would. This reduces the opportunity for employees to walk out with company product.

LANDSCAPING

Bushes and trees that can grow in front of windows give burglars the opportunity for concealment while burglarizing the building through the window. To reduce the concealment advantage, all ground landscaping should be kept trimmed to a two-foot maximum height and trees should not be allowed to hang below seven feet.

PUBLIC RESTROOMS

Would-be burglars have been known to enter a business during open hours, go into the restroom, climb up onto the toilet privacy walls and lift the drop ceiling panels. They then gain entry to the ceiling and replace the ceiling panel. After the business has closed they re-emerge and burglarize the business. Not until they exit the store do they trigger the perimeter alarm system.

If new construction or remodeling is being done, all restroom ceilings should be solid drywall or the interior concrete block walls should extend up to the roofline and locks installed as described below. For existing structures with block walls extending to the roofline, double cylinder deadbolts should be installed on all restroom doors. These locks have key operated cylinders on both sides of the door. After business hours restrooms should be checked for occupancy and then locked. Any burglar secreted in the ceiling will have to spend the night in the ceiling or the restroom. In the event the burglar has free access to the entire ceiling area, interior motion sensors must be installed in the store. However, if an alarm occurs, the key holder will have to respond to allow interior inspection by the police or security officer response force.

HALLWAY MAINTENANCE DOORS

In large commercial complexes, public hallways have maintenance closets. Burglars have used these closets to conceal themselves just before closing hours. Later they will exit the closet or storeroom to burglarize offices. In some instances, personal assaults on employees have even occurred when these employees have stayed to work late. All hallway closet and storage room doors should be equipped with locks that are always in the locked mode.

OFFICE EQUIPMENT

Burglars and even employees will steal unsecured electronic office equipment. All such pieces of equipment should be secured to their workstations by specially designed anti-theft devices. These locking devices range from padlocks and cables to specially designed lockdown plates as well as alarm cables attached to every separate piece. The goal is to either delay the theft or create an alarm when the cable is disconnected. These devices all serve a purpose. However, the greatest deterrent is to visibly engrave or indelibly stamp the company name on every single piece of valuable electronic equipment. It is difficult to re-sell a stolen item when it is clearly labeled with someone else's name. When engraving the object, it is wise to record the serial number of the item and a short description so that if it disappears the business will have proof of ownership and a number that can be entered into a national stolen item police database.

SERVICE VENDORS

Some burglars are brazen enough to enter a restricted business complex under the guise of being a service repairperson. They may pretend to be there to fix a telephone, computer problem or photocopy machine. They might refer to a fictitious copy of a work order and, if refused entry by the receptionist, would indicate that any negative ramifications will be the responsibility of the receptionist. This may tend to fluster some receptionists who would then allow the person entry. Industrial spies have also been known to use this ploy and then attach discreet monitoring devices to corporate phone, fax and computer lines. Always check out every service employee. Ask to see a work order, company identification and who requested the service. Call for the affected person to escort the individual into the building and then have someone monitor the person's work until they are finished.

Discovering a Burglary

If, after all the best efforts to prevent a burglary, a business owner arrives at the business and discovers a burglary has occurred, the building should not be entered. Leave immediately and, if possible, post another employee in the parking lot to prevent others from entering. The business owner should go to a neighboring business, payphone or cell phone and call the police. It is a remote chance, but burglars, especially drug addicts, have been known to fall asleep in the burglarized business, or sometimes, to simply lose track of time. Employees risk personal injury if they surprise a burglar inside a business. Let the police check out the building before entering. After the formal police investigation would be a good time to ask the officer for advice on how to better the secure the point of entry. Another burglar may find the same weakness.

Summary

While it is true that nothing will stop an absolutely determined burglar, a clearly target hardened building presents a less than desirable target for the burglar. Following the suggestions in this chapter offers the first step in deterring the burglar.

Note: this unit continues on the next page with Residential Burglary considerations.

Part Two

Residential Burglary

This section of Burglary Prevention concentrates on residential burglary. Many of the aspects of burglary prevention overlap with the previous building prevention information. In this section the focus will be on conducting a security survey of a house and some of the unique issues to homes.

Residential Security Survey Form

At the end of this textbook, in the Appendixes, is a Residential Security Survey checklist form. This security survey form is a convenient and time effective means to survey almost any size home. Note, however, that if the contents of the home are very valuable and might attract the attention of skilled burglars or the resident would be considered a high-profile business or public official a professional security consultant should be called in to offer additional advice and recommendations. The police officer or security professional must be confident of their skill level and experience in these situations.

The form covers the physical security needs of any home. By critiquing the survey items from top to bottom and noting deficiencies and recommendations in the boxes below each item the homeowner will have the opportunity to understand the vulnerabilities to his/her home and understand what corrective actions will need to be taken to add security to the home.

As the Residential Security Form in your book may not copy well you can request an electronic copy by emailing the author at Jerry.Antoon@gmail.com.

A basic review of the items follows. Note, the topics are presented in the order in which they appear on the Residential Security survey form.

LANDSCAPING

The basic premise is denying concealment to a burglar who is working on a window or door that might be secluded behind vegetation.

LIGHTING

All burglars, rapists, prowlers, and other criminally minded individuals are repelled by light. Illuminating a backyard will deter these individuals from completing their criminal activities at the rear of a home. High Pressure Sodium lights in a 35 watt version will illuminate any standard residential rear yard. The advantage of these lights is two-fold. First, they will retrofit mount on any existing outdoor lighting fixture. Secondly, these fixtures are so efficient that using average electrical rates these fixtures only consume $20.00 of electricity over the course of one complete year based on an average of 12 hours use per day. Most of these fixtures come with a dusk to dawn sensor and thus can be left on all the time. Finally, the bulb for HPS fixtures will last over five years before burning out.

A front porch light using a 25 watt small appliance bulb will cast enough light to discourage most criminals from attacking a door or window on a porch for fear of being seen. A screw-in dusk to dawn sensor will negate having to worry about turning the light off in the morning.

DOOR LOCKS – ALL

One of the most overlooked aspects of door security is the failure to rekey door locks when the new occupant moves in. It is not a matter of trust of the former occupant. It is a matter of lack of control on how many other keys to the home exist. A child of the former homeowner may have given a key to her now ex-boyfriend. Dog sitters, domestic help, neighbors, care givers may all have had a key or access to one. You cannot be certain that these same people do not currently possess a key to your house. Considering the possibilities of that should motivate any new occupant to immediately contact a locksmith.

Because some locks may not be intuitive as to their operation (double cylinder deadbolts) it is imperative that those people who temporarily or permanently live in or use your home understand how to escape in an emergency. What may seem a simple operation to the homeowner may confound a person who is not mechanically inclined.

A note regarding life safety must be addressed here. Homeowners are not subject to commercial building codes. However, some fire codes relating to double cylinder residential door locks may be in existence in a particular community. Before installing or recommending a double cylinder deadbolt on a residential door check with a local locksmith or fire code official for the legality of the lock. Note that an opinion of a double cylinder door lock may not mean it is illegal. Ask for the code or ordinance that might forbid a double cylinder lock on a home. Also, any code may only prevent a licensed professional from installing it but would not forbid a homeowner from putting one on a door.

FRONT DOOR

The common theme of deadbolts, strikeplates, and 3" screws begins with this door. It will continue for all entry doors. Note that the only way to determine if the screws are actually 3" is to remove at least one of them to verify. Just because a four-hole strikeplate is present does not mean the proper screws were used. Also note that a door with a side window (called a side lite) that only has a center frame of 2" will not accommodate a 3" strikeplate screw. Inserting a 3" screw will certainly penetrate and break the glass. While this may seem obvious it has been done!

The only other additional information is the use of door viewers (peepholes) to identify a guest prior to opening the door. Home invasions are increasing across America. Opening a door prior to identifying the guest may allow a criminal to force his way into a home as the door is now standing open. A door viewer allows visual identification without opening the door. Making sure that children who are home alone can see outside without opening the door requires the installation of a second door viewer at their height.

ATTACHED GARAGE – RESIDENCE ENTRY DOOR

Homes with attached garages should consider the garage entry door as an exterior door to their home. It must be secured in the same manner. Entry into a garage means that a burglary now has concealment and tools available to him as he works on your entry door. What is even a greater consideration is the number of residents who fail to lock this door or install a deadbolt on this door. An easy entry into a garage means an even easier entry into the house, day or night if the door is not locked.

Fire codes today require that these doors do not contain any glass. Therefore, that option does not exist in this form. If residents do have glass in their doors it is recommended that the door be replaced with a standard exterior, non-glass door.

ATTACHED GARAGE – DIRECT BASEMENT ENTRY

Some homes have a secondary basement entry directly from the attached garage. The same principle of all doors applies here. Once again, fire codes prohibit the use of glass in these doors. Therefore, the assumption is that there is no glass in the door.

You will find these doors installed in both in-swinging and out-swinging versions. In-swinging doors are installed at the basement floor level. Typically, concrete stairs lead down to the basement and the door which opens into the basement. No hinges are exposed and the bolt is concealed behind the door stop trim.

Out-swinging doors are usually found at the garage level. Opening the door toward you leads to normally wooden steps leading into the basement. This door will have exposed hinges and a bolt. Therefore, the recommendation for security hinges and a latch guard plate.

REAR DOOR – HINGED PATIO DOOR

These types of doors, sometimes referred to as French Doors, may come in two forms. These are single pane glass or individual panes of glass. Because the single pane of glass will be tempered glass (by Federal code) it will completely break into small pieces when broken. This would allow the burglar to walk right into a home bypassing the lock. Therefore, a single cylinder deadbolt is acceptable. Note that breaking these types of windows is very unusual due to the loud noise generated by this entry, except in rural areas.

REAR DOOR –SLIDING GLASS DOORS

These doors are normally found on residences and converted businesses. They are of two types: aluminum framed and wood framed. The aluminum framed and some wood framed sliding doors have a common installation method that makes them prone to burglary. Once the doorframe is installed and the non-sliding door fixed in the frame, the sliding door is put in. This is done by first inserting the top of the sliding door into the upper track and lifting the entire door up. There is extra space built into the top door header that allows the door to be lifted higher than normal. This lifting action allows the bottom of the door to move over the bottom track. The installer then lowers the door into the bottom track and the weight of the door keeps the door in place. Many of these door systems come with a special insert that is supposed to be installed in the upper track of the sliding door. This prevents burglars from lifting the door out of the frame. However, some installers either forget or choose not to install this anti-burglary insert. In the event the door would ever need repairing, the opposite process would allow the door to be lifted and out of the track and allow for its removal. It is in the removal process that the burglar has the advantage.

From the exterior side of the door, the burglar may insert a pry bar or large screwdriver into the bottom door track. The burglar then applies lifting action on the door and moves the door up into the hollow track. When the door clears the lower track the burglar simply pushes the bottom into the house and lowers the door onto the floor. The burglar then grabs the door and pushes it aside. This works even when the standard door lock is 'locked'. All aluminum-framed doors are installed this way, but not all wooden framed doors. Some wood framed doors are installed by simply inserting the slider door into the bottom track, pushing it into place and then nailing a wooden casing around the door-frame to keep the door in place. These cannot be lifted. To discover which type of door a specific home may have look into the upper track to see if there is extra clearance or simply lift the door up and see if it clears the bottom track. If the door is of the latter type it cannot be defeated in the manner we have just discussed.

Residents have always been told to lock their doors and put wooden dowels in their sliding door tracks to prevent the door from being slid open by burglars. However, as we have just examined, the wooden stick is of no value in this attack. The typical door lock on sliding glass doors will not prevent this entry either. Many hook locks on these doors do not lock into a positive stop action like a deadbolt does. Subsequently, the hook will move out of the frame-locking slot as the door is being lifted into the house. The door is now out of the track and the dowel as no effect.

Wooden doors that do not install in this manner are not, however, immune to burglary. Burglars have defeated the wooden dowel in the track as well. This is done by taking a normal metal coat hanger and straightening it. Then the burglar bends one end into a hook shape and files it to a sharp point. Inserting the hooked end into the space between the doors that allows the doors to pass each other, the burglar extends the coat hanger over the wood dowel. The burglar will now manipulate the coat hanger hook over the far end of the dowel and pierce the end or even the surface of the dowel with the sharpened hook. With that accomplished the dowel can be lifted out of the track and dropped onto the interior floor. With the pry bar, the burglar then proceeds to pry open the sliding door by breaking the inexpensive lock on the door. Note that doors built since about 2000 have a built-in channel along the trailing edge of the door that blocks the insertion of such a device.

Prevention solutions are relatively simple for all sliding glass doors. For doors that lift out of their tracks one must first open the door and look up into the track. Notice the extra 1 ½ to 2 inches of space above the top of the door. In the upper track of this door four small holes should be drilled. In these holes insert 2" or longer screws that will protrude down into the upper track. The idea is that with the door closed the door cannot be lifted into the extra space because it hits the heads of the screws. This will take some minor testing and adjusting as the screws are installed but by simply moving the door to each screw the homeowner can visually see if the door will clear the screw. If the door would ever need to be repaired or removed, the screws would simply be removed first and the door can be removed in its normal fashion.

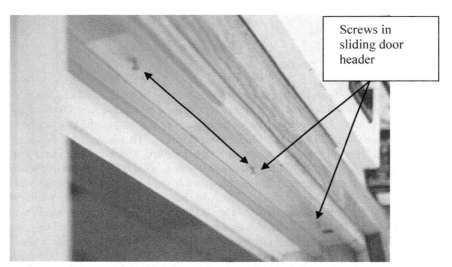

Screws in sliding door header

Screws Inserted into Header to Prevent Lifting from Outside

An alternative prevention method is to drill a hole in the doors where their two edges overlap in the center. At the top of the door edges that overlap the hole would be drilled completely through the movable door and halfway into the fixed door edge. A nail inserted into the hole will now stop the doors from sliding. The sliding door cannot be lifted out either because the non-moving door anchors the sliding door in place. The best nail to use is a duplex (double-headed) nail. This nail gives the homeowner a piece to grab onto when the nail is to be removed.

Yet a third method involves the use of a sliding barrel bolt. These bolts are the inexpensive type that a person might use on a garden gate or dog kennel door. The bolt is attached to the top lip edge of the sliding glass door. A hole is drilled into the upper track directly above the bolt. It is drilled the length of the bolt. Then, after attaching the bolt lock to the rear edge of the door, the bolt is pushed up and into the upper track and turned to the locked position. In this locked position, the door cannot be slid open or lifted. The bolt in the upper track prevents the sliding action and the top of the bolt hitting the upper track as it is being lifted, prevents the door from being lifted any further.

Sliding Glass Door with Barrel Bolt Solution

Exterior Sliding Door Bolt Mount

Some door manufacturers are making sliding patio door units with the sliding door on the outside of the unit. The theory is that when the wind blows against the door it will force the sliding door against the interior door and create a natural draft block. However, this design makes it difficult to secure the door in the manner which has been described. Some creativity may have to be taken to secure this exterior door from burglary. It may be possible to use the barrel lock described above by mounting it sideways and inserting the barrel into a hole drilled into the face of the sliding door. Use caution to not drill into the glass edge. As has been stated in the beginning of the textbook, think like a thief on how this door might be bypassed and then concentrate on the solution.

Sliding doors can also be purchased with interlocking deadbolts installed from the factory. These are very good locking systems, but they are expensive. They are manufactured to meet building codes for sliding door systems that will be installed in upper stories of multiple level apartment complexes. The downside is that they must be ordered this way when the home is being built or with remodeling.

Finally, if the decision on what type of patio door to purchase and install is being made during the design stage the home or building owner may want to consider a French style door that swings in and is constructed like a normal door. These doors can be fitted with traditional deadbolt locks which are still the best option for any door. Pending a review of fire codes, they are also best for business doors.

REAR DOOR – STANDARD IN-SWING

These items contained in this section replicate those from the front door, as they will for the remaining entry doors.

EXTERIOR CELLAR – GROUND LEVEL DOORS

These types of doors can be found on rural farm homes. As implied they lead to either an enclosed cellar or a basement. The doors are angled at about a 30-degree tilt. They lift and over to fall back toward the ground. For security they require a concrete foundation with hardware that is in good condition. The bolts that connect the hardware to the doors must be of the carriage type. These bolts, sometimes called stove bolts, must have round heads to prevent a burglar from simply unscrewing the bolts from the exterior. The same bolts must be on whatever locking device is securing the doors. As the locks on these doors can be of various formats thinking like a thief as you view the lock is the best method of determining if it is an adequate lock.

WINDOWS – SINGLE OR DOUBLE HUNG

Single or double-hung windows are the slide-by up and down windows. Only the lower window moves on single-hung windows while double-hung allow both windows to move. Their locking mechanism is usually the turn latch located in the middle of the window on the sill. Burglars have defeated this standard factory lock from the outside by inserting a butter knife in between the center window frames. The blade is forced against the thumb latch and worked back until it is turned completely past the locking point. The window can now be raised relatively silently. Supplemental window locks will lock securely and keep a burglar out, but the locks must be engaged for them to work. Key operated locks work fine but are not needed if a good non-locking supplemental lock is installed. A window that is painted shut and cannot be opened by the homeowner from the inside is also not secure. A burglar can easily force this window open by inserting a screwdriver into the lower frame and prying up. While this damages the wood frame this does not concern the burglar.

Single Hung Window

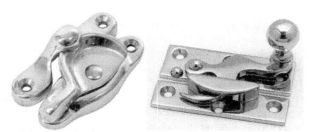

Standard Window Lock   **Secure Window Lock**

If the addition of supplemental locks is not desirable or possible there is another option. That prevention recommendation is the same as for the sliding glass doors. Where the two windows meet in the center, at each frame end, the homeowner should drill a hole. The same type of duplex nail can be inserted to 'lock' the windows in place. For ventilation, the lower window can be opened about four inches and a new hole re-drilled into the new height. You would then move the nail to this new hole. This allows ventilation without the risk of the burglar opening the window any further. Caution must be exercised to prevent the drill bit from drilling into the actual glass within the window frame. However, be aware that this recommendation will only work for hung windows that do not tilt in for cleaning. These newer style tilt-in windows can be forcefully pulled inward, right out of the frame, by the homeowner. But this very design means that the nail in the sash will not work. That's because if the burglar pushes on the window frame from the outside the window and nail will simply pop right out of the frame and into the house. Furthermore, the burglar, anticipating the crashing window, can react quickly enough to grab it before it crashes inside. One solution for this is the installation of supplemental keyed locking hardware on the center sash. This locking hardware would secure the two window panes together and prevent the opening of either unit. However, the ventilation option is also eliminated.

Hole Drilled in Corner of Window   Ventilation Hole Drilled 4" Up

There is another higher tech solution. Inexpensive standalone alarm sensors can be attached to either side of the window frame with double sided tape or even Velcro. When the window is opened even an inch a loud piercing sound emanates from the device alerting the homeowner and scaring off the intruder. The sensor is attached to either the window or the window frame. The other component, the small magnet, is attached to the opposite window part. When the window is opened the separation between the sensor and the magnet creates the alarm. The sensor should be attached at the top of the lower window unit (in the same area as where you would drill a hole for a nail when using that option).

For protection with the window open for ventilation the following solution is offered using the same alarm device. First, the window should be opened no more than 4" to allow for ventilation without burglar access to the device. That means that either the magnet or the sensor attached to the window has also moved up the same distance and is no longer aligned with its mating part on the window frame. However, if the mating part on the frame were attached using a piece of Velcro that part, either the magnet or the sensor, can easily be removed and reattached 4" higher to match up with the piece on the window, offering the same degree of protection even in a ventilation mode. Sensors like this can be found online (search for Window or Door Alarm) and at larger home improvement retailers.

Window and Door Alarm

A variety of commercial locking devices also exist for this type of window. They can be found at larger hardware stores and retail locksmiths. Newer windows of the single or double hung type may be adequately protected with manufacturer's hardware. However, burglars have used brute strength to force the window past these protection devices, defeating their intent. Using additional add-on security devices is the best way to protect entry through these windows.

WINDOWS – CASEMENT

Casement windows are windows that crank out. They are the most secure form of operable window when they are in the closed and latched position. The latching portion is concealed in the window frame and cannot be easily accessed from the exterior. They are, however, the least secure when they are even slightly open. This slight opening allows the burglar a handhold with only his fingers inserted. Then, with little effort, the burglar can pull and strip the turning gear that operates the window. With the gear stripped the window swings open, allowing complete access. Entry can be made without any damage by simply grabbing the open window and vigorously jiggling it. This action will turn the gear and allow the window to slowly open. With one exception there are no commercial retrofit locking devices for these windows and nothing that would be attractive enough to be acceptable to most homeowners. The one exception is a device made in Europe. Readers can research it at www.jackloc.com. The photo, below, shows an example of the Jackloc. In the author's opinion it would be very effective on both the single and double hung windows (need two for double hung) and would also work well on the casement window. The Jackloc or alarm sensors would offer ventilation for casement windows.

Casement Window

Jackloc Window Lock

WINDOWS – SLIDING

These types of windows are very difficult to properly secure. Like sliding glass doors, they lift out and are easily removed. Unlike sliding doors both windows are movable and thus cannot be secured by simply locking the center mullions onto each other. This means that a burglar can easily pry up on either window unit and remove one or both from the exterior. There are no after-market devices that will properly secure these windows. The only physical security measure is to replace this window with one of the other types described above. However, using an alarm sensor, as previously described, would protect this window by detecting an intruder entry.

Sliding Glass Window

Ventilation pinning would NOT prevent these windows from being lifted and out of the track as both window units would simply lift and out together as one unit. It should not be recommended to any client or homeowner on the ground level of a structure.

WINDOWS – LOUVERED (JALOUSIE)

Jalousie windows are frequently found in warmer climates and on summer cottages. These windows are narrow, horizontal, overlapping panes of glass that crank out at a 45-degree angle. Frequently found on exterior doors, they are inserted in grooves and held in place by bent metal tabs. Opening the tabs allows the pane to be pulled out of its frame, which is what burglars do. As the tabs are on the outside of the window they are readily available to the burglar. Prevention can be as drastic as replacing the door to as simple as removing the panes of glass, running a bead of glue in the groove and re-inserting the pane of glass. This requires the burglar to break the glass, something most burglars wish to avoid. In the event of a broken window the glass and glue can be chiseled out with a screwdriver.

Jalousie Window

WINDOWS – TILT/TURN

This is a very common window in Europe but is seldom seen in the U.S. However, the benefits of this window may allow it to become more popular in our area. This window has hardware that allows it to work in two positions. First, by a twist of the handle it can be tilted in from the top about 6" for ventilation. Turning the handle, the opposite way allows the window to be swung completely into the home on the side mounted hinges. The design of the tilt function makes this a naturally effective security barrier. The opening denies a burglar entry while still allowing ventilation. To swing it into the interior of the house the window must first be closed. While they cost more than traditional windows the improved security side benefit may make this window an attractive option for new or remodeled homes. Note that no window, by itself, is burglar proof. Even tilt/turn windows can be manipulated from the outside using a tool (such as a coat hanger) over the top of the open window and grabbing the handle and turning. Therefore, anytime a window is going to be left open for ventilation purposes a form of alarm sensor is always recommended.

Tilt Turn Window Configurations

WINDOWS – BASEMENT

The first thing to understand about basement windows is that they are only designed to allow light into the basement. At the same time juvenile burglars have found basement windows to be an ideal entry point. Standard basement windows are also not intended to allow egress in an emergency. Our security solutions are not intended for egress either. However, that option is offered in the security survey checklist.

If recommending security bars, the escape key is designed to still allow the occupant an opportunity to escape if needed. The 40" distance matches the distance specified for deadbolts. However, don't place it too far away that smoke would overcome the person before they could reach it.

Glass blocks are a very good option for security as they are cemented in place and still allow light to penetrate. Polycarbonate, a plastic material that is 300 times stronger than glass is also a good solution provided it is properly anchored. Obviously, no one is going to escape out of this window if these options are used.

Basement Glass Block Window

HOUSE NUMBERS

This simple item makes sure that emergency response personnel can find the homeowner more quickly. They should be at least 3" high. However, check with local ordinances as some local jurisdictions require 4" high letters.

WINDOW AIR CONDITIONER

Window air conditioners are installed from the inside of the house. They are placed on the window sill and then the edges are supposed to be screwed into the window frame to keep it from falling back into the home. Many people simply pull the window down to hold the appliance in place and forget about the screws. Burglars know this installation technique. With a push of their shoulder they can drive the screws out or simply push the air conditioner into the room allowing easy access.

Using an eyebolt secured to both the A/C unit and the house wall, connecting them with heavy chain and a padlock, will prevent the unit from being pushed into the house. Other security options are displayed below.

Custom Cage **Fasten Additional Screws to The Top Rim**

GARAGE – ATTACHED

Because attached garages lead to entry doors into the home they need to be secured like any other doors. This includes deadbolt locks, high security strikeplates, and 3" screws.

TELEPHONE ACCESS BOX

If there is no alarm system connected to the house there really is no security issue other than someone cutting the phone lines prior to a physical attack, not the normal issues facing homeowners, and thus a remote situation. However, the phone box on the rear or side of the home can be opened with a screwdriver and accessed. Thus, a neighbor or prowler could open the box at 2:00 am and plug his own phone into the jack inside the box. This would allow him to dial toll numbers or pay per call numbers and have them charged to the homeowner with no evidence left behind. The phone jack is there for the phone company and the resident to check their lines during trouble calls. Simply installing a padlock will prevent this access.

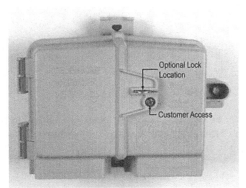

Telephone Access Box

If an alarm system is tied into the phone system the stated recommendations in the survey form should reduce the chance of someone accessing and cutting the phone lines prior to a burglary.

Note: While not all items on the survey forms that are included at the end of the book have been covered in this textbook they have all been worded to allow a basic interpretation of the required minimum standards. This should allow the reader the ability to complete a basic physical security survey based on the textbook content and the forms included at the end of this textbook.

Also, even with the implementation of all suggested recommendations there is no guarantee that an intruder will not gain access to any home.

References

http://www.wbdg.org/resources/bollard.php

http://www.wikihow.com/Burglarproof-Your-Doors

http://www.businesssecurityinformation.com/2011/05/security-lessons-learned/

http://www.jewelers.org/retail/r_educationtraining/elearning/jewelry-articles/security/detail.php?ID=1688

http://learningcenter.statefarm.com/safety-2/work/protect-your-business-from-burglary/
I got robbed. Oberbeck, E.B. // Cosmopolitan; Oct90, Vol. 209 Issue 4, p122

Profitability through facility protection.
Hertig, Christopher A. // Security: Solutions for Enterprise Security Leaders; Feb98, Vol. 35 Issue 2, p54

Make Sure To Secure Your Home First.; Furger, Roberta // Tennessee Tribune; 12/2/2010, Vol. 21 Issue 48, p3B

Home security.; Story, Richard David // New York; 4/18/94, Vol. 27 Issue 16, p48

Protect Your Business From Rooftop Cat Burglars; by Paul Davis

Protect Your Business from Professional Burglars; by Paul Davis

Thinking Like A Burglar; By Harold Achiando; EzineArticles; April 27, 2012

http://www.securityforsmallbusiness.com/blog/access-control-for-small-business-owners.aspx
Security Systems: Protection Against Burglary; by: Chris Lontok

15 Steps to Achieving Business Burglary/Theft Prevention; By Jerry T.

Home Guides; How to Fortify a Door; by Herb Kirchhoff, Demand Media

Chapter Six

Robbery Prevention

Robbery Prevention Performance Objectives:

- Identify proper opening hours procedures
- Explain proper operating hours procedures
- Identify proper closing hours procedures
- Explain the issues and solutions related to bank deposits
- Explain how to handle after hours emergency calls
- Explain the different robbery alarm options
- Cite and explain the appropriate robbery reactive measures
- Describe the issue associated with a business owned weapon
- Explain what retailers should do while waiting for law enforcement arrival
- Cite the two keys to surviving a robbery

Introduction

Robbery is defined as the theft of property from a person by force or the threat of force. Often the media, and even some law enforcement officers, incorrectly identify a burglary as a 'robbery'. This confusion is even greater for the general public. The main difference between the two is that burglary generally involves taking property from a structure while in a robbery property is generally taken from a person by use of or threat of force. As a building is an inanimate object it cannot be robbed through a threat of force. (Think about trying to threaten a house with violence unless it dumps out its valuables). Likewise, a person cannot be 'burglarized'.

Robbery is a crime that is impossible to prevent. If we choose to live in a free and open society we will live with this threat. However, this does not mean that we cannot reduce the opportunity for robbery situations to occur. The remainder of this unit will focus on various prevention methods and on suspect identification and apprehension techniques.

Prevention Techniques

OPENING HOURS PROCEDURES

Prevention of robbery begins with opening the business in the morning. Robbers have been known to wait around a corner or even inside a burglarized building and attack when the owner enters. The following procedure should be part of any routine opening of a business.

When the first employee arrives at a business, that employee is thinking about the day ahead and is not necessarily concentrating on the surrounding environment. The robber may take advantage of this and ambush the arriving employee. Escorted into the business, the robber may force the employee to hand over the money or open the safe. Alternatively, the robber waits with his hostage for the employee with the secure box keys or safe combination to arrive. All employees unwittingly walk into the situation. Under the circumstances, the best outcome is if the robber takes only the money and no one is harmed.

Employees can control such a scenario by implementing a pre-planned opening hour procedure. The first step is to never open a store by oneself. Two employees must always be present. If an employee arrives early then that employee should wait in their vehicle with the doors locked until the second employee arrives. When both are in the parking lot the business opening process can begin. A suggested format would operate like this.

Both employees meet briefly before one enters the business and the other remains in his/her vehicle. At this meeting they both agree on an "all clear" signal. This step is the most critical part of the procedure. It involves identifying a specific gesture that tells the waiting employee that everything is okay. Some businesses, financial institutions, currently use such a procedure. The problem with their procedure is that it is rarely altered. The same signal is used daily for as long as a year before being changed. A robber who is "casing" a business can quickly figure out that the waiting employee leaves his/her vehicle only after the same drapes are opened or light turned on. Having knowledge of the "all clear" signal the robber will burglarize the building sometime during the night. Once inside the building the burglar will wait for the first employee to enter the building in the morning and force the employee to give the correct "all clear" signal. Thus, using the same "all clear" signal continuously, defeats the whole purpose of having a signal.

Proper "all clear" signals begin in the parking lot. They are decided on the spur of the moment by the two cooperating employees and are different each time. It may be as simple as touching the right ear, waving the left arm, holding up a notebook, or carrying a coat over the shoulder. The critical part is that it be unpredictable. The employee enters the building through an entrance that is visible from the waiting employee's position. Should the entering employee be accosted the waiting employee would, of course, immediately call the police. If a cell phone is not available then the waiting employee should know where the nearest public telephone is located. (911 calls are always free). Before such a call is made, the waiting employee should have memorized the address or cross streets of the business location.

Employee Entrance Hidden Behind Storage Area
Employee Was Robbed at Entrance Opening Restaurant

Once the entering employee is inside, the employee should quickly scan each room and area for signs of burglary or intruders. Once the building is deemed to be secure the pre-arranged daily signal can be given. *Where* the signal is delivered is also a critical element. If the entering employee were accosted inside the business, the waiting employee would not know this. The robber could have a gun pointed at the first employee's head and be threatening to shoot if the wrong signal is given. Prudence for one's life would dictate that the correct signal be given and the unsuspecting waiting employee would also enter the business, negating the entire all-clear signal process. As such, the all-clear signal needs one more aspect added to it. That is that the signal must be given *outside* of the business building. The entering employee should *always* step away from the building at a distance from 3 to 6 feet and then give the signal. This should occur regardless of the weather conditions outside. If the robber has cased the business prior to the robbery he will see this action repeatedly. This alone may well prevent a robbery from occurring.

In the event the robber recognizes that all-clear signals are used he/she may tell the hostage/employee to use the correct signal or the employee will be harmed or killed. The employee should indicate to the robber that the correct signal involves stepping outside the building. The robber should be told that if this part of the signal (stepping outside) does not happen then the waiting employee would call the police. The robber might be reminded that if he/she is aware of an all-clear signal then he/she has previously watched this routine. The only way the robber can gain cooperation is if he/she allows the signal to be given correctly, outside the door. Of course, the armed robber will likely reinforce his/her threat of harm if the employee giving the all-clear signal does not immediately re-enter the business. The hostage/employee should readily agree and then, with the robber's permission, step outside. He/she should position him/herself to give the signal and then immediately run diagonally away from the entrance to the closest building corner or position of cover, out of sight. The robber must now make an immediate decision. Does he/she attempt to follow up on this threat (now that the hostage is gone) or does he/she make their own escape? This is also a decision that must be evaluated by the hostage/employee at the time of the incident. It must be made clear to the reader that employing this tactic may result in personal danger to the hostage/employee. Running from the scene will certainly increase the hostage taker's anxiety and anger. Their response may not be a rational thought of escape but rather a violent reaction toward their hostage who has run away. Common sense and an individual evaluation must be made before exercising such an escape attempt. The employee must consider their physical condition as well as the potential restrictions of clothing and high-heeled shoes. Additionally, the running surface must be evaluated. If there is snow, ice, or gravel present the prudent thing to do may be to not attempt an escape on foot. Finally, if the hostage/employee does decide to risk the chance of running the employee waiting in the car should immediately drive off as well. That employee should either call the police and/or pick up the other employee if he/she is hiding behind cover and it can be done safely.

In the event a robber has *not* cased the business first, and the first employee is accosted inside the business, the robber may not know the second employee is waiting. The second employee should recognize that the normal clearing time is overdue and should call the business phone number. If there is no answer the employee should call the police. If there is an answer the outside employee should call the inside employee by the wrong name to see how the employee reacts. No reaction indicates a problem. The outside employee should then immediately call the police.

These prevention techniques reduce the possibility of a robbery in most situations. However, each occurrence is unique in its nature and variations in responses may be required depending on circumstances. The overall goal is survival during the robbery.

BUSINESS HOURS PROCEDURES

The most common time for a robbery to occur is during the regular work hours. Businesses are concentrating on operating their business and are not focused on the possibility of a robbery. The following guidelines offer prevention assistance.

Store Windows

Robbers do not want to be seen from outside the business. Stores that have their windows covered up with sale banners and posters run a greater risk of robbery if the robber thinks passing pedestrians or patrolling law enforcement may not see him/her. All windows offering a view of the cash register should remain clear always.

Cluttered Store Windows Obscure Vision from Outside

Cash Register Placement

The cash register should be located next to a front facing window. This requires a robber to commit the act in front of potential passing pedestrians and witnesses. While the argument can be made that it allows the robber a faster exit, the possibility of visibility is a much greater threat to a robber.

Cash Register Directly Inside Entrance

Money Handling Procedures

Even if a robbery occurs, the loss of money can be reduced through pre-planning. The first consideration is the storage of cash. Several things can be done. The first is to not keep all spare cash in one location. Keep only enough in the register to handle typical transactions and make sure that all large bills are immediately put into a safe. Larger cash reserves can be kept locked in the office for quick access. (However, this money should be kept under lock and key always to prevent office looting during staged gang type customer disruptions.)

Cash that is to be taken to a financial institution or cash not needed for customer use must be placed in a safe. The best type is a drop safe. This allows cashiers to bundle the cash and drop it in a slot in the top of a safe. The safe is locked always and the cashier does not have the combination. In the event of a robbery, a sign with bold letters on the front of the safe should announce that the cashier does not have the combination to the safe.

Drop Safe with Money Slot

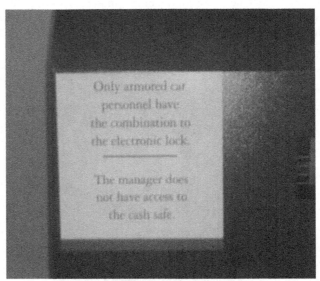

Only armored car
personnel have
the combination to
the electronic lock.

———————

The manager does
not have access to
the cash safe.

Sign on Safe Indicating Employees Do Not Have Combination

Bank Deposits

Either in lieu of or in addition to storage of cash in a safe, frequent bank deposits should be made. This transfers the risk to the financial institution. However, there is risk in the transfer as well. Robbers who are watching the business may identify a pattern of deposits. Therefore, deposits should be made at different times of the day. Additionally, your traffic route should be varied. Both precautions will make it difficult for a robber to plan an attack based on prediction. If a business has a consistently large deposit it would be wise to consider the services of an armored vehicle service.

The final note on deposits is the use of financial institution deposit bags. Using these bags in public advertises the contents. When carrying the bags in public areas they should be placed inside a normal business shopping bag. This would appear no different from any other customer exiting the store.

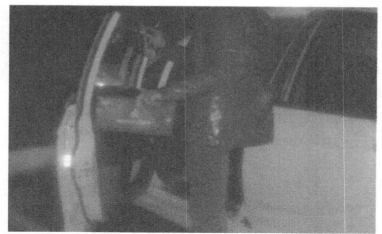

Actual Covert Photo of Employee Leaving Business with Bank Bag

CLOSING PROCEDURES

In closing a business for the evening, the same basic opening hour procedures, without the signal, should be followed, but in reverse. One person precedes the last person out of the business and is watched while they safely enter their vehicle. The second person then vacates the business and the person in the vehicle watches while they enter their vehicle. Should the second person be approached after exiting the business the person in the vehicle should sound the vehicle horn to attract attention and possibly deter the potential robber. However, the first person should not exit their vehicle in an attempt to assist the second person. That simply puts two people in danger. Sounding the horn and turning the headlights on to illuminate the scene should drive off the trespasser. Afterwards, they can render aid as needed, as well as be a witness to the act.

AFTER HOURS EMERGENCY CALLS

On occasion the owner of a business may receive a late-night phone call from the police about a burglary or incident at their store. The owner may be asked to respond to secure the business or assist in the investigation. There are legitimate calls such as these that do occur. However, robbers pretending to be the police may also place these calls. Their hope is that in one's sleep induced state a business owner will not think clearly and will respond quickly to his/her business. Once the business owner arrives he/she is accosted and forced to open the store and the safe. On occasion high profile businesspersons have been kidnapped for ransom and even murdered when lured out of their homes in this manner.

Prevention procedures require that the original caller not be questioned. However, after hanging up the business owner should call the police department, explain the situation, and verify that the police did call. The dispatcher should be able to verify the legitimacy of the call or have the police investigate it. Even with a legitimate call a person should not exit the vehicle until a marked police car is present. Potential robbers may simply get the business owner's name out of the phone book or, during business hours, they may have copied the name and number from a list of employees that is posted in plain view next to the business phone. The owner or manager's name is frequently listed first. On occasion this task is made even easier by posting the name and emergency number in plain sight in the window at the front entrance, something that is strongly discouraged.

Public View Emergency Phone Numbers

IDLE CONVERSATION CAUTIONS

Many business employees enjoy a time of mutual companionship after working hours and will congregate at a local pub to relax before heading to their homes. If a person were to enter one of these establishments for the express purpose of listening to the conversations around him or her they would find that many of the patrons would be discussing their employer. It seems to be a fact of human nature that, at times, these conversations would also be critical of their workplace. Talking about the negative aspects of one's job frequently encourages other employees to speak about their concerns with their employer. Problems arise for the employer when employees speak about issues that may attract the attention of would-be thieves.

Items that attract thieves relate to anything about money. At times employees may complain about their meager salaries and compare it to the amount that is kept in the safe. Or the complaint may relate to extravagant spending on original artwork in executive offices or the seeming lack of concern for employees who make large money deposits from their private vehicles. Maybe the talk is about the lack of security in securing prescription drugs in a medical field or the non-secured storage of money. Any talk relative to money will attract the attention of those who are interested in relieving the company and/or individual of that money. This means the taking of the money may occur in the form of a burglary, or may directly affect the employee in the form of a robbery during business hours. There is also the possibility of being kidnapped and taken hostage for the money or property. Identifying where the employee works is as simple as following the employee home and then to work in the morning or simply befriending them at the drinking establishment and innocently asking them where they work.

Prevention methods are more difficult to control in these situations. The employer will appear overbearing if after-business hours conversational topics are restricted. However, identifying the risks to the employee as the primary concern of the employer may give some credibility to any such suggestion.

ROBBERY ALARMS

Robbery alarms are only useful in notifying the police of a robbery in progress or that has just occurred. It is rare to have the robber still at the premises when the police arrive. However, the quick notification and arrival of the police increases the potential for a quick apprehension if the robber or his/her vehicle were clearly visible.

Robbery alarms are available in three forms. The first is the typical central station or police monitored alarm. A concealed robbery switch is activated by hand or foot and a silent signal is transmitted to the receiving central station. Few law enforcement agencies monitor private businesses today, with the possible exception of financial institutions. The private central monitoring station receiving the signal relays it to the police department who then dispatches a police vehicle in response to the alarm. The business with the alarm must pay a monthly monitoring fee to the central monitoring company for this service.

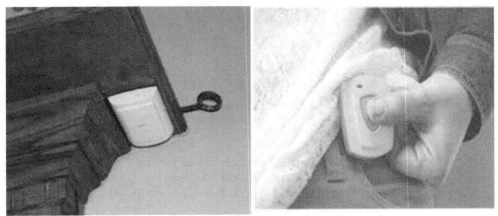

Two Types of Robbery Alarm Activation Devices

Another form of alarm signal is fee free. It is called the "buddy alarm". A robbery alarm is installed in each of two adjacent businesses. When the alarm is activated in one business the signal travels to the neighboring business instead of to a monitoring company. The received signal may be a flashing light or buzzer or combination of the two. The important thing is that the neighboring business employees know that they are to contact the police and inform them of a robbery next door. This does require that the businesses share the same business hours. The only cost is the installation of the alarm system.

The final form of alarm is a police stakeout alarm. Typically called a "Varda" alarm, after a common manufacturer's brand, this alarm is used when a series of robberies has occurred and there is an emerging pattern. The system is owned by the police department but many agencies do not own one.

Once the police can identify the next likely target the police install the Varda alarm inside the business. This alarm is directly connected to police patrol vehicle radio frequencies. When the alarm is activated the signal is immediately dispatched over the police radio frequency. Area patrol vehicles can respond much more quickly and are more likely to apprehend the robber at the premises. Because these alarms tie up a police frequency, however, they are used only when the next crime target can be accurately forecast.

SURVEILLANCE CAMERA SYSTEMS

Security camera systems offer a deterrent to robbery by their ability to later identify a robber. The most effective of these systems includes a monitor at the cashier's station that clearly shows the customer. This verifies the validity of the camera system to any potential robbers. The actual recording unit must be secured against theft or damage and the recording format should be compatible with common playback units for police evidence.

Security Video Monitor for Customer Viewing

Increasingly, robbers, recognizing the damaging evidence, are demanding the disk or recording device. Therefore, a dummy DVD player should be installed under the store counter. It should be turned on and a blank DVD inserted. During a robbery, this is the DVD that should be ejected and offered to the robber.

Reactive Measures

When the preventative measures fail to stop a robber from entering a business, there are still employee reactive factors to be considered. The following list of items attempts to address these concerns.

REMAIN CALM

While this sounds difficult to do, in a real situation it is possible if you can concentrate on remaining passive. Some people panic in the immediate moments of the situation because their survival instincts take over. It is when these instincts are ignored, or employees begin to think about how to stop the robbery, that people are hurt. The robber is usually already nervous. Any hesitation on the part of the employee whether because of nervousness or bravado may provoke violence on the part of the robber.

OBEY COMMANDS

Listen carefully to what the robber requests and follow his/her instructions exactly. The robber has some plan in his/her mind and expects that it will be followed. If the victim does not exactly comply with the request the robber may suspect some form of trap. Remember that this is a frequently fragile ego desiring to be in charge. As an example, if the robber requests only the five, ten and twenty-dollar bills from the cash register, do not hand over the single dollar bills to be more cooperative. In the robber's mind the single bills may be tied to the alarm system and as a result the employee just activated the alarm. This may provoke the robber to potential violence.

DO NOT RESIST

Robbers have hurt many robbery victims because they have attempted to resist the robber. While occasional news accounts can be found describing how a victim successfully fought off a robber, the reports are news precisely because of how infrequently this succeeds. Physically resisting a robber is one of the surest methods of getting injured or killed. No piece of property is worth a life.

DO NOT VOLUNTEER INFORMATION

Sometimes in an attempt to be overly cooperative victims will volunteer the location of excess funds or a hidden safe. While this may please the robber, it increases the loss to the business and lengthens the time that the robber remains in the building. This exposes arriving customers and the clerk to additional danger. However, if the robber specifically asks for hidden money, it should be handed over. Having inside information about the source of hidden funds will be a clue to the robber's identity and assist the police in their investigation.

OBSERVATIONS

In an attempt to identify the robber, it is helpful to have the clerk observe specific features of the robber. This can be done without directly looking at the robber's face. Such items as tattoos on the hands or arms, unique rings or hand deformities may later be useful for identification purposes. Other items like thick glasses, a shaved head, earrings, scars and speech differences are all important identifying items. Height estimates can be made against the clerk's known height or a measuring scale on the doorframe. The type of container the money was put into is also helpful if the police later stop the robber and the container is visible on the seat or floor. While clothing can be changed, a description of what the robber was wearing at the time can lead to a possible suspect shortly after the crime has occurred. Finally, unless told to lie down or stay in place, following the robber to the door may help identify any vehicle that the robber may be driving.

CALL POLICE

As soon as practical, the police should be called. Many victims, after dialing 911, do not wait for questions on the phone. As soon as the phone is answered they insist on forging ahead with a convoluted explanation of the robbery. This ultimately delays the police response, as the critical items are not answered. After the police answer the telephone, the victim should simply inform the dispatcher that a robbery has occurred. The police will likely ask for the address first and any possible vehicle information. Then the victim may be put on hold. This is because the dispatcher must first alert patrol vehicles to the crime so that they may begin responding to the location. The dispatcher will then come back on the line to get additional information. The victim should wait for the questions to be asked before offering additional details. It would be helpful if the victim knew the directions of the street in front of the business. This would assist responding officers in searching for the suspect.

BUSINESS OWNED WEAPON

Occasionally, a victim who has been previously robbed decides to take things into his or her own hands. The victim may have purchased a gun for protection purposes against any future robberies. When the next robbery does occur, the victim finds him/herself with no opportunity to use the weapon while the robber is standing in front of him/her. The victim, in frustration, may run after the robber carrying the gun in their hand. What the victim would not know is that a passing pedestrian, witnessing the robbery, has possibly called the police. When the police arrive at the business they see a person with a gun running down the street and away from the crime scene. The police, thinking this is the suspect, order the running person to stop. The victim hears the identity of the police and turns for help. Tragically, the victim might now be pointing a gun at the police who, thinking they are about to be fired on by the robber, may shoot and possibly kill the victim. This factual incident could easily have been prevented if the victim had stayed off the street with his or her own weapon.

Waiting for Police Arrival

While waiting for the police to arrive, the victim should lock the business doors. This prevents customers from coming in and creating diversions that may cause the victim to forget essential details.

Next, the victim should write down any details that they observed. The details can be written down on anything that is nearby. Even a store paper bag will work.

Anything touched by the robber should be preserved for fingerprint inspection. If a merchandise item was picked up, it should be left in place and covered with a bag. A folded bag could be placed over the counter where the robber placed his/her hand.

Any witnesses in the store should refrain from talking to each other. Sharing details with other witnesses of the robbery can contaminate memories. Witnesses should only speak to law enforcement officers.

Police Report

The initial amount of loss should not be reported to the police. It is the initial crime report that the media will report, including the amount lost. If another robber reads the news account and sees a large amount of money lost, along with a specific time and day of the week, it may encourage another robbery. Save the exact loss information for a follow-up police report that can be submitted the following day.

Summary

While robberies cannot be prevented, business owners can pre-plan strategies. The keys to surviving a robbery are simple: remain **calm and cooperate**.

Note, sample Robbery or Suspect Description Form, like those that follow, can be found on the internet via a search engine by using the same phrase. That would allow the reader to print a clean copy that could be used for duplication and training purposes.

Suspect Description Form

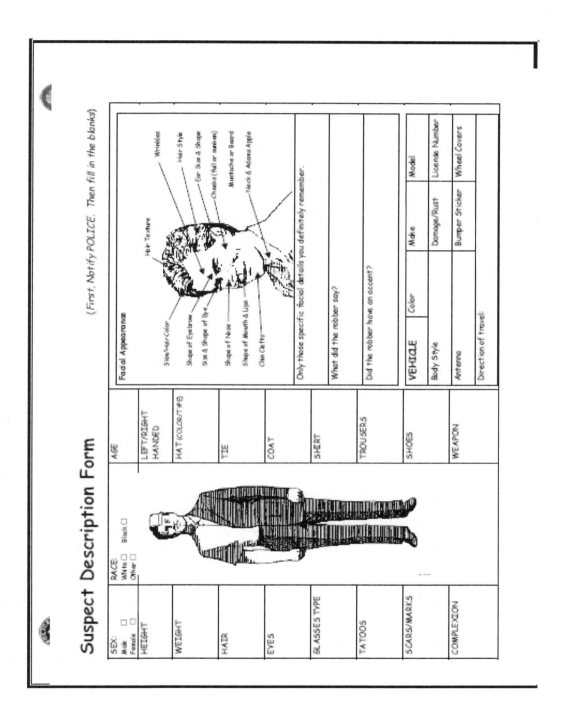

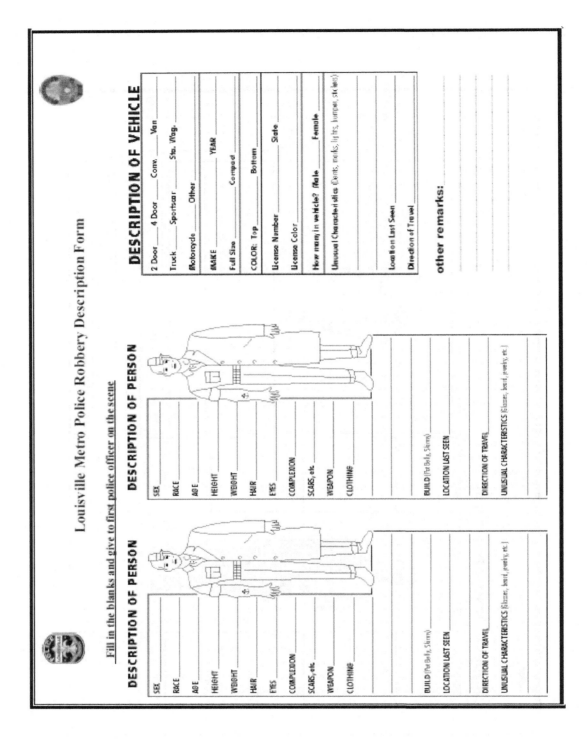

Louisville Metro Police Robbery Description Form

Fill in the blanks and give to first police officer on the scene

Courtesy of the Louisville Metro Police Department

References

"Robbery Prevention, Response and Aftermath Techniques." Security Education Systems <
http://www.nvo.com/ses/robberyprevention1responsesaftermathtechniqu/>

"Robbery Facts." Crime Doctor <http://www.crimedoctor.com/robbery1.htm>

http://learningcenter.statefarm.com/safety-2/work/protect-your-business-from-robbery/

"Robbery Reaction Tips." Rutgers University
<http://crimeprevention.rutgers.edu/crime/robbery/business%20robbery/reactiontips.htm>

Robbery Prevention Tips for Businesses "Making Your Business Safer"
By Charles Montaldo http://crime.about.com/od/prevent/qt/prevent_robbery.htm

Texas Department of Insurance Division of Workers' Compensation
"Small Business Crime Prevention Guide" (pg. 3-4)
http://www.tdi.texas.gov/pubs/videoresource/ghspscrimepreventi.pdf

Forsyth County Sheriff's Office Crime Prevention
"Business Watch"
http://www.forsythsheriff.org/units-mainmenu-121/crime-prevention-mainmenu-130/business-watch

Montaldo, Charles (2012). Robbery Prevention Tips for Businesses. Retrieved 4/27/12 from
http://crime.about.com/od/prevent/qt/prevent_robbery.htm.

City of Tempe Crime Prevention Unit (2012). Robbery Awareness Tips. Retrieved 4/27/12 from
http://www.tempe.gov/cpu/robbery.htm

School of Criminal Justice at Rutgers University (2012). Robbery Prevention Tips. Retrieved
4/27/12 from http://crimeprevention.rutgers.edu/crime/robbery/business%20robbery/preventiontips.htm

Armed Robbery Awareness . N.p., 2011. Web. 20 Apr. 2012. <http://armedrobberyawareness.com/>.

Montaldo, Charles. "Make Your Business Safer." Robbery Prevention Tips for Businesses. Los Angeles
Police Department, Sept. 2011. Web. 22 Apr. 2012.
<http://crime.about.com/od/prevent/qt/prevent_robbery.htm>.

"What all Employees Should Know." BUSINESS SECURITY. Kansas.gov, n.d. Web. 20 Apr. 2012.
<http://www.accesskansas.org/kbi/info/docs/pdf/Business20Robbery%20Prevention.pdf>.

Montaldo, C. (2012). Robbery prevention tips for businesses, make your business safer. Retrieved from
http://crime.about.com/od/prevent/qt/prevent_robbery.htm

U.S. Department of Justice, Federal Bureau of Investigation. (2012). Uniform crime reporting statistics

Sheriff Bradshaw, R. (Writer) (n.d.). Robber prevention and awareness training [Web] PowerPoint
Presentation.

http://bjs.ojp.usdoj.gov/ucrdata/Search/Crime/State/TrendsInOneVar.cfm?NoVariables=Y&CFID=48500
335&CFTOKEN=12341737

http://www.securitydefensesolutions.com/

http://law.jrank.org/pages/1986/Robbery-Characteristics-offenders.html

http://blogs.ajc.com/view-from-cop/2010/08/18/robbery-prevention-tips-for-business-owners/

http://crime.about.com/od/prevent/qt/prevent_robbery.htm

www.pbso.org/.../RobberyUnit/BankRobberyPrevetion - ROBBERY PREVENTION AND AWARENESS TRAINING

http://law.jrank.org/pages/1986/Robbery-Characteristics-offenders.html

http://www.adt.com/small-business-security/learning-center/security-tips/robbery-prevention

www.pbso.org

http://www.portlandonline.com/police/index.cfm?a=31555&c=29869

Chapter Seven

Intrusion Alarm Systems

Intrusion Alarm System Performance Objectives:

- Describe the components of an alarm intrusion system
- Explain the concept of building protection layers
- Explain the concept of a property threat analysis
- Describe the types and operating principles of perimeter alarm intrusion sensors
- Describe the types and operating principles of area intrusion sensors
- Describe the types and operating principles of point detection sensors
- Identify appropriate alarm intrusion sensor applications

Introduction

Commercial businesses are increasingly relying on burglar alarm systems in the protection of their property. This chapter will educate the reader on the basics of building alarm systems and sensors that are most commonly installed in businesses. Additionally, there will be a study of how much protection to put into a building related to building content value and the sophistication of the expected burglar.

Prior to an in-depth discussion of alarm systems, it is important to note one thing. Alarm systems have no function in the actual protection of property. Their entire purpose is the detection of intruders. If alarm systems function properly it is only because the physical protection of a building failed. The first line of defense should never rest on alarm systems alone. Proper physical security may deter or allow detection of an intruder because they are committed to spending time outside of the building and in the public eye as they attempt to defeat the physical measures. That being said, some buildings are too old, too large, too remote, too complicated in their features, or would simply cost too much to properly secure by physical means alone. Additionally, the contents of these buildings may be of such high value that they would attract the attention of professional burglars. It is at that point that an alarm system should be considered to supplant the existing physical security.

Alarm System Components

There are four main components of any burglar alarm system. They are 1) Control Panel, 2) Communication Transmission, 3) Sensor, 4) Annunciator.

CONTROL PANEL

The control panel is the heart of the system. All other components are connected to it and interact with each other. The control panel houses all wire connections, a backup power system failure battery, telephone or radio communications circuitry, and processes authorized users. When an intruder enters a protected premise, it is the control panel that determines which sensor is in alarm and communicates the entry to the outside world.

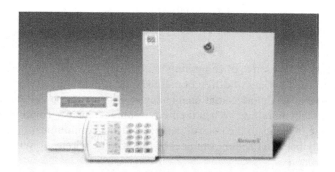

Intrusion System Key Pad and Control Panel

An integral part of the control panel is the keypad or key switch that arms or disarms the alarm system. A keypad allows the authorized user to arm the system at the close of business and disarm it when they arrive to open the business. Keypads, like a digital phone dial, typically have a standard 12 button configuration. Additional functions are performed through buttons variously labeled 'enter', 'panic', 'function', 'clear', etc.

Keypads also allow the use of different entry codes to later identify who made entry and on what date and time. While it may be mounted directly to the face of the control panel the keypad is usually mounted on a wall somewhere near the employee entrance/exit and connected by a direct wire. This location allows the employee to enter the door and disarm the system within a prescribed time before the system sends out an intrusion alert.

The most common form of arming and disarming a system today is via a keypad. However, in very simple or older systems a key switch performed the same function. The key switch would be mounted in the door frame, usually on the exterior. The employee would turn off the alarm system from the outside prior to entering the premises. The key switch is rarely used today because of the susceptibility to attack or defeat on the exterior of the building.

COMMUNICATION TRANSMISSION

The control panel communicates with the intrusion sensors through either a **hard wire** or **wireless radio frequency**. A hard-wired installation means that each sensor, regardless of its location within the building is physically connected back to the control panel by multiple pairs of wire. The downside of this installation method is the labor cost associated with the running of the wires. Each wire must be run through ceilings and walls and around obstacles to connect the two components. This is usually the most time-consuming portion of the installation of any alarm system. Unforeseen internal wall obstacles can drive up the price or reduce the profit of the installer. The positive side of hardwired installations is they are usually extremely reliable when properly installed.

Wireless communication between the control panel and the sensors means that each sensor must have a radio transmitter built into it or connected to it to transmit its status back to the control panel. The control panel must also be fitted with a radio receiver to monitor each sensor in the system. The use of radio frequency sensors adds to the overall cost of each sensor and the control panel. However, the reduced installation cost brings the price of wireless alarm systems back into line with hardwired systems. The disadvantage of wireless systems is in two forms. First, some sensors are larger in size because of the additional electronics contained in the case. Secondly, signals can be blocked by metal building construction or by long distances from sensor to control panel. The advantage of wireless systems lies in their rapid installation time. One person can install an entire system in an average home in half a day. Similar labor cost savings are found in a business building. However, practical limitations on wireless signals mean that they are usually relegated to homes and small business buildings.

SENSORS

In general, sensors detect the presence of something or someone that was not there when the alarm system was armed. They do this in a variety of different methods; door or window opening, motion inside a room, breaking glass, and other unique situational changes. However, they all detect a change in the state of the environment inside the building. When their environment changes (motion, noise) they communicate that change in status to the control panel. Like the communication transmission, sensors can also be hardwired directly back to the control panel or they can be wireless. We will examine different sensors in the next section.

ANNUNCIATOR

The annunciator is nothing more than a signaling method to communicate an intrusion alarm to the outside world. The exact method of annunciation is at the discretion of the business owner. The various methods are described below.

The least complex of the annunciator signals is a simple **bell, horn, or siren**. Called the local alarm and connected to the control panel its only function is to blare out a loud sound indicating that the alarm system has been activated. Such a device would be attached to one or more of the exterior walls of a business high enough to not be reached by the intruder. The intent of the noise making annunciator is to draw the attention of the surrounding public and hope that someone will call the police to investigate. The one advantage of this system is that it does not cost the business owner any money in fees. The main disadvantage is the distinct possibility that the noise may be ignored and thus the burglary is never reported. So many people have tuned out audible alarms that many simply no longer bother to call at all and others may wait for 30 minutes or longer, after their patience level has worn thin, to report the alarm which has long ago allowed the intruder to escape.

Bell in Housing and Siren Annunciators

Another option for annunciation is a **central station alarm**. Once again, the control panel sends out a signal indicating that the alarm system has been activated. However, this signal is sent out over the business telephone lines to a 24-hour monitoring station that exists for the sole purpose of monitoring alarm systems. In this situation the monitoring station receives a signal that is displayed on a computer screen. The display indicates the name and address of the business. More sophisticated systems may indicate the location of the sensor that has gone into alarm. Also on the screen will be instructions on who to call and in what order. For instance, the owner may have the system programmed to read that the central station monitoring personnel must first call the business phone number to verify that the owner is not present and accidentally tripped the alarm. If someone answers inside the business a pre-arranged code word must be shared to clear the alarm or the police automatically called. In other situations, the owner has listed his or her cell phone number first. They may choose to personally investigate the alarm at their business prior to calling the police. If they do not answer a second number may be listed. If no one answers either phone the instructions may say only then shall law enforcement be called. Some security companies offer private security patrol and response services for an extra fee. In this case they would respond to the alarm location. If they discover a burglary then they would call law enforcement.

Central Alarm Station

The advantage to the monitored system is that the building owner is guaranteed that someone will be notified to respond and investigate the alarm. The disadvantage is that there is always a monthly fee for this service starting at $50 a month and up. Higher fees allow for 24-hour monitoring for robbery or panic alarms as well as burglary. Another option is monitoring of your closing and opening hours. If you close at 10:00 pm and you always activate your alarm by 10:15 pm any deviation from that would alert the monitoring station to call your business and inquire as to your status. If you were being held under duress during a robbery you would give a duress code word and the monitoring station would dispatch the police.

The final option for monitoring of alarm systems is a direct result of the availability of cellular smart phones. Increasingly business owners are programming their control panels to directly dial their cell phones during an alarm. The advantage to this system is that there are no monthly monitoring fees to be paid. Their cell phone operates as the monitoring company. The disadvantages relate to cell phone reception, distance from the business for response purposes, vacation travel, and a powered down cell phone. A hybrid version of this system now allows a business owner to monitor the interior of his business using interior business cameras connected to the internet. In response to an alarm notification on a smart phone the owner would type in an internet URL address into the smart phone or internet connected computer and thus would be able to view and direct a camera view right from the phone or computer keyboard. If someone were observed inside the building the owner could call the police directly and inform them of the burglary in progress.

There are several reasons for the existence of the various options. The local alarm option is obvious. It costs the owner nothing beyond the initial installation expense. The monitored alarms are more involved. The central station alarm has been around for decades and has proved its value in identifying burglaries many times. The monthly monitoring fees are a reasonable business expense but false alarms have driven change. Law enforcement agencies have determined that a great deal of their time is spent responding to burglar alarms that are false. In response to this some police agencies have begun to charge business owners false alarm fees. In some cases, they are even refusing to respond to any unverified burglar alarms. The impact on businesses is a direct hit to their profit margin. While the monitoring fee may be $50 a month the false alarm fee can start at that point and go up to $300 per incident upon the third false alarm. No response at all means no protection against burglars from alarm system notifications.

What is the solution? Alarm sensor manufacturers are engineering better sensors. Alarm installation companies are doing a better job of educating the end user/customer. End users are being held more accountable for forgetting to disarm their systems or for erroneous keypad entries. Alarm monitoring companies are calling their customers whose businesses or residences have incoming alarms before they call the police. Cameras and microphones in the alarmed business and connected to the monitoring company assist in verification of an intrusion before police are called. All of these measures are reducing the false alarm problem.

However, the solution of having the business owner respond to alarms is simply never recommended. While not common, owners have been found murdered at their business after responding to such alarms. Even when they respond with the intent of simply looking for evidence of a break in, encounters with burglars can still occur and the personal reactive emotion of finding evidence of a burglary can cause the owner to overreact with the result of taking things into their own hands. Ultimately law enforcement and the individual business owner must meet and come to some consensus on how to handle this issue at the local level.

Building Intrusion Detection Layers

Building interior alarm sensors are divided into three classes or layers. They are 1) Point, 2) Area, 3) Perimeter. This allows the store owner or alarm company system designer to concentrate the appropriate level of protection on those items or areas that are deemed most valuable or most vulnerable to attack or theft by an intruder. Planning out the proper design saves the end user money by not having to install unnecessary sensors and beefs up protection on more sensitive items or areas.

Let's take a simple example. Picture a retail store with typical doors and windows on the exterior, the inside public shopping portion of the business, and a private, internal office area, maybe containing a safe in the office. If the safe is one of the areas that are determined to be a likely target of the burglar then we would naturally want to devote more protection to it. We would do that with the class of sensors called *point* sensors. The purpose of point sensors is to concentrate on sending out an alarm if a specific object is moved or touched. Safe sensors exist for just that purpose.

However, we also have leather coats hanging on racks in the store. *Area* sensors would detect a person who hid inside the clothing racks until after closing and then emerged to steal the coats without breaking in.

Perimeter sensors would detect the typical burglar who breaks a window or pries open a door to gain entry. One or all levels of sensors may be needed or used depending on what kind of property we have in our building.

There is one consideration that must be kept in mind with detection zones. The earlier an alarm is sounded the more time security or law enforcement has to respond. If the only sensor used is inside Zone 3, the intruder may already be gone by the time someone responds. So, this must be considered when designing a building alarm system.

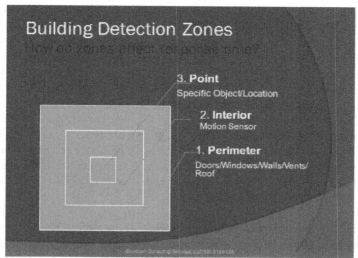

Building Alarm Detection Zones
Response Is Longest from Zone 3

Property Threat Analysis

Prior to suggesting or designing an alarm system or sensors on a building it is important to evaluate the type of property being protected. From the outside a warehouse looks much the same regardless of where it is located or what it houses. However, the warehousing of digital cameras would require a considerably different level of protection than would a warehouse containing handheld garden implements. It is important to ask questions of a building owner/lessee regarding current and future types of retail goods or property that will be housed inside of a building. Then the person designing or suggesting an alarm system can perform a more accurate threat analysis of the building and of the alarm system that should be installed or recommended. This is another example of wearing the three hats. An experienced or otherwise educated system designer, police officer, or security professional will have the background to better advise the building owner of the potential methods of burglary entry, the sensors best designed to detect such an entry, and the relative cost of goods being protected to the alarm system cost ratio.

During the analysis the anticipated type of burglar must also be examined. The higher priced the merchandise or property and the greater the amount of that property on one site the more likely a sophisticated burglar(s) will target the site. A diamond exchange or bank vault can expect such a burglar and should be analyzed as such. An auto repair garage would not be the target of sophisticated burglars and would not need a sophisticated alarm system. Aberrations do occur, however. The author recalls a burglary investigation of a standalone clothing store building. The business sold only pants jeans but had thousands of pairs in stock at any one time. The business was burglarized over a holiday weekend and the entire store was emptied of the clothing contents. The building was alarmed but only the doors had sensors on them. The burglars chopped a hole in the roof and with some form of container pulled up every pair of jeans through the hole including themselves after the burglary, effectively bypassing the alarm system. It was not a business that would have made it on the radar of most experts analyzing a high threat situation. Yet the complete loss of inventory lost many customers and ultimately caused the business to close. The question to ask is how much the business can afford to lose compared to how much they are willing to spend on a security system.

Sensors

As already discussed intrusion alarm sensors come in three categories; **point, area, and perimeter**. There are two additional categories that are beyond the scope of this textbook. However, for purposes of thoroughness let's briefly identify them. Beyond the building perimeter is a class of exterior alarm sensors that are designed to detect an intruder walking across the property toward the building. They are appropriately called 'Exterior Area Detectors'. These detectors can be located above ground, and thus be a deterrent, or hidden underground and thus unknown to the intruder. Applications would include the residences of Fortune 200 CEOs and high-level government and judicial officials. Should you ever visit the White House you will not see any above ground alarm sensors for esthetic reasons. However, there are underground sensors. If you look carefully you might spot the above ground control panel boxes hidden in groups of bushes. (Water infiltration keeps these panels above ground). The sensors themselves are underground. Once a year someone will prove the point by jumping the low fence and running toward the White House. If you can get close to many prisons with double fence lines you might see examples of the above ground sensors between the fence lines.

The other exterior category of sensors is 'Perimeter Property Detectors'. The most common of these sensors are fence mounted. They detect the climbing and cutting of a fence while having the ability to disregard a wild animal rubbing against the fence. There are other sensor formats but they are all designed to offer early detection of an intrusion onto protected property. You might see these sensors at nuclear power plants and many military installations. On occasion an industrial plant may have such devices. You can expect to see more private industrial applications in the future as the war on terror continues.

For the much more common application of building protection and detection we would begin at the physical building perimeter and move inward to protect specific objects. Let's examine the three building areas more closely and the applicable sensors available for each area. We will begin our examination from the point of intruder entry into the building.

PERIMETER INTRUSION SENSORS

This class of sensors detects entry to all six exterior sides of a building. The obvious points of entry are windows and doors. However, any part of the perimeter can become an entry point for a burglar. Roof hatches, vents, skylights, old basement coal chutes, utility tunnels, air conditioning units, the roof, floor, and the penetration of walls themselves have all been used in the past by enterprising burglars. From a police and security perspective the more quickly an entry is detected the more time there is to respond and capture the intruder. Building perimeter alarm sensors offer this early detection opportunity.

Magnetic Switch

Magnetic switches are contact switches used to detect the opening of a window or door. Their operation depends on the intruder physically opening the door or window to activate the alarm. Magnetic switches are composed of two parts; a magnetically activated switch mounted on the interior frame of the door or window and a magnet mounted to the interior surface of the moving door or window. When the door or window is closed the magnet lines up with the switch. The magnet pulls the adjacent switch closed which creates a closed alarm signal loop. Upon arming the alarm system, small electrical current flows through the alarm wires and the closed switch. When the door or window is opened by an intruder the removed magnet causes the spring-loaded switch to open, breaking the electrical circuit and creating an alarm.

Wired Magnetic Switch

Magnetic switches come in two forms. The first is surface mounted. They are rectangular shaped, approximately 2"x1/2"x1/2". Much smaller sizes are manufactured for residential applications. The switch will typically have a pair of wires permanently attached or terminal screws to attach wires. The magnet has an identical housing as the switch but without the wires. They can be attached with screws or two-sided tape. They are manufactured in brown, white, and grey colors to match the frames they are attached to.

Wireless Window/Door Magnetic Switch

The other format is a recessed mounted or flush sensor. Designed so that they are not visible when the door or window is closed they are esthetically more pleasing and not as easily tampered with. The cylindrical switch would be installed in a hole drilled into the top or non-hinge side door frame and the same configuration magnet would be pushed into a hole drilled into the door edge opposite of the switch.

Recessed Concealed Switch

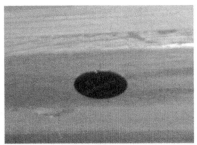

Recessed Commercial Magnet Installed in Door Header

These switches can create false alarms under certain conditions. Poor fitting doors or windows can rattle during windy or stormy conditions. The movement of the door or window in the frame can create enough movement that an alarm is created. Because of the door movement and severe environmental factors overhead garage doors and pull-down security doors in shopping malls will have specially designed contact switches.

Overhead Door Magnetic Alarm Switch

Defeat techniques of these sensors include the inside employee/intruder substituting a higher strength magnet taped over the switch, putting a metal object across the exposed screw terminals, and removing the magnet casing screws while duct taping the magnet to the switch so that the magnet stays in place when the door is opened. Also, any intruder can cut a large hole in the door thereby bypassing the switch.

Glass Breakage

Glass break sensors monitor glass that is likely to be broken during a forced entry. They come in two types; acoustic and shock. A third type, dual technology acoustic/shock sensors combines these two technologies. Either sensor will typically only cover about 100 square feet of glass.

Acoustic glass breakage detectors have a microphone that listens for and detects the high frequency sound wave typically created when glass is broken. An internal processor filters out unwanted sound frequencies and only allows frequencies at certain ranges to be analyzed. The analysis compares the frequency to those associated with breaking glass and, if a match occurs, sends out a signal to the control panel. These sensors are typically mounted on the ceiling 10' to 20' in front of the protected glass. They can be of various shapes from rectangular to circular. Most have a small, 1/8" orifice in which the microphone is installed.

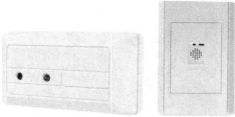

Wall Mount Acoustic Glass Breakage Shock Sensors

Shock glass sensors detect the shock wave created when glass is broken. They are mounted on the adjacent window frame, wall, or sometimes on the glass itself. These sensors detect the specific frequency shock wave that is created when glass is broken. They are usually about 1" square.

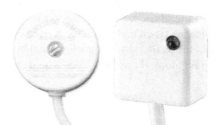

Glass Surface Mount Glass Break Shock Sensors

Ceiling Mount Acoustic Glass Break Sensors

A dual technology glass break sensor simply combines the technologies of both acoustic and shock sensors, requiring both technologies to 'verify' the intrusion before activating an alarm signal. They are useful in reducing false alarms.

Another form of glass break detection that is rarely used any longer is worth mentioning as it is still visible in very old buildings and on occasion may be found on newer buildings. Foil tape is a silver colored lead based tape that is glued to the surface of glass, usually along the outer edges. Its ends connect to alarm wires and an electrical current is pulsed through the tape. When the glass is broken the tape tears in half breaking the electrical circuit and creating an alarm. High installation labor costs and continual maintenance expenses have relegated this sensor technology to a practical museum status.

Foil Tape Glass Break Sensor

Glass breakage sensors are susceptible to stray radio frequency and high-pitched sound frequencies. Jet engines, squealing tires, worn brakes, train whistles, ringing bells, sirens, and even jingling key rings have been known to activate these sensors. Dual technology sensors dramatically reduce these issues.

Glass breakage sensors can be defeated by muffling the breaking sound of the glass with duct tape on the window or a blanket pressed against the glass. Cutting glass works well in movies but, would still trigger a glass breakage sensor. This is because when a glass cutter is used on glass it really on scores the glass to allow for a controlled break. Thus, unless the, usually professional burglar, also uses duct tape on the glass, the impact of breaking the glass along the scored lines would still create a vibration and noise.

Window Screen

This form of alarm sensor is normally found on residences but can be used on business windows that are operating windows; that is, they open and close.

The obvious security measure on operating windows is to have them closed and locked when the building is not occupied. However, humans being who they are windows are sometimes overlooked and left open. In homes, of course, they may be open for days and nights for weeks in a row. In either situation it is an open invitation for a burglar to either remove the screen or cut the screen to access the open window.

Window alarm screens overcome this issue by sounding an alarm if they are either removed or cut while installed on the window. These window sensors have two features. First, they have a built-in magnet that matches up with a flush magnetic switch in the frame of the window. The second method of protection is a very fine wire that is woven into the fabric of the screen itself. This is a single thin wire that enters through the window screen frame, weaves through the screen and exits at the same location. The wire is then connected to a 24-hour alarm loop in the alarm system. If the burglar attempts entry by cutting through the screen he will also have to cut the thin wire which activates the alarm. Removing the screen brings about the same result.

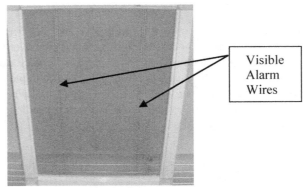

Visible
Alarm
Wires

Window Alarm Screen

Due to the great variety of window sizes and shapes alarm screen companies do not actually manufacture alarm screens. Alarm installing companies will remove the existing screens from the building or home and send the entire screen to the alarm screen company. There the screens are taken apart, the alarm wires and magnet installed, the screen is reassembled and sent back to the alarm company.

Wall Vibration

Vibration sensors are mounted on walls, ceilings, and floors and are intended to detect mechanical vibrations caused by chopping, sawing, kicking, ramming, or drilling of the physical structure to which the sensor is attached. These sensors have transducers that detect the vibration energy that is generated during the attack. Better sensors are attached to an inline processor or have similar technology built into the sensor. This processor acts as a filter by counting the number of impacts, thus eliminating someone accidentally bumping the wall while backing up their car. Other processors will analyze the vibration properties consistent with the nature of the structure to which they are attached. Therefore, a concrete floor will have different properties than a sheetrock wall or plywood roof. Manufacturer's specifications must be carefully followed in the installation of the various sensors.

Wall Mount Vibration Sensors

These types of sensors are best mounted on rigid supports of the structure. Exterior sources of vibrations will cause vibrations that create false alarms. Trains, heavy traffic, a passing truck will all cause vibration issues.

Defeat of properly installed vibration sensors is not easy. Insider knowledge of uncovered areas can occur. However, many repetitive deliberate false alarms initiated by an intruder can cause the actual entry alarm to be ignored, as is true for any alarm sensor.

Trip Wire

This sensor is used in areas where an intruder might crawl through a ventilation hole or other opening through the perimeter shell. It is basically a wire attached to a switch on one end. Mounted across a hole or inside a ventilation shaft, when the wire is pulled or pushed out of the way it dislodges the circuit in the switch creating the alarm. Cutting the wire would also break the circuit and activate the alarm.

False alarms are uncommon in these sensors. However, if the switch is located inside an active ventilation shaft it is subject to debris contamination and failure. Frequent testing must be done to verify its operation. A better installation is to have the switch mounted on the outside of the ventilation shaft with the wire running through the shaft.

Defeats are also uncommon due to their construction. However, given enough time an intruder could detach and move the sensor up or down as a single unit allowing passage without triggering the sensor.

AREA INTRUSION SENSORS (MOTION SENSORS)

This is the second of the three levels of sensor protection. These sensors protect the interior of a building by detecting intruders moving around inside. It functions as either a secondary level of detection for intruders who have bypassed the perimeter sensors or an initial form of detection as it detects the intruder who was hidden inside the building during the closing of the business and the arming of the alarm system.

Passive Infrared (PIR)

Passive Infrared sensors, as the name implies, are passive and thus do not emit a signal or any energy. PIR sensors detect a change in the temperature baseline of their environment. Specifically, these sensors look for the heat of an intruder and, comparing it to the surrounding environment, activate an alarm. The sensor, typically a rectangular box shape varying in size from 2 square inches to 3"x 5", has a face that is covered with a lens that is divided into sections or zones. These lens sections create fields of vision for the PIR that look much like the fingers on a hand. When the heat source crosses over two or more of the zone boundaries (or fingers) an alarm is initiated. Given this detection pattern these sensors must be installed so that the intruders' likely path of travel is perpendicular to the sensor face, crossing over and through the sensor fingers.

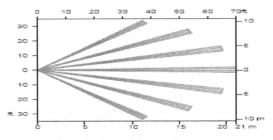

PIR Field of View – Top View

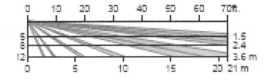

PIR Field of View – Side View

When a PIR is first armed the sensing element inside the PIR adjusts itself to the existing environment and associated thermal image from walls, furniture, carpet, objects, etc. When an intruder enters he would typically cross through this thermal environment and change the parameters to which the PIR had previously adjusted itself. These changes are sent through a built-in processor and creates an alarm when the parameters are exceeded.

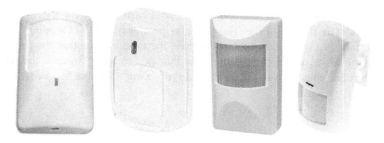

Wall Mount PIR Sensors

PIRs are the most common motion sensor in the intrusion alarm industry. It is reliable, inexpensive, does not drain a backup battery in power failures as do active sensors, and has the fewest false alarms in its group of sensors. Sensor designs allow it to be wall mounted in box formats or ceiling mounted in circular formats with lens configurations that can spread 360 degrees from the ceiling and 180 degrees for 40' from a wall, or 30 degrees for 150' down a hallway. Covert models exist in the form of wall thermostats and there are residential models for homes with pets that do not sense below three feet.

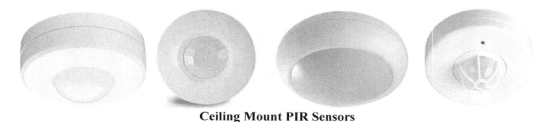

Ceiling Mount PIR Sensors

The same operating principles that work for a PIR sensor can work against it. In environments where the ambient temperature is 80 – 100 degrees F. a PIR may not see an intruder because the background temperature does not offer enough of a contrast.

False alarms can occur with PIR sensors. Insects nesting inside the lens area will appear human size when walking over the lens or sensor element. Space heaters, hot water pipes, and hot air vents positioned above the PIR will trigger an alarm as they turn on and the heat rises or blows on the sensor. Additionally, unless special filters are installed, visible light from headlights, security flashlights, and even sunlight intermittently covered by clouds can set off an alarm due to the sudden intrusion of heat in the light.

PIRs can be defeated in several manners. The most common method is known as 'sloth' movement. Moving very slowly across a room allows the PIR to slowly adjust to the presence of this new thermal source as being a normal environmental change. Walking directly into the view of the PIR can permit the intruder to walk into the dead area between two zones. If a PIR is set to activate on three or four zones it is even easier to walk directly into the path of a PIR as you are likely to only trigger two adjacent zones. An insider who has access to the PIR can defeat it for later entry by rubbing petroleum jelly on the outside of the lens, blocking the view without creating an obvious covering. Higher quality PIR sensors have built in technology to detect this restricted view and signal a tamper alarm.

Microwave

Microwave sensors are active energy sensors that generate radio waves as their energy source. These generated radio waves reflect off solid walls and objects in a room and reflect back to the sensor to be analyzed for motion changes. Microwave sensors transmit a signal at an 'X' frequency which bounces off solid objects and returns to an internal sensor antenna that measures either a consistent frequency or a change in the frequency (frequency shift). The process operates off of the Doppler frequency shift principle (as does a radar gun). When an intruder enters the field of detection the radio waves reflect off him and back to the microwave sensor antennae. The intruder, moving closer to the sensor, would cause a shorter frequency shift and thus activate an alarm. Moving away from the sensor would also cause a shift, just a different frequency return.

New Style Commercial Grade Microwave Sensor

Old Style Microwave Sensor

Proper placement of this sensor must account for the likely path of travel by the intruder. As this detector requires a sufficient reflection pattern to occur the intruder is best detected when traveling parallel to the energy path, as in directly into or away from the face of the sensor.

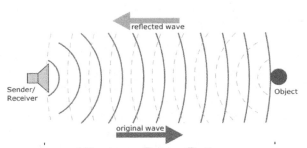

Microwave Energy Pattern

Since microwaves are a form of radio waves, like any standard radio signal, some of the emitted waves will penetrate solid materials. In relative terms microwave signals are passed or blocked in the following manner:

Material	Degree of Signal Penetration
Glass	100%
Sheetrock	75%
Plywood	50%
Masonry Block	25%
Concrete/Metal	0%

Relative to both protection and false alarms this unique penetrating characteristic can work for and against the end user. On the positive side if the end user wants to protect two adjacent rooms with a single sensor, thereby saving on installation costs, a microwave sensor pointed at the separating sheetrock wall would easily detect motion in either of the secured rooms. Hiding a sensor in a drop ceiling would also conceal the sensor making it all but impossible to 'sloth' defeat this sensor as its presence is unknown to the intruder.

However, the same characteristic can create false alarms if improperly installed. A sensor installed pointed toward an exterior wall will likely pick up normal motion outside of the wall, creating an alarm. Even when the microwave sensor is properly mounted on the exterior wall but pointed inward there may still be a reflection problem. This occurs when something metallic is placed against the interior wall. The microwave energy is reflected off the interior item, through the exterior wall on which the sensor is located, bounces off a passing semi-trailer (large reflection pattern) back into the protected premise and finally to the sensor creating a false alarm. Such internal reflections have occurred with shoplifting mirrors, foil backed wallpaper, and a series of metal file cases placed against the interior wall. Foil backed drop ceilings would likewise prevent above ceiling use.

It is interesting to note that water is also an ideal radio signal reflector. Therefore, aquariums later introduced into a protected premise might reflect microwaves back through an opposite exterior wall creating false alarms. Also, a newly installed sensor ostensibly installed correctly and with no exterior walls around it might be triggered by an unseen flow of water. Such was the situation when a sensor introduced to a new system was activated by water flowing down pipes from a flushing toilet located in an unprotected office area on the floor above. Finally, a microwave sensor installed on a rainy day might be inhibited by a moisture laden wall, only to have stray signals pass through the wall when the sun later comes out and dries the wall. An understanding of the unique characteristics of microwave signals and site testing must be done to verify the proper operation of this sensor and any dual technology sensor using microwaves.

Additional areas of false alarms relate to strong electromagnetic fields such as electric transformers, generators, industrial pumps, etc. Fluorescent lights can generate interfering signals and should be located at least 20 feet from the nearest sensor. Sensors mounted on loose, vibrating walls will create their own signal shift and cause false alarms. Finally, loose floating balloons in a retail application and sale ad banners moving in front of an air flow register may create a false alarm signal.

Intruders may defeat these sensors in one of two ways. The first is by use of sloth motion. Moving very slowly allows the signal to self-adjust to what it perceives as a natural, slow change in the environment. The intruder need only reach the wall or area below the sensor to be out of detection range. Additionally, an intruder with normal unrestricted daytime access to the protected area can 'map out' the actual sensor footprint by walking the protected area during non-alarm times and observing the illumination of the sensor trip LED when the edge of the protected area has been breached. This test would determine the parameters of the protection curtain.

Microwave sensors as standalone sensors are no longer common due to the false alarm issues from penetration of exterior walls. However, they are very common when paired with a PIR sensor in the same housing. These combination sensors are called Dual Technology sensors and are addressed later in this chapter.

Ultrasonic

This active energy sensor emits energy in the form of sound waves. These sound waves are above the human hearing range (ultrasonic). It must be noted that, due to the great number of false alarms, ultrasonic sensors are rarely installed anymore, replaced by PIR and microwave sensors. However, prior to the early 1980s ultrasonic sensors were the leading form of area protection and therefore are readily found in many buildings constructed and alarmed prior to that time frame. Many of these sensors continue to operate as a part of those alarm systems.

Old Style Wall Mount Ultrasonic Sensors

Ultrasonic Room Occupancy Light Shut Off Sensor
Not a Security Sensor

The ultrasonic sensor uses air as its medium. It transmits energy using sound waves. The sound waves are transmitted into an enclosed area, typically a room, with the energy pattern in the shape of a light bulb. The sound waves reflect off the walls and solid objects in the room and are returned to the sensor. Like the microwave sensor a Doppler shift determines if the sound wave frequency has changed. A moving person will alter the sound wave pitch and the returning sound waves would be different, signaling an alarm. Like the microwave sensor the most likely detection occurs when the intruder is walking into or away from the source of the sound waves. Envisioning a light bulb shape would point out the obvious dead spots under the sensor and in the corners.

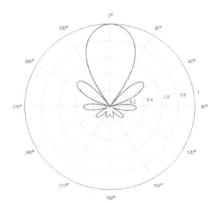

Ultrasonic Detection Pattern

Ultrasonic sensors are characterized by a narrow, 12-14-inch-long housing with a cloth or foam front. Behind the front are two transducers; one for transmitting a signal and the other for receiving the signal. It can be mounted horizontally or vertically in a corner. Even older units used two separate components mounted on the ceiling or on adjacent walls approximately 10' apart. One unit would transmit and the other unit would receive and analyze the sound waves. The originating sound waves would reflect off the floor and back up to the transceiver. Residential models were designed to look like a bookshelf speaker and were self-contained with an AC power cord, motion detection sensors, electric socket for an auxiliary lamp, and electronic siren annunciator. The degree of shock to a burglar when the alarm sounded might be envisioned through the author's experience. In investigating an office burglary, the alarm sensor was found to be smashed on the floor. In another residential burglary the entire alarm device was stolen along with the more typical loss of items.

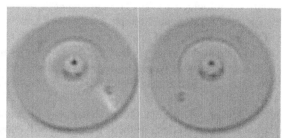

Old Style Ceiling Mount Ultrasonic – Transmitter and Receiver Units

Ultrasonic energy is easily captured within an enclosed room and cannot pass through any solid surface area. However, it can thus be blocked by shelves, furniture, and stacked items creating dead spots behind these objects.

Ultrasonic sensors calibrate themselves to their environment upon startup. Later environmental changes can alter their detection sphere. Heavy humidity in a room not air conditioned can reduce the area of protection by as much as 40%, creating a large unprotected area on the perimeter of a room.

False alarm situations are common with this detector. Air movement from heating, air conditioning, and ventilating systems, and drafts from poorly fit doors and windows can create enough air turbulence to disrupt the transmitted wave pitch. Leaking radiator pipes in older buildings, ringing telephones, air horns, train whistles, screeching tires and brakes can all create noise that is in the ultrasonic spectrum disrupting the original sensor sound wave and triggering a false alarm. Space heaters located below sensors that turn on during the evening hours can create rising hot air currents that may disrupt the sound waves. In warehouse applications flying birds can also trip this sensor. All these false alarm potentials and the advent of the PIR created the rapid demise of the ultrasonic sensor.

The most common defeat measure against ultrasonic sensors is the sloth motion. Slow horizontal movement by an intruder across the area of coverage is often difficult motion for an ultrasonic sensor to detect.

Photoelectric

This is the only mainline sensor that has two operating components. The photoelectric sensor transmits a beam of invisible infrared light across a space to a receiving unit. When the beam is broken by an intruder walking through the area the alarm is signaled. This sensor pair is often used to cover a doorway, hallway or center of a room. It is normally installed between 16" and 24" high.

Photoelectric Sensor Pair   **Interior View of Dual Beam Lens**

The transmitter uses an LED light source to transmit a modulated, or pulsed, light beam to the receiving unit which focuses the light onto a photoelectric cell. The modulated light is intended to prevent the introduction of artificial light by an intruder in an attempt to defeat the sensor. If the receiver part of the pair fails to receive at least 90% of the beam, or if the beam received by the receiving unit is not modulated at the same rate as the transmitter unit, the sensor will go into alarm. This sensor can be spaced up to 1000' apart but a realistic response focus would limit practical distances up to 350'. Mirrors can be used to focus the beam around corners or in a zigzag pattern to better block an entrance.

Potential problems affecting this sensor mostly relate to disturbance of the light transmission. Dust and smoke will refract the light beam. Dirt on the lens of the sensor units will cause it to go into alarm if more than 10% of the beam is disrupted. Sunlight streaming into a room and falling on a sensor may trigger an alarm or reduce its sensitivity. An insect crawling inside the unit and walking over the lens can block the signal and cause an alarm. The latter issue is prevented by sealing the units with caulk after installation. All other issues require careful installation planning and regular maintenance.

The primary defeat technique for this sensor is the simple act of stepping over or crawling under the sensor beam. As these units are rarely concealed during installation an alert intruder will spot it and simply bypass it on his way to the targeted property. In the realm of motion sensors and the author's experience with burglars who have bypassed this sensor, photoelectric sensors should be considered a backup sensor only.

Dual Technology Sensor

Dual technology sensor is a generic name for a single housing sensor that combines two motion detection technologies. Almost exclusively those two technologies are passive infrared and microwave and are typically referred to as 'dual-tech'. This sensor requires that BOTH technologies be tripped before an alarm is signaled.

Dual Tech Sensors
Typically with Multi Color LEDs

This sensor was created with the primary intent of reducing false alarms. It works well in this regard because the false alarm factors of each technology are different from the other. As an example, a microwave signal that inadvertently is picking up outside motion will go into 'pre-alarm'. The PIR portion of the sensor, however, is still looking for the heat signature of an intruder. Finding nothing it will not validate the microwave alarm signal and thus no intrusion alarm is sent out. After a short amount of time both sensors will go back to their original un-alarmed state.

Some of these Dual Tech sensors come with multi-color LEDs. The LEDs provide the installer the ability to monitor which of the technologies is detecting movement during the installation process.

While the reduced false alarm rates are making this a very popular sensor with installing alarm companies there is a dark side. Intruders who attempt to defeat this sensor with sloth motion and end up tripping one of the technologies can freeze in place and not activate the alarm. Waiting a short time period will reset the sensor and allow a continued intrusion attempt. Thus, the intruder will continue his progress toward the goal in the protected area. For this reason, dual tech devices should not be used in high security situations. Separate technology sensors and multiple sensors that have been properly analyzed for application and installation location are a much better approach for anything beyond standard unskilled burglary detection.

Note that most dual tech sensors today are very sleek in design and appear to be identical to that of PIR sensors. Sensors with multiple LED indicator lights would signify a dual tech sensor. However, other dual tech sensors only have a single light. The only definitive method of identifying such a dual tech is to remove the cover and look for the microwave sensor component.

POINT DETECTION SENSORS

Point sensors are designed to protect a specific item or location from being moved or entered. Point sensors detect the motion or removal of an item, the touching of an item, or the walking within a very defined point of space. Examples would include art displays, retail displays, electronic components, a safe, stairway, or portal entry way.

Pressure Switch

A pressure switch is a simple mechanical switch with a center compression leg or ball. The switch is attached to the underside center of a cabinet shelf, table, or podium with the ball extending through the top of the mounting surface. The item to be protected is placed directly on top of the ball which is compressed by the weight of the object and completes an electrical circuit inside the switch. The action of lifting the protected item opens the switch and creates an alarm. For items that would not normally be moved a 24-hour circuit can be incorporated allowing around-the-clock protection.

Roller Ball Pressure Switches

While there are no environmental issues with this sensor it can be defeated. Should the intruder be aware of the point sensor underneath the object he can slide a piece of plastic or cardboard under the protected object prior to lifting the object which would continue to maintain pressure on the ball. A brick placed on top of the substituted plastic piece would defeat the switch.

Pressure Mat

Also called a Tape Switch this sensor looks like a flat rubber mat. It is placed under carpet or a rug for concealment purposes. Inside the mat is a series of ribbon switches. Ribbon switches are two long pieces of very thin and narrow metal rails stacked upon each other and separated by an equally thin piece of foam rubber. Each piece of metal is attached to one of a pair of alarm circuit low powered electrical wires. The separating foam piece prevents the metal rails from touching each other and completing an electrical circuit. However, when a person steps on the hidden mat he compresses the two strips of metal which would then touch and create the needed electrical circuit to activate the alarm signal.

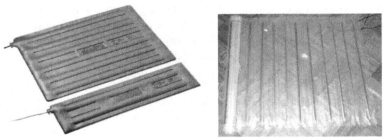

Pressure Mats

Mats like this would normally be placed in front of high value items or likely points of remote entry. Examples would include in front of art displays, in front of a safe, under a remotely located window, and inside the doorway of a high security room. A variation of this sensor is a stairway mat (photo above right.) This is a mat constructed in lengths of 10' or 15' that are installed on stairs under the carpet. This might be an application for seldom used stairs when the likely intruder path would take him up those stairs. For residential installations there is a special 'pet mat' that requires 40 pounds of pressure to activate the mat, enough for a person, but not enough for a smaller pet.

Problems with this sensor come from inappropriate installations. Mats that are installed inside main entrances are likely to wear out from excessive foot traffic and fail to function when needed. Inadequate concealment of the alarm wires going under the rug or carpet to the mat is an example of a poor concealment problem. Replacement of a worn-out mat under carpet means the removal of the carpet to access the mat which can be an expensive proposition. Proper installation of this sensor would make this sensor immune to defeat.

Flex Sensor

This unique sensor is designed to detect the weight of an intruder as he walks across a floor or up a flight of stairs. The sensor is installed on the underside of floor or stair construction joists. As the intruder's weight settles and displaces the floor around a flex sensor the sensor itself will flex signaling an alarm. All wood floor and stairs will flex under the weight of a person and this is considered normal. This sensor is designed to take advantage of that factor.

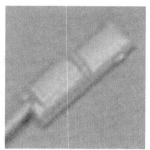

Flex Sensor

No problems typically exist with this sensor with a few exceptions. Train or heavy truck traffic in the area will create false alarms as will local heavy construction. A poorly laid foundation that is settling or moving a lot will also affect reliability. This sensor is normally not defeated as it is unseen.

Capacitance Proximity

The primary purpose of this sensor is the protection of money and fire safes. In essence this sensor creates a field of static electricity around the safe. Penetrating this field creates an imbalance in the field and activates an alarm.

The sensor panel itself is mounted on a wall next to the safe. A wire leading from the sensor panel is welded or screwed into a leg or top of the safe. A small electro-static charge of electricity is generated in the sensor and fed down the wire to the safe. Much like the static electricity built up on the human body walking over carpet in a dry atmosphere, the static electricity is built up around the entire perimeter body of the safe. The safe is insulated from the floor by use of plastic or rubber discs. Hockey pucks work well in this application. Proper operation requires that the safe be kept away from the rear wall and surrounding objects to about 12". The capacitance proximity detector measures the amount of static electricity around the safe and maintains it during the alarm period. If the safe were to be touched by an intruder the static electricity would immediately drain away onto the intruder's body. This action would cause an imbalance in the monitoring sensor and would create the alarm.

Capacitance Alarm Control Panel

This sensor is also used in some unique applications. When used with metal screens mounted behind it, wall mounted museum art work can be protected in this manner. Metal desks and file cabinets can likewise be protected. A most unlikely candidate is a jet fighter. However, the U.S. Air Force uses this technology to protect rows of parked aircraft. Already mounted on rubber tires they are built with specially insulated electronics that allows the use of static electricity around the entire aircraft without damaging the internal components. Yet, anyone approaching or touching any part of the plane would immediately activate an alarm.

Problems with this sensor include the use of wooden insulating blocks. Floor cleaning liquids eventually seep into the wood and create a short to the floor. Uncontrolled humidity environments will disrupt and reduce the effectiveness of this sensor. Electrostatic electricity needs a dry atmosphere to properly function. Finally, if the protection strength is set too high it can extend to 18" to 24" around the protected item. This would cause the static charge to penetrate a nearby wall and inadvertently create a field into an adjacent, unprotected room. Normal movement in that room would activate a false alarm. Proper set up and monitoring would prevent this.

Under normal circumstances this sensor would not be subject to defeat.

Industry Updates

Two new forms of detectors have recently come on the market. They are not intrusion detectors but do relate to the security/safety field.

The first is an 'aggression detector'. Quoted statistics by the manufacturer state that "90% of physical aggression is preceded by verbal aggression." This detector is touted to intelligently detect that verbal aggression and automatically send notifications to first responders. It allows monitoring staff to review the recording of the actual sounds that triggered the alarm. (Real time monitoring might violate eavesdropping laws.) The alarm can also be linked to video cameras to highlight the location of the aggressive conversation. Applications would include schools, workplace locations, prisons, check-in counters, banks, healthcare institutions.

The second detector is a 'vaping' sensor. It is designed to alarm upon the detection of chemicals emitted by a person using a vaping device or e-cigarette. The standalone vaping detector could be used in employee restrooms or related public facilities.

A unique, related, detector incorporates both vaping and bullying detection. It will detect both chemical composition and aggression sounds. This is specifically designed for school systems with applications in bathrooms, under stairwells, and other hidden locations where illegal activity might occur.

There is another detector that has been, and now is increasingly, installed in homes and businesses. This sensor is not new but, in today's privacy concerns world, should be addressed and explained. It is the 'verified audio intrusion' detection sensor. First this sensor has, and is, being used in communities where, typically, local laws require alarm monitoring companies to verify that there is an actual intruder in a building or home before law enforcement will respond. In operation, an alarm company receives notification of an intrusion. The alarm monitoring employee will then activate the sound sensor to listen into the interior of the home or building for sounds of burglary or voices of non-building occupants. The noise or conversation must be of a criminal nature to convince the monitoring agent that the sounds relate to an illegal activity. The agent then notifies local law enforcement.

The issue, of course, is that the agent can listen in on actual, real time conversations inside the home or building. The author has verified this during his consulting work. While there are strict policies in effect to prevent employees from doing so the potential exists for abuses to this policy. In some cases, it is also possible that a computer hacker could access this sound sensor and monitor conversations taking place inside a business during business hours. Confidential conversations could be overheard. If 'verified audio verification' is required in your jurisdiction prudent placement of these sensors is advised. Note that other jurisdictions might allow 'verified video verification' without the use of sound sensors. Of course, the possibility of the video being hacked is also a threat.

Another update relates to the remote monitoring of an intrusion alarm system. Historically, standard (non-high security) alarm systems have been connected to the internal phone system of a home or business. When an intrusion is detected inside of a building the control panel dials a phone number and electronically notifies the monitoring company of the intrusion. Burglars have been able to easily prevent the outgoing phone call by cutting the phone cable located on the exterior of many homes and small to medium sized businesses. This effectively disconnects the alarm system to the outside world.

While residences may no longer have 'landline' based phone lines this is not the norm for businesses. However, there is now a reasonable solution for both homeowners with phone lines and businesses. It does assume that you are connected by internet (broadband) cable. The technology is termed by the generic phrase of 'pay on demand cellular monitoring'. This concept offers the best of both worlds for security customers. It combines the already present wi-fi internet connection with the always-on, reliable protection of cellular. Wi-Fi, already paid for, can occasionally become unavailable. The 'pay on demand' concept is a standby wireless cellular device that is installed inside the alarm panel and is only used if the internet cable is cut. Then, and only then, will you pay for the cell phone call to the alarm monitoring company ensuring that alarm signals are always transmitted to the central station.

Summary/Miscellaneous Considerations

Several additional points must be addressed to have a complete crime prevention understanding of alarm sensors.

Alarm system control panels must be mounted on interior walls. Should an intruder have inside knowledge of the placement of the control panel on an exterior wall he could simply knock a hole in the wall next to the panel and disable the panel from inside without setting off an alarm.

For the same reason every control panel should be protected by its own motion sensor mounted above the panel. A PIR works well in this situation. Should someone hide inside a business and reach the control panel without walking through any motion sensors they will be forced to enter this protection field while approaching the panel, thus activating the alarm before it can be disabled.

Finally, how long can an alarm system expect to last? Most people think of turning an alarm system on and off. In fact, alarm systems and their respective active sensors are always 'on'. Motion sensors, in particular, are always detecting and working 24/7. What happens at night, when a business closes, is that the system is switched to an 'armed' mode. In the morning it is 'disarmed'. Given the fact that these sensors are continuously operating it is suggested that they be replaced by new and better technology replacements every 10-15 years. A convincing argument can be made that a brand-new color television that is kept on for 24 hours a day, seven days a week would not offer the same picture and quality 10 years later as when it was new. Alarm sensors must operate at peak performance all the time. Replacement of sensors or the entire system is not unreasonable in the suggested time frame.

TYPE OF EQUIPMENT	PURPOSE	PRINCIPLE OF OPERATION	COMMON CAUSES OF FALSE ALARMS	GOOD APPLICATIONS	COMPONENT COST RANGE (INSTALLED)	POTENTIAL CONFIGURATIONS
ULTRASONIC SENSORS	SPACE PROTECTION	EMITS INAUDIBLE SOUND-WAVES THAT ARE SENSED BY A RECEIVER. INTRUDER ALTERS WAVE PATTERN ACTIVATING AN ALARM.	AREAS CONTAINING: • ROTATING OR MOVING MACHINERY • ESCAPING AIR OR STEAM • LARGE GLASS WINDOWS OR THIN WALLS THAT CAN VIBRATE • RADIO TRANSMITTERS • MAGNETIC FIELDS FROM MOTORS OR GENERATORS • FLUTTERING DRAPES	ROOMS WITH UNBROKEN LINE OF SIGHT. LARGE OBJECTS SUCH AS STACKS OR FURNITURE CAN CREATE SHADED AREAS ON THE SIDE AWAY FROM THE TRANS-CEIVER. MULTIPLE UNITS TO BE USED IN THESE APPLICATIONS.	$150 - 275	SINGLE ROOM / LARGE ROOM WITH STACKS
PHOTO ELECTRIC BEAM (ACTIVE INFRARED SENSORS)	SPACE PROTECTION	DIRECTS INVISIBLE IN-FRARED LIGHT BEAM AT A RECEIVER. ANY INTERRUP-TION OF THE BEAM RESULTS IN AN ALARM.	• ALIGNMENT BETWEEN TRANSMITTER AND RECEIVER CRITICAL. FREQUENT CHECKS REQUIRED. • HEAVY DUST, HEADLIGHTS	• DOORWAYS • LOADING DOCKS • AISLES • CORRIDORS • ALONG INVENTORY STACKS A LINE OF SIGHT SENSOR USING A PENCIL ZONE OF PROTECTION.	$155 - 199	OFFICE CORRIDOR / INVENTORY STORAGE
MICROWAVE SENSORS	SPACE PROTECTION	TRANSMITS AN ELECTRO-MAGNETIC FIELD INTO THE AREA TO BE PROTECTED. IN-TRUDER MOTION ACTIVATES ALARM.	AREAS CONTAINING: • SMALL OPENINGS WHICH CAN ALLOW ESCAPE OF MICROWAVE ENERGY TO OUTSIDE AREAS • FLUORESCENT LIGHTS • HEAVY MACHINERY • WALL VIBRATION • THIN WALLS OR GLASS • RADIATED OR CONDUCTED ELECTRO-MAGNETIC RADIATION	LONG CORRIDORS, AISLES OR TOTALLY ENCLOSED AREAS OR AREAS IN WHICH SENSOR CAN BE DIRECTED AWAY FROM WIN-DOWS AND THIN WALLS. IN WELL CONSTRUCTED BUILD-INGS, GOOD FOR LARGE SPACE PROTECTION. NOT AFFECTED BY AIR CURRENTS OR TEMPERA-TURE DIFFERENTIAL.	$225 - 460	LARGE WAREHOUSE OR STORAGE AREA
PASSIVE INFRARED SENSORS	SPACE PROTECTION	COMBINATION OF HEAT GENERATED BY A BODY PLUS MOTION OF THE BODY ACTIVATES THE SENSOR.	• OBJECTS IN A ROOM HEATED BY SUN-LIGHT THROUGH WINDOWS • SPACE HEATERS • RODENTS AND ANIMALS HIGH RESISTANCE TO COMMON FALSE ALARMS.	ROOMS OR AREAS WITH HIGH AIR TURBULENCE. ALL INTERIOR SPACES. SENSOR SHOULD BE MOUNTED SO THAT DIRECT SUNLIGHT IS NOT IN THE SEN-SOR'S DIRECT FIELD OF VIEW.	$160 - 240	ROOM OR AREA COVERAGE / SHIPPING/RECEIVING AREA
SONIC (AUDIO) SENSORS - ACTIVE -	SPACE PROTECTION	FILLS THE AREA TO BE PRO-TECTED WITH SOUND-WAVES. DISRUPTION OF THESE WAVES BY INTRUDER ACTIVATES ALARM.	MAY BE ACTIVATED BY EXTRANEOUS SOUNDS FROM OUTSIDE THE PROTECTED AREA. OBJECTS WITHIN A ROOM WHICH CAN MOVE SUCH AS FANS OR EQUIPMENT. SOUNDWAVES CAN BE DISTURBING TO PER-SONS IN ADJACENT AREAS.	INTERIOR SPACES WHERE STAY-BEHINDS ARE A THREAT OR IN WHICH ITEMS IN THE AREA MAY BE IN DIFFERENT LOCATIONS FROM DAY-TO-DAY. SUCH AS WAREHOUSES OR SHIPPING AREAS.	$200 - 260	ROOM COVERAGE / WAREHOUSE COVERAGE
AUDIO/REMOTE (LISTEN IN) - PASSIVE -	SPACE PROTECTION	USES LEASED TELEPHONE LINE AND MICROPHONE TO PROVIDE REMOTE LISTENING CAPABILITY TO DETECT IN-TRUDER MOVEMENT.	EXTRANEOUS NOISE MISTAKENLY CLASSIFIED AS AN INTRUSION. (PASSING VEHICLES, MACHINERY, NOISE IN ADJACENT AREAS, ETC.)	PROVIDES A MEANS TO VERIFY OTHER INTRUSION SYSTEMS PRIOR TO RESPONSE.	$35 - 80 PER UNIT	LARGE ROOM COVERAGE

TYPE OF EQUIPMENT	PURPOSE	PRINCIPLE OF OPERATION	COMMON CAUSES OF FALSE ALARMS	GOOD APPLICATIONS	COMPONENT COST RANGE (INSTALLED)	POTENTIAL CONFIGURATIONS
INTERIOR CAPACITANCE PROXIMITY SENSORS	POINT PROTECTION	USED IN CONJUNCTION WITH METAL OBJECTS SUCH AS FILES. THE METAL BECOMES PART OF THE TUNED CIRCUIT AND ANY CHANGE IN THE CAPACITY OF THE TUNED CIRCUIT (I.E. BODY TOUCHING THE OBJECT) CAUSES AN ALARM.	RELATIVELY FREE OF FALSE ALARMS. • PROTECTED ITEMS MUST BE KEPT CLEAN AND MOUNTED OFF THE FLOOR ON BLOCKS.	• FILE CABINETS • SAFES • METAL GRATES OR SCREENS • MACHINERY • HARDWARE	$200 - 230	
VIBRATION SENSORS	POINT PROTECTION	SENSORS ARE MOUNTED WITHIN OR UPON WALLS TO DETECT FORCED ENTRY VIA VIBRATION	• VIBRATIONS CAUSED BY LARGE MACHINERY, HVAC EQUIPMENT • THUNDER OR HEAVY WIND	• STORAGE AREAS • VAULT-LIKE ROOMS • CONTROLLED ACCESS AREAS	$125 - 160	
DOOR AND WINDOW SENSORS (1) CONTACT SWITCH	ENTRY/ POINT PROTECTION	RECESSED AND SURFACE MOUNTED SENSOR WHICH ESTABLISHES AN ELECTRO-MAGNETIC CONTACT BE-TWEEN THE FIXED FRAME AND MOVABLE DOOR OR WINDOW UNIT.	NORMALLY LOW SUSCEPTABILITY TO FALSE ALARM. POOR INSTALLATION OR MAIN-TENANCE CAN LEAD TO REDUCED EFFEC-TIVENESS OR BYPASS.	• INTERIOR & EXTERIOR DOORS • WINDOWS • OVERHEAD DOORS	$50 - 150	
(2) FOIL	ENTRY/ POINT PROTECTION	SURFACE MOUNTED ON GLASS. INTRUSION BY BREAKAGE OF GLASS BREAKS CONTACT AND AC-TIVATES ALARM.	• POOR INSTALLATION • OLD VARNISH BREAKS DOWN • CLEANERS BREAK FOIL • CORROSIVES ON CONNECTORS	ALL WINDOWS AND GLASS DOORS	$30 PER STANDARD WINDOW	
(3) GLASS BREAKAGE DETECTORS	ENTRY/ POINT PROTECTION	SURFACE MOUNTED ON GLASS. USES ULTRASONIC SIGNAL GENERATED BY GLASS BREAKAGE TO SIGNAL AN ALARM.	SOME PRODUCTS CAN BE ACTIVATED BY WINDOW VIBRATION.	ALL WINDOWS AND GLASS DOORS	$45 EACH	
SWITCH MATS	POINT PROTECTION	PRESSURE SENSITIVE FLOOR MATS ACTIVATED BY IN-TRUDER'S BODY WEIGHT.	LOW FALSE ALARM POTENTIAL. MOISTURE COULD CAUSE SHORT CIRCUIT.	• IN FRONT OF SAFES, FILES AND CASH REGISTERS • IN DOORWAYS AND STAIRWELLS • UNDER WINDOWS • UNDER CARPETING IN EXECU-TIVE OR OTHER OFFICES	$125	
WIRELESS DURESS ALARMS	POINT PROTECTION	WIRELESS ALARM ACTIVA-TING SYSTEMS ARE USED TO SEND ALARM SIGNALS OVER THE AIR TO A REMOTE CEN-TRAL RECEIVER.	ACCIDENTAL ACTIVATION BY THE USER. WALLS AND OTHER BARRIERS WILL REDUCE EFFECTIVE RANGE.	• GUARDS ON PATROL WITHOUT COMMUNICATIONS • AS A MONEY CLIP IN RETAIL OR CASH DEPOSITORIES • LOCAL COURIERS	$140	

References

ISC (International Security Conference) West, 2018

Security Dealer & Integrator Magazine, January 2016

How Stuff Works; How Burglar Alarms Work; by Tom Harris

Service Magic; Protect your Property with a Burglar Alarm System; by Jon Nunan

Central-Station Alarm Services; UL 827

Business.com; Security and Alarm Systems for Small Business

The Free Library by Farlex; Tips in Setting up Burglar Alarm Systems

Security Sales and Integration Magazine; Burglar Alarm Systems Booooring? Pleeease!
July 2012

WebmasterEngine.com; Burglar Alarms Install Guide - 4 Steps to Install an Alarm System

Brickhouse Security; What is an Alarm System?

False Alarms Down Sharply In Los Angeles; ERIC HARTLEY; SOURCE: DAILY NEWS, LOS
ANGELES   CREATED: JULY 5, 2012

Commercial Security: Burglary Patterns and Security Measures (with M. A. Gaffney). Security Industry
Association, Washington, D.C., February 1994

Burglar Alarms and the Choice Behavior of Burglars: A Suburban Phenomenon" (with A. Buck and G.
Rengert), Journal of Criminal Justice, Vol. 21 (5), October 1993: 497-507.

Burglar Alarms: What do we know about them? (With A. Buck) 1990. Security Journal, Vol.1, Number
2:101-108.

Entrepreneurship Flourish in the Alarm Industry, Security Sales, August 1997: 114-118
ArticleSnatch.com

Why Do I Need A Commercial Alarm System For My Business. By: Tanya Wiseman

Consumer Reports magazine: June 2011; Alarm-company gotchas

Ezine Articles; Three Things We Ought To Know From Security Firms
By Fernando Severns

American Journal of Economics and Sociology, The / Oct, 1996
Spatial and temporal patterns of commercial burglaries: the evidence examined
by Simon Hakim, Yochanan Shachmurove

Security Sales and Integration; Intrusion Detection Can Work Magic; July 2012
Bob Dolph

Chapter Eight

Check Fraud Prevention

Check Fraud Performance Objectives:

- Explain who is the maker on a check
- Explain who is the payee on a check
- Describe a two-party check
- Explain the concept of 'good as gold'
- Explain the difference between a forged check and a counterfeit check
- Cite and explain the seven check examination points to be performed by a retail clerk
- Describe and explain the acronym MICR
- Cite specific prevention actions that can be taken by retailers to reduce losses to check fraud

Introduction

Checks are not as prevalent a method of payment for the purchase of goods in America as they once were. However, for those with poor credit, and no bank cards they are still the only method of payment rather than carrying a lot of cash. This means the opportunity for check fraud continues to be an issue for some people. In fact, a J.P. Morgan, 2014 report on Payments Fraud indicates that checks continue to lead as the payment type experiencing the most fraudulent attacks, ahead of bank card fraud.

Previously limited to the illegal use of legitimate checks, today check fraud criminals with easy access to computers are creating fictitious checks based on information taken from actual account holders. This has created a whole new set of criminal investigation issues for those responsible for investigating and stopping check fraud. This unit will assist the business owner or loss prevention professional in identifying those checks that may be forged, altered, or counterfeited.

Extent of Fraud Problem

Recent surveys by the American Bankers Association and the Federal Reserve Board indicate that check fraud is a huge problem in America. While the use of paper checks in the U.S. is declining, check fraud is actually on the increase. An estimated $900 million annually is lost to businesses and financial institutions. These losses represent the more than 500 million checks that are forged each year. Additionally, the 2013 ABA Deposit Account Fraud Survey Report showed that 24% of check fraud losses were a result of counterfeit checks. Clearly it is a problem that continues to grow as the sophistication of the criminal increases. The solution lies with each person who receives a check for payment for any goods or services. Diligence on the part of the recipient in examining each check is the best tool in the fight against this rising problem.

Types of Checks

There are many different forms of checks used in America. To better understand how the different check frauds occur one must first understand how each check is legitimately used.

PERSONAL CHECK

This type of check reflects a personal account typically recorded in one or two individual (joint account) names. It is written out and signed by the person offering it for payment. The person who is writing (making) the check is known as the *maker*, and the person who is receiving the check (who is going to be paid) is known as the *payee*.

TWO-PARTY CHECK

This form of check is not an official check as authorized by a financial institution. However, it is commonly used and thus is addressed here. This check is normally a personal check that is issued for payment of services or goods. The payee, as in any other normal transaction, would endorse the check. However, the person who receives and endorses the check changes its status to a two-party check by signing it off to a second party on the back of the check. This is done by simply endorsing the check with the original payee's signature. Then, below this signature, the payee writes this statement: Pay to the Order Of. Then a second party's name is added below this statement. This now allows the check to be cashed by the second payee listed on the reverse side of the check. This is a perfectly legal procedure. Most financial institutions will cash this form of check after verifying that there are funds in the account.

The problem arises when the original maker stops payment on the check to the first payee. This might occur because of a dispute over the purchase between the original maker and the original payee. The second payee is not aware of the dispute or the stop payment on the check. This second payee deposits the check only to have it bounced back without payment. When this second payee contacts the first payee, he is told that the first payee did not issue the check and therefore cannot maintain control over the check and that the problem is with the original maker of the check. Because the original maker of the check has no control over who finally cashes the check there is no legal relationship between the maker and the second payee. The second payee, then, must try and recover the amount of the check from the first payee, not the original maker. Because of this triangular problem with second party checks, disputes involving these checks are rarely of a criminal nature. The original jurisdiction involving two-party checks is in the civil court system. The only exception would be if there was intentional fraud involving the maker of the check.

The business application of two-party checks usually involves retail stores. Some party type stores and grocery retailers will accept payroll and, sometimes, personal checks written out to their customers. The customer wants to pay for their purchases with these checks made out to the customer. The retailer, wanting to both make a sale and not lose a paying customer, accepts the check as payment. At that moment the check becomes a two-party check with the store as the second payee. Of course, the same issues explained above can now affect the retailer. The best policy for retailers is to simply refuse to accept two-party checks.

PAYROLL CHECK

This check is issued to an employee for employment services rendered. A payroll check is normally identified by the words 'payroll' stamped or printed somewhere on the check. This is what makes these checks so vulnerable to fraud. The person who receives this check for encashment sees the 'payroll' on the check and mentally identifies this as a 'good as gold' type of check. That is, a check that is virtually guaranteed not to bounce because of its origin.

TO: AL MILWAUKEE & METRO AREA STORES
Managers, Assistants, Cashiers

FROM: Elayne Schmitz
Return Check Department

DATE: October 12, 1993

COUNTERFEIT

STATE OF WISCONSIN

MADISON

FIRST WISCONSIN National Bank Account No. 11851 019

NOTE: These checks are printed on excellent quality check paper and are perforated at the bottom. They have a blue check pattern with a white background and say "Bi-Weekly Payroll". The original State of Wisconsin payroll check has a red check pattern with a white background. Over 51 of these checks have been cashed in two days. All checks have been payable to:

BENJAMIN J. SMALL JR.
5318 N. 29th Street, Apt. 1
Milwaukee, WI 53209

Being presented as Identification is: **WID S540-0706-9202-07**

ALL STORES: Do a system inquiry for the name Benjamin J. Small, Jr. Report any card numbers issued under that name to the Return Check Department immediately. Stores who are not on Universal Check must put the above Wisconsin ID number in the negative system immediately! If one of the described checks is presented, call the police!

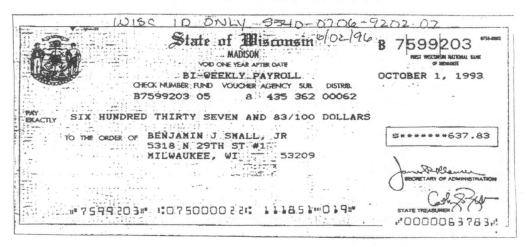

Example of How Much Can Be Lost to a Counterfeiter
51 Checks Passed in Two Days

When examining payroll checks one finds that they are nothing more than a regular company business check with 'payroll' printed on the check. If a crook can get a blank copy of a business check he/she can easily make it a 'payroll' check. This is done by either typing or stamping the word 'payroll' on the check. Blank copies of a business check may be stolen directly from the business itself or even counterfeited. Check software programs can also create exact replicas of legitimate business checks. Some business burglars will leave the checkbook behind but will take several checks from the back of the checkbook where they will not be missed until much later.

For retailers, payroll check fraud prevention efforts may be as simple as questioning the existence of the company listed on the check. Is the company a well-known and established business? If so, it is probably safe to take the check. If the company is not from the area or is unknown to the person accepting the check, then a phone call to the business is in order. If the business is no longer in operation then the telephone number will likely also be out of service. Call the number on the check or contact information for the number. Obviously, if the phone number has been disconnected, the business no longer exists and the payroll check is likely fraudulent.

GOVERNMENT CHECK

Government checks are issued by federal, state, county, or some local form of a public entity. They are issued for salaries, tax refunds, welfare payments, veteran's benefits, and many other forms of payment. These checks share the common misconception with payroll checks in that the receiver of a government check has the same 'good as gold' mentality while looking at these checks. In their minds, if the check is from the government it will be honored. While this is normally true of legitimate checks and legitimate holders of these checks, the concern is for the check that has been stolen or counterfeited.

These checks are frequently stolen from apartment and other residential mailboxes and forged. All too often the party cashing the check does not know the payee of these stolen checks. The cashing party simply sees a government check and the 'good as gold' syndrome occurs. The check is accepted for encashment and deposited. Frequently the cashing entity is a retailer of some form. They cash checks as a courtesy to their customers in the hope that the customer will spend some of the money at the store. When the check is returned for non-payment due to forgery or counterfeiting, the store cashing the check is victimized for the amount of the check.

Prevention efforts in this area require the retailer to either know the customer or require two forms of identification to cash checks. A much better policy would be to not act as a banker in the first place. Essentially the retailer, in accepting these two-party government checks, risks losing the full amount of the check and even the cost of the goods that were purchased with the fraudulent check. In requiring identification, the retailer puts the check forger in the position of having to produce two more pieces of paper that have the same name and information on them that the check and the true check payee possess. If the check was stolen from the mail, the forger will not likely have these additional items. While it is possible for the criminal to obtain counterfeit items to back up the stolen check, this requires time and more expense for the cashing of one check. More likely the thief is going to leave the store and go to another store that is less security minded. Of course, the retailer with the stricter policy saves money while other locations are being victimized to an even greater degree.

TRAVELER'S CHECK

These checks are used by people who anticipate traveling to areas where their personal checks may not be accepted and they do not want to risk carrying large amounts of cash. They are sold with a preprinted dollar amount on face of the check. These checks are discussed in detail at the end of this unit.

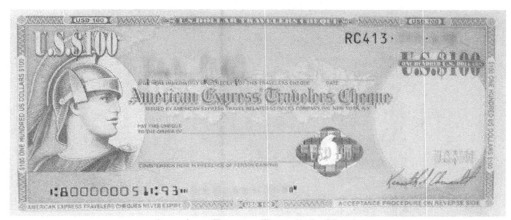

American Express Traveler's Check

MONEY ORDER

These financial instruments, processed as checks, are purchased for a customer-determined amount at different retailers. Users of money orders pay a fee on top of the value of the money order. Users of money orders may not have their own personal checking account or they may be purchasing the money order at the request of the recipient. Typically used to send payments through the mail, they reduce the risk of fraud to the recipient because the sender has already paid the full amount of the money order. This means the recipient need not worry about a bounced check or closed account. This is another case of where the recipient views the check as being 'good as gold'.

While money orders continue to be valid for mail order purchase and payments, it is not recommended that retailers accept these instruments for payment in face-to-face transactions. The retailer needs to ask him/herself about the logic of this type of transaction. If cash was paid for the money order, plus a money order fee on top of the face value, then why did the customer not pay the cash directly to the retailer? If the answer to this, or any other check related question cannot be satisfactorily answered, fraud should always be examined as a possibility.

Money orders are available at many businesses. Grocery stores are a popular place to purchase money orders. Grocery stores sell money orders from their customer service desks. If you watch or ask to purchase one, you will see exactly where they store them. It is usually from an unlocked lower cabinet or drawer. The thief can ascertain where the checks and imprinter are stored. After business closing, the thief may return, smash out the front window, jump the counter, remove the blank checks and imprinter and be gone before the police arrive. With the imprinter and blank checks, the thief is now free to imprint as many of the fraudulent, 'good as gold' checks as desired. This will not work, of course, with the electronic money orders. However, there are enough of the manual types available. The simple prevention policy is to not accept money orders in retail transactions.

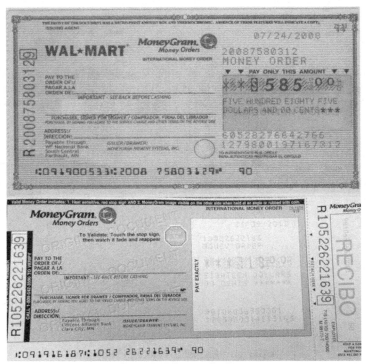

Sample Money Orders

CERTIFIED/CASHIER'S CHECK

This classification of check is used when large expenditures of money are being spent and everyone wants a risk-free transaction. Typical applications might be home mortgages, business acquisitions or automobile purchases. These checks operate in a similar manner to money orders. They are obtained, sometimes for a fee, at any financial institution. One pays the full amount of the check to the bank, which is supposed to guarantee that payment has been made, and then the bank issues the certified or cashier's check. These bank checks are identified by the word "cashier's" or "certified" stamped or typed on the check.

The fraud problem comes into play when a counterfeit bank check is produced on a computer and is identified with a stamped or typed in "certified". When the word is printed or stamped in red ink it is even more believable. The recipient financial institution or product supplier looks at the check, sees the type of check and once again assumes the "good as gold" attitude in accepting checks. This is exactly what the thief is hoping for in passing on these usually large dollar worthless checks.

The prevention technique for this potential fraud is simple. Before accepting the payment or passing on the purchased goods a phone call to the issuing financial institution is in order. They will tell you if the check is valid and if the funds are in the account listed on the check. This simple procedure could save a business thousands of dollars.

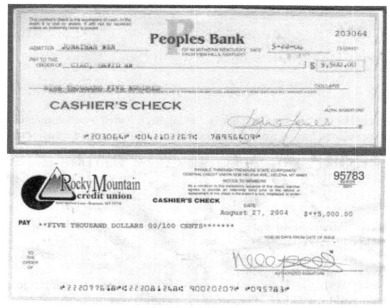

Cashier's Checks

Check Examination Points

Checks are returned to retailers for a variety of reasons. Non-Sufficient Funds (NSF), and Account Closed (AC) are two categories that any retailer can be victimized by and for which there are no known easy solutions. However, two additional categories can be reduced by careful examination of a check. They are *forged* and *counterfeit* checks. Both types of checks have clues associated with them that can tip off a retailer.

Before examining these frauds one thing must be understood. Sales clerks, the best defense against check fraud, are rarely trained to examine checks and very few do anything but give checks a cursory glance before putting them away. Every worthless check must pass through the hands of a sales clerk before being put into a cash register. The criminal cannot bypass this step. Yet, failure to examine the check is exactly what happens in the clear majority of purchases made by check. If retailers ever hope to reduce their losses in this area they must do a much better job of training their clerks for more than just reading/scanning prices and punching numbers on a machine. The following examination points should be taught to every retail sales clerk. Note: 'Bad Check' graphic is in full size at end of chapter.

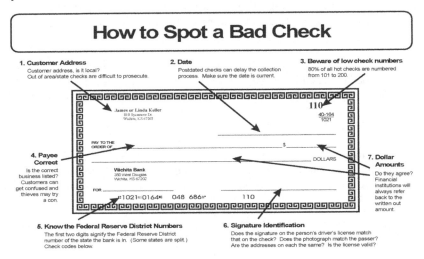

FORGED CHECKS

Forged checks are checks that are genuine checks, having been issued by a legitimate financial institution to a customer. They become forged when a thief either takes possession of a customer's check book and removes a blank check and fraudulently completes it, or alters a check legitimately made out to them or someone else. The following examination points will reduce the successful passing of forged checks.

Customer Address

Checks that are accepted from out-of-state customers and are returned by the bank for non-payment are extremely difficult to collect on. Prosecuting attorneys simply do not have the time, money or resources to pursue prosecution across state lines. This means that the retailer must be diligent in enforcing policies regarding the acceptance of out-of-state checks. While businesses that cater to tourists must accept these checks as part of doing business, this is not true of most other retailers. If retailers do not depend on tourist dollars then they must ask themselves what the gain is versus the potential loss in accepting out-of-state checks. If the check is fraudulent it is virtually impossible to collect on it. The loss would be much greater than the modest markup profit on the now stolen merchandise. Retailers should create a simple policy of not accepting out-of–state checks and enforce the policy.

Date

There are two considerations regarding the date on a check. It can either be postdated (a future date) or predated (a past date). Either situation can create potential cashing problems for the retailer.

Postdated checks are not legally enforceable until the date on the check. In this way, checks are like business contracts. When a person walks into a retailer and purchases an item for sale, it must be paid for at the time of the sale. While cash may be preferred, the retailer will take a 'promise to pay' in the form of a personal check. Essentially, this check has just become a legal business document in the form of a contract, with all the legal ramifications of a contract. And, like any business contract, the applicability date and thus enforcement date of a business contract is the date written on the contract and agreed to by both parties.

To clarify this process: with the retail purchase in hand the con artist approaches the clerk. The con completes the check for the amount of purchase. On the check (which is the '**offer**' in official contracts) are all the business related contract elements: the names of the agreeing parties (maker and payee), details of the agreement (I owe you X dollars for merchandise, optionally stated on the memo line; this is the '**consideration**' in an official contract), the date of the contract (the maker (or con) controls this on checks), and two signatures (the maker on the front and payee's stamped or electronic signature on the rear; this is the '**acceptance**' of an official contract). The maker (con artist) fills out all the lines on the check/contract (this keeps the con in control) and signs the check with his signature. The clerk (an employee of and therefore official contract agent for the retailer) reviews the check (contract) for accuracy and then indicates acceptance by the retailer of the conditions on the check (contract) by endorsing it on the back with the retailer stamp (the second signature).

What typically happens is that the clerk has only looked at the numeric dollar amount on the check. Rarely is the date examined. This is the con artist's goal. The con may postdate the check by 6 to 12 months or more. After the check is accepted by the retailer the con leaves and calls their financial institution and agrees to pay a small service fee to put a hold on the check. The stated reason for the hold is because of the post date. (It is true that if you do not call, the financial institution can and will legally process the check regardless of the date. The call puts the responsibility to hold back on the financial institution). When the check is forwarded by the retailer to the con's financial institution for payment, it is held for payment until the due date or returned to the retailer for non-payment due to the hold. The retailer now spends valuable time tracking the maker (con) down on the phone. When they finally do connect, the con artist simply tells the retailer that he/she will honor the check (contract) on the agreed upon date on the check (contract). Because the sales clerk (contract agent) was authorized to accept checks (make contracts) the entire process is legal and not enforceable until the date of the check. This means that the con has use of the retailer's property free of charge until the check comes due. The retailer may contact their attorney, at an additional expense, but they will be told that this is, first, a valid contract, and that any issue the retailer has with the transaction is a civil contract issue and not a criminal complaint. Of course, failure to pay when the check becomes due is a criminal issue. However, the con is betting that this will never occur. The reason is that the retailer must keep track of the paper check for the next 6 to 12 months and then remember it, locate it and process it. The con artist is hoping, logically, that the check is likely to have been lost in the paperwork of the retailer and will never be cashed. The purchase then becomes free to the con artist. If the check is located and cashed, the con is out nothing by honoring the check when it comes due. The con must be prepared, however, for a hold on all his/her future checks at that retail store. Of course, opening a new checking account means that he/she can do the entire process all over again.

For all that inconvenience and potential loss, the prevention of this fraud is simple. The clerk should examine the date on the check and make sure it is the current date.

The next issue is *predated* checks. This is a check with a date in the past. The issue here is that a financial institution that may notice the "stale" date and not process it. Many financial institutions refuse to process checks that are more than six months old. Some even have a time limit of 60 or 90 days, while others will go up to 12 months. If spotted, the check would be returned to the retailer without benefit of depositing it into the retailers account. The retailer must now locate the maker. Once again this is an extra cost to the retailer. The major difference here is that failure to honor the check, in this past date case, is a crime.

Once again, wasted time and expense can be saved by proper examination of the date before accepting the check.

Check Number

The FBI is responsible for collecting crime reports from all law enforcement agencies in the U.S. One of the interesting statistics that comes out of those reports relates to check fraud. Fully 90% of all fraudulent checks have a check number that is below the number 200. The reason for this anomaly is that check fraud criminals open new checking accounts wherever they travel. They present false identification credentials, offer $50.00 in cash and wait for their new checks to be sent to a post office drop box address. They then begin writing as many checks as they possibly can in a three-day period. With quick work they can easily write 100 to 200 checks worth tens of thousands of dollars. Of course, with only $50.00 in the account, all the checks are returned uncashed and the retailers lose their money. Meantime, the criminal has moved on to another community.

There are several prevention efforts aimed at stopping this problem. The first is at the retailer level. While it may inconvenience some legitimate new customers, any patron who presents a check with a check number below 200 (some retailer's state 500) should be asked to show two forms of local identification. When the criminal opened the account they probably had an out-of-state counterfeit identification card or driver's license that would not necessarily be obvious to the bank personnel. However, if the person is shopping in a local store, with a local address printed on the check, he/she should have a local identification matching the information printed on the check. Few criminals plan on staying in the community they are stealing from and so do not bother trying to get a state or local identification card. Also, if a counterfeit state identification card were to be used at the retailer there is always a chance that someone may spot it and call the police. This should discourage most criminals from continuing the transaction.

Another option for retailers would be videotaping of the transaction. A clearly posted sign would announce to customers that for their safety and security all sales transactions are being videotaped. Then do it! No criminal wants to leave his/her face behind as evidence during the crime.

Financial institutions themselves are assisting retailers with this problem through legislative action. In many states (32 at this printing) there is a law called the '101' law. It states that any new checking account opened at any financial institution in that state must start with check number 101 if a personal account and 1001 if a business account. In addition, only 200 checks will be mailed with the first order. This is designed to assist the retailer in identifying new accounts with the low check number, and to better examine the passer and his/her ID.

In the absence of such a law some financial institutions will let customers choose any number desired to start on their account but they will print a coded account opening date on each check. (This is optional at the discretion of the financial institution). The date code will look like 6-12 or 612 to indicate that the account was opened in June of 2012. The code will either appear to the right of the printed name on top of the check or above the signature line. Thus, regardless of the check number the sales clerk will know that this is a recently opened checking account and can ask for additional identification or call for a manager.

Payee

This is not normally an issue created by a check fraud artist, but rather by accident. However, it can still result in potential losses. If a harried maker writes the wrong payee on the check, the financial institution may process the check incorrectly. Why take a chance? Simply verify the correct payee on the check.

Signature Identification

The first step required in a signature examination is to make sure the signature is present. It may seem obvious, but many worthless checks have been accepted by sales clerks without having been signed by the customer. The next step is to make sure the check has the same name on the signature line as is printed at the top of the check. Some check fraud artists enjoy playing a game with the sales clerk. It is a game of catch-me-if-you-can. As an example, worthless checks have been signed with the signatures of Mickey Mouse and Donald Duck. The legendary 'John Hancock' has even signed some checks. One check signer even went so far as to leave a clue in the form of the signature. It was signed, "*I. Screwed You*". Of course, it was returned to the retailer, unpaid. Checking the signature can pay off!

Dollar Amounts

There are two amount lines on all checks. While sales clerks are supposed to cross check each amount, the reality is that the numerical amount is the line almost always looked at for purchase amount verification. This means the thief can easily pass checks with two different amounts on the same check. This may be due to simple lack of concentration on the part of the check maker, or it could be the work of a check fraud artist.

The first examination point should be of the two amounts. First, the inks on the two amounts should be the same to prevent altering the amount of the check. This is a quick sign of a stolen check that a criminal is trying to cash. Secondly, there should be no erasures on the amount lines. Next, they should be legible and clear as to the amount. And, finally, the two amounts should agree. But what if the sales clerk missed the last point and the check is processed?

So, how do financial institutions handle two different amounts on checks? When customers bring check amount disputes to their attention, financial institutions will always accept the written-out amount rather than the numbers themselves as the legal amount of the check. This is because the numeric figures are easily altered to a higher amount. A one can easily become a seven or four. A three or seven can become an eight, etc. The very reason for the written out numeric amount is to avoid any dispute over the "true" amount of a check.

Once again, the con artist will take advantage of this. The criminal, knowing that the average sales clerk will only look at the numeric dollar amount, will write the correct sales figure on this check line, say $500.00. However, on the written out amount the dollar figure will be hundreds of dollars less, or possibly even "$ Fifty dollars and zero cents". The check will likely be processed for the $500.00 figure as the clerks who process checks also usually look at the numeric amount. However, after the check has been returned to the criminal customer he/she will dispute the amount of the check and claim that someone else in the store must have raised the dollar amount and raided the cash register for the difference. Unless every purchase is on a store audit tape listing the day, date, account number, check number, and purchase price, the fraud artist will beat the retailer on this one.

Retailers who follow all the preceding six simple check examination points should be able to dramatically reduce their losses from check fraud. While all the examination points taken together may initially be a bit overwhelming, with very little practice they can all be accomplished in five seconds. Once a clerk is properly trained in these points the process becomes automatic and checks fraud losses drop proportionately.

COUNTERFEIT CHECKS

Counterfeit checks differ from forgeries in that forged checks are legitimate check stock forged by a thief. Counterfeit checks are created from blank paper stock using either legitimate, but stolen information, or fictitious information. This information is transferred to the blank check stock to be made to look like a genuine check. In addition to the standard forgery check points, there is one examination point for counterfeit checks that is addressed below.

Federal Reserve District Numbers

This examination point concentrates on reading and interpreting the first two MICR (Magnetic Ink Character Recognition) numbers (also called routing numbers) of a personal check. The numbers and characters appear as follows at the bottom of all checks used in the United States:

0123456789 ⑈ ⑆ ⑇ ⑉

They are called MICR because the ink used to print these numbers and characters is actually magnetically encoded. Thus, the equipment used by the Federal Reserve and financial institutions across the U.S. actually 'read' the characters based on their magnetic shape, not on the number or character.

It is the first two numbers of the total MICR line of characters (second set of numbers of Business Checks) that counterfeiters *may* alter when they counterfeit checks. By altering the first two digits it is possible to gain additional time before the check is identified as a counterfeit. The additional time is used to pass a greater number of these bad checks. Note that not all counterfeiters are sophisticated enough to understand the system and others simply do not care about having additional time to pass these bad checks as they will simply create new counterfeits to pass when these are identified. So, while spotting this aberration will catch some counterfeit checks it will not catch them all.

The first two numbers in the MICR identify which one of the twelve U.S. Federal Reserve districts will ultimately clear the check. Each Federal Reserve is geographically situated in the U.S. and each is assigned a number.

The 12 regions and 12 Federal District numbers are as follows. Note that the second number listed identifies Credit Unions and Savings Bank financial institutions. These separate entities and their unique district numbers are further explained at the end of this section.

- Boston-01 (21)
- New York-02 (22)
- Philidelphia-03 (23)
- Cleveland-04 (24)
- Richmond-05 (25)
- Atlanta-06 (26)
- Chicago-07 (27)
- St. Louis-08 (28)
- Minneapolis-09 (29)
- Kansas City-10 (30)
- Dallas-11 (31)
- San Francisco-12 (32)

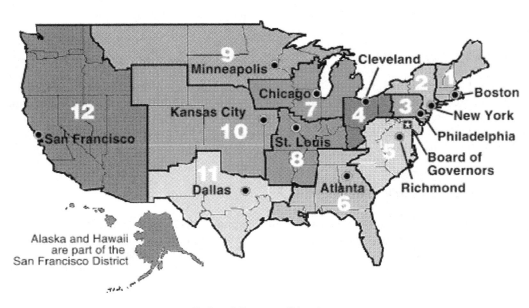

Federal Reserve Districts

The Federal Reserve officially identifies Districts by number and Reserve Bank city.
In the 12th District, the Seattle Branch serves Alaska, and the San Francisco Bank serves Hawaii. The System serves commonwealths and territories as follows: the New York Bank serves the Commonwealth of Puerto Rico and the U.S. Virgin Islands; the San Francisco Bank serves American Samoa, Guam, and the Commonwealth of the Northern Mariana Islands. The Board of Governors revised the branch boundaries of the System in February 1996.

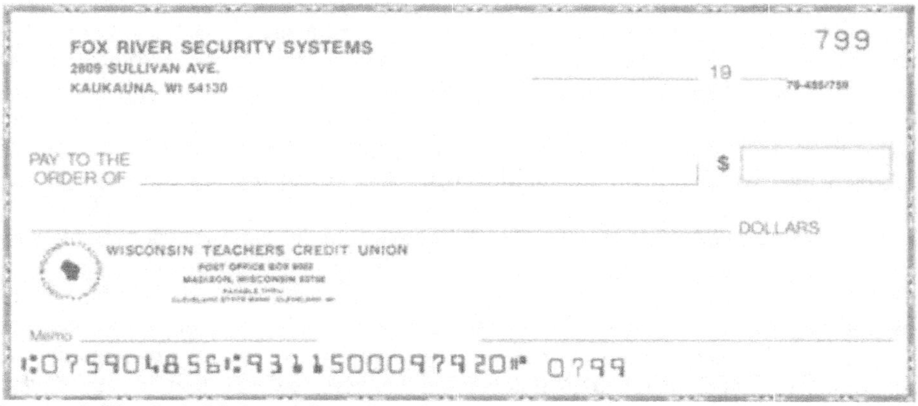

Personal Check (with home based business name) with Federal Reserve Number 7
This is an example of a Credit Union check with a non-Credit Union Federal Reserve number

As identified in the chart above, the 01 as the first set of numbers in the MICR, indicates the Federal Reserve Bank of Boston. 07 indicates Chicago, while a 12 identifies San Francisco. (*Business* checks have the routing numbers placed as the *second* set of numbers in the MICR sequence. The first set of numbers on business checks is the check number; see following example).

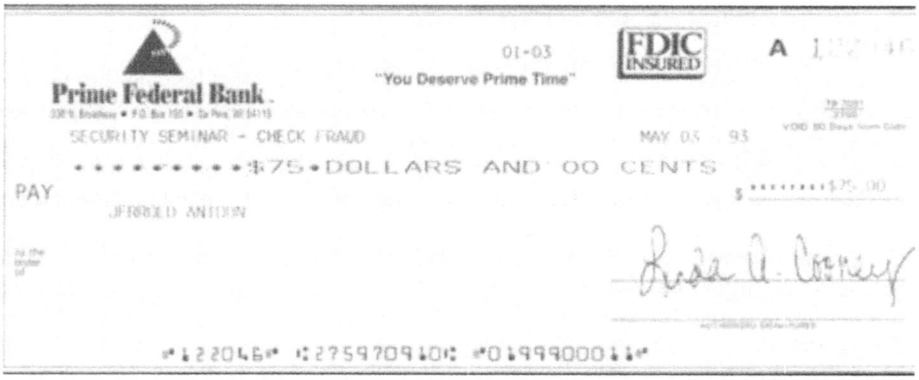

Business Check with Federal Reserve Routing Numbers as Second Set of Numbers
Note, this is a 'Savings Bank', thus the 20+ MICR number

A careful study of any current or future check you may have or receive will best demonstrate the exact placement of these MICR numbers. Regardless of the type of check, personal or business, the Federal Reserve District number will always follow the 'sideways smile' character, which looks like this:

⑈

As an example, in the MICR routing number sample, below, the Federal Reserve number is 1 for Boston. (First set of two numbers after the smiley face). Single digit Federal Reserve numbers will always begin with a 0, as in 05 for Richmond. Always look for the first two numbers following the 'sideways' smiley face to identify the Federal Reserve Number for that check.

⑆0123456789⑆⑈⑇⑇

The numbers after the Federal Reserve digits identify the home bank of the check and additional routing information that is not relevant to this discussion.

To better understand how a counterfeit check criminal takes advantage of the check routing system, a short primer on how a legitimate check works in the system is in order. For example, let us use a fictional check drawn on a maker's financial institution. For discussion purposes we will call the check maker's bank the First Bank of Boston. This check is passed in a Boston store for payment of merchandise. The check will first be routed through the *retailer's* financial institution for crediting to the retailer. Let's call the retailer's bank the Freedom Bank, Boston Massachusetts. Freedom Bank must now get the maker's check back to the First Bank of Boston. To accomplish this task for the Freedom Bank, and every other bank in the U.S., the U.S. Federal Reserve system takes over. In this case, Freedom Bank is going to send the check to the regional Boston Federal Reserve (01). The Boston Federal Reserve receives all the area checks and forwards them all to the Atlanta Federal Reserve. Atlanta is responsible for sorting through every single check in America. (A task that used to be done by all 12 districts but the declining use of checks no longer justifies that). The Atlanta Federal Reserve sorts them out by using high speed magnetic ink (MICR) readers to read the magnetic MICR routing numbers on the bottom of every check. The Federal Reserve of Atlanta sends the check back to the originating bank, in this case the First Bank of Boston. The First Bank of Boston processes it, deducts the amount from the holder's account, and sends out the monthly statement documenting the transaction.

In the event the check is counterfeited with the correct Federal Reserve District number the process would be the same and the fraud would not be detected until the account holder notices the loss, typically within two days. However, if the Federal Reserve number was changed it would be routed to the wrong bank and would cause additional delays as the discrepancy was 'corrected' at the Federal Reserve level. Even at that point the fraud would not necessarily be uncovered. The Federal Reserve only reads the MICR, it does not interpret correct or incorrect numbers. Therefore, the counterfeiter could have as much as four days to write out counterfeit checks before leaving the area.

The solution to this problem is education and awareness. Sales clerks must be taught to be aware of the Federal Reserve district number in their area and make sure it is the correct district number on the check. The incorrect number in their home state or area is an indicator that the check is counterfeit. Again, not all counterfeiters will alter the Federal Reserve number. The examination process just explained will only catch those counterfeit checks in which the Federal Reserve numbers have been intentionally altered.

There is one exception to the use of the numbers 1-12 for U.S. Federal Reserve banks. The number exception applies to credit unions and savings banks. Because these financial institutions were not part of the original founding of the U.S. Federal Reserve, and did not contribute to their financial base, they are treated slightly differently.

These institutions are allowed to use the Federal Reserve system to process their checks, which are legally called 'share drafts', not checks. The Federal Reserve banking system then charges them a fee for each share draft that goes through their system. To make sure that the fee is collected, a separate set of numbers is assigned to these financial institutions. Fortunately for retailers it is an easy system to de-code. Each of the 12 Federal Reserve numbers had the number 20 added to it. So, a Boston credit union share draft (check) would have a Federal Reserve number 21. (1+20=21). Chicago becomes 27 (7+20) and San Francisco would be 32 (12+20). In some cases, you will see a credit union check with a 1-12 Federal Reserve number on it. The Federal Reserve implemented this policy some years back in the interest of efficiency. So, the check could have either number listed as the first two digits in the MICR routing line and either would be correct.

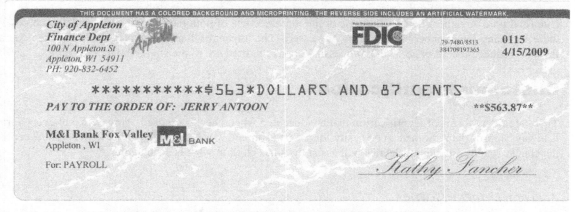

FOX RIVER SECURITY SYSTEMS
PH. 766-2664
2809 SULLIVAN AVE.
KAUKAUNA, WI 54130

19____   800

79-7914/2759

PAY TO THE
ORDER OF _____ $ _____

_____ DOLLARS

WISCONSIN TEACHERS CREDIT UNION
POST OFFICE BOX 8003
MADISON, WISCONSIN 53708

MEMO _____

⑆275979144⑆01000979022⑈ 0800

Credit Union Federal Reserve Number of 27

Check Printing Software

The ability of individuals to print their own checks on their home computer printer is commonly available through both online vendors and office supply stores. Once the software is loaded anyone can print checks with their own financial institution MICR numbers and even copy and paste the logo onto their checks. Some ink cartridges even come filled with magnetic ink to prevent hang-ups in the banking system.

However, these same software programs can be programmed by counterfeiters to print a check with any MICR numbers and in any amount from any check holder. Of course, the check is not valid and would be considered a counterfeit if passed on to a retailer. However, it would not be discovered as a counterfeit until the account holder notifies their financial institution. At that point the check charge would be reversed and the retailer will suffer the loss. Thus, retailers will continue to be victimized by accepting paper checks given this scenario.

THIS DOCUMENT HAS A COLORED BACKGROUND AND MICROPRINTING. THE REVERSE SIDE INCLUDES AN ARTIFICIAL WATERMARK.

City of Appleton
Finance Dept
100 N Appleton St
Appleton, WI 54911
PH: 920-832-6452

FDIC   79-7480/8513   0115
384709197365   4/15/2009

**************$563*DOLLARS AND 87 CENTS**

PAY TO THE ORDER OF: JERRY ANTOON   **$563.87**

M&I Bank Fox Valley M&I BANK
Appleton, WI

For: PAYROLL   _Kathy Fancher_

⑈0115⑈ ⑆322759340⑆ 054184078472⑈

Counterfeit Check Printed with Check Printing Software
Note the '32' Federal Reserve Number for Wisconsin

CHECK CLEARING FOR THE 21ST CENTURY ACT

On October 28, 2004 a new law took effect that makes the alteration of MICR Federal Reserve District numbers much less profitable for the criminal. The Check Clearing for the 21st Century Act was not passed to combat check counterfeiting, nor was that its intent. Nevertheless, the result is that it will affect professional check counterfeiters.

This new law creates a new legal instrument called a 'substitute check' which allows financial institutions to remove the actual paper check from the check collection and return system within the Federal Reserve, and replace the check with an electronic check file image. Operating very much like a checking account debit card, or the electronic processing and immediate return of your check directly at the retailer's location, your paper check is converted to a digital format. That allows your check to be processed as computer bits and bytes rather than in paper format. Your paper format check may well be stopped at the retailer's bank and converted right there to digital form. The digital version of your check would bypass the Federal Reserve paper processing system and would immediately be processed at the maker's bank based on the MICR routing numbers.

The paper check would be destroyed and only the electronic image would remain. In the event of a legal dispute over the amount, signature in a forgery, or other issue with a check, the digital copy of the check, called a 'substitute check' (a front and back paper reproduction) would become the legal representation of the original check. Courts, retailers, and other financial institutions are all required to accept this substitute check as proof of payment just as they would the original check.

Counterfeit checks then, will be affected as well. This is due to the rapid electronic processing of any counterfeit checks that would be spotted and, presumably, stopped immediately by the maker's bank. This would negate the attempting passing of the typical 500 counterfeit checks. However, the passing of individually counterfeited checks could still occur at the retailer level, making examination of the MICR numbers just as important as before this new Act was passed.

An interesting side note to this 21st Century Act. It was the banking industry itself that pushed for this federal legislation. The impetus was the terrorist acts of September 11, 2001. On that day all commercial aircraft nationwide were immediately grounded in mid-flight at the nearest airport. Many of those planes were carrying checks that were in the process of being shuttled around to different Federal Reserve check processing systems. The resulting loss of the use of those funds and interest income to the banks by the grounded checks led to the concept of electronic copies of paper checks and the reduction of handling of millions of paper checks every day.

One final note on paper checks. Because of the increased use of both bank credit cards and debit cards there are many fewer paper checks being processed. The impact of this change is that in 2007 the Federal Reserve reduced the 12 paper check processing centers in the U.S. to the single Atlanta Reserve.

Customer Identification

There are many forms of identification that are accepted when checks are used. However, not every form is always appropriate. Some can be easily forged and some may not be recognizable to the clerk accepting the check. The following guidelines will assist the sales clerk in what is acceptable.

ACCEPTABLE IDENTIFICATION

Driver's License

The most universally accepted, and typically most authentic form of identification, is the state issued driver's license or identification card. This card can certainly be altered or even falsely issued using fictitious information, but both require some effort under tightly controlled circumstances. Compared to other forms of identification, it is still the best. Here are some things to look at on state issued identifications.

The first item to examine is the picture on the card. Comparing the picture with the person will at least eliminate the thief who is the wrong race, age or gender. The physical data can then be compared. While people may gain or lose some weight, an excessive amount over or under what is printed on the identification is a ground for further scrutiny. Also keep in mind that a person's height does not normally change. The clerk should compare his or her own height to what is stated on the customer identification. Is the person taller or shorter then indicated on the identification? The best piece of identification on the card is the signature. If stolen, it will probably not match the signature on the check. Clerks should compare signatures from the check and the identification as a matter of routine. The best method of comparing is to lay the identification card above the check signature line for comparison. Turning both items upside down for comparison is an excellent method of verifying signatures. That way you are not reading the signature but truly comparing the actual lines. If there is not a match, the sales clerk should call for a supervisor to check the signature and handle the sale refusal. If the driver's license is from another state or country in North America, then the clerk should be prepared with a published identification book from those areas. Check the Internet, library or local law enforcement agency for referrals on where to purchase these identification guidebooks.

Local Employee Identification

These can be accepted with reservations. Local employee identification cards can be effective but this means that the employee ID cards must be well known to the clerk due to frequent exposure to the cards. Employee ID cards from a company some distance away will not be recognized by the clerk and should not be accepted. He/she may not be able to differentiate between an authentic card and a fraudulently created one.

Bank Cards

This is another form of ID with reservations. Many stores that require identifications will identify a major bank card as an acceptable form of ID. This can be a source of concern. The reason any ID is requested in the first place is so that the ID number recorded on the check can be used by the police to trace it back to its owner. If the presented ID is a bank card, it could well be the card that was in the purse or wallet that was stolen with the checkbook. It may also be a counterfeit card. Even if legitimate, when the police contact the bank card company and ask for assistance on a check fraud case the likely response will be that a warrant is needed in order to gain the information. Because the bank card company is not the victim they may not be able to legally pass on any information they have on the account holder.

Fingerprint

Probably the best form of identification is a fingerprint on the check. This is not widely used in most states in America, but in those areas where it is being used bad check losses have been dramatically reduced. With non-visible ink being used, there is no mess involved in the process. The check passer is asked to place their thumbprint on the face of the check. The special invisible ink allows the fingerprint to show up on the check. If the check is returned as not payable, the police have a ready piece of evidence to use in their investigation and the thief is aware of this. Financial institutions using this tool are realizing its power and are beginning to implement it.

UNACCEPTABLE IDENTIFICATION

While some forms of identification should never be taken, the check passer may be convincing enough to con the sales clerk into accepting it. The following forms of identification should never be accepted.

Social Security Cards

Social security cards should never be accepted. A new number can easily be obtained using a fake birth certificate and baptismal certificate, both of which are different for each county of each state. By claiming recent immigration status, a new card and number are issued to each requester. Social Security cards may also be obtained through the theft of purses or wallets. But the real question is why accept the card at all? There is nothing on the card except the person's typed name and a dated signature. The card could be counterfeit printed on a computer and the name typed on it. Even if it was legitimate, the 1974 U.S. Privacy Act forbids the U.S. Social Security Department from releasing any information about the person, even to law enforcement, except under court order.

Business Cards

People, in the course of introducing themselves to others, routinely use business cards. These cards have become an accepted form of identification in business or social gatherings, but lack the needed identifiers for check acceptance. They have no numbers or signature or physically identifying data.

Military Identification Cards

Those who are in the U.S. military use military identification cards. Unfortunately, most people outside of the military would normally never see a military ID and so could not recognize a legitimate card. Indeed, when the various legitimate military dependent, police, retired, reserve, medical personnel, and active cards are placed together they create a rainbow of different colors and designs. A sales clerk can easily be fooled into thinking that a counterfeit card has been issued by the military. In fact, even an authentic military identification card may be in criminal hands as past burglaries of military installations have procured blank identification card stocks.

Immigration Cards

Immigration cards are frequently referred to as 'green cards'. However, U.S. immigration cards are white, not green. How does a sales clerk keep all this straight? With proper education and resources. The resource manuals listed below should assist.

IDENTIFICATION CHECKING MANUALS

When a form of standard identification is given to a sales clerk, but it is not immediately recognized, there is a way to both accept the check for the sale and have a reasonable certainty that the ID presented is legitimate. Two books are widely published that print full color samples of most public government identification cards. The first is called the ID Checking Guide. This annual paperback guide contains a color replica of every current and immediate past driver's license and identification card for each of the fifty U.S. states and all the provinces of Canada. Pictorial representation of U.S. Federal documents and financial institution bank cards are also included.

The second guide is called the United States Identification Manual (USIM). It is a spiral-bound hard cover guide that lists everything the above listed guide does, but goes into much more detail on each item. All U.S. federal documents are portrayed as well as traveler's checks, current and past. For a subscription fee it will also be updated on a quarterly basis. Note that the USIM is only sold to legitimate law enforcement agencies and related enforcement/investigative entities.

ID Checking Guide can be obtained from:

Driver's License Guide Company
PO Box 5305
Redwood City, CA 94063

United States Identification Manual can be obtained from:

U.S. Identification Manual Division
1492 Oddstad Dr.
Redwood City, CA 94063

www.idcheckingguide.com

Traveler's Checks

Traveler's checks were created to provide the safety of checks without the cashing problems associated with passing personal checks out of the maker's home area. However, con artists have created frauds with these checks as well. Retailers are the most susceptible to these frauds. Being aware of the types of frauds involving traveler's checks is the best defense. Note that the Traveler's Check companies are offering Electronic purchase cards (debit cards) as an option to paper checks. It is likely that this option will reduce the number of paper traveler's checks used by travelers.

CHECK PURCHASE PROCEDURES

Traveler's checks are purchased at financial institutions, travel agencies and a few other select locations. Basically, the purchaser buys a number of standard end-bound checks in fixed denominations. At the location of purchase the purchaser must sign his/her name (on some checks two parties may sign) at the top of every check. Later, when a traveler's check is used for a purchase, the holder of the check will again sign the check at the bottom. The sales clerk will then compare the two signatures and, if the signatures match, will accept the check.

Traveler's check companies have instituted a short method of remembering how to properly accept these checks. It is simply called *"Watch and Compare"*. The "watch" part means that the store clerk should actually observe the signature being signed. "Compare", of course, is the comparing of the signatures. If the signing was observed and the signatures compared and matched, the traveler's check company will honor the check. If the signatures do not match the company returns the check, uncashed, to the retailer.

FRAUD TECHNIQUES

There are four common frauds associated with traveler's checks. They are always used in retail settings at a loss for the retailer. In the first three of these frauds the checks have been stolen and taken to a professional forger to be pre-signed. The passer must then convince the clerk that each check to be passed on to the retailer is being signed in their presence. The last fraud does not involve a professional forger, but is signed by the thief passing the stolen check.

Fraud One

The first fraud involves placing the check on the counter and covering the signature line with the non-writing hand. The thief is pretending to use the non-writing hand to hold the paper in place. The passer then pretends to sign the checks, which have, of course, already been pre-forged. The clerk only thinks they have witnessed the signature.

The prevention of this fraud is to actually watch the check being countersigned. This means to literally observe the ink flow onto the paper.

Fraud Two

In the second fraud, the thief allows you to observe the signing of the first, blank check but, lifting that check, pretends to sign the remainder of the checks. They are actually already forged. In passing them to the clerk, the passer palms the top check and presents the forged ones.

The prevention technique is the same: observe *every* check being signed.

Fraud Three

In the third fraud the thief purchases a second set of traveler's checks in the name of the person whose name is actually on the stolen checks in his/her possession. The passer purchases merchandise and signs all the checks he/she purchased in the presence of the clerk. The checks are then accidentally dropped by the passer and, when bending down to pick them up, are switched for the stolen ones that have already been forged. This works when the passer is wearing a jacket with inside pockets. The legitimate checks purchased by the thief will be returned for a refund.

Prevention efforts require the clerk to remember that if the checks are ever out of sight, for even a moment, to have the passer re-sign the check on the back and then compare all three of the signatures.

Fraud Four

The last fraud is an attempt by the passer to not have to pay a forger for his/her work. The passer has traced over the original signature on the stolen checks with a felt tip pen thus obliterating the original signature. In the presence of the clerk he/she then countersigns the check in the proper location. However, by writing slowly the thief may be able to emulate his/her own tracing of the original signature as though it was his or her own. Many clerks will not press the issue for fear of angering the "customer".

The prevention aspect requires the clerk to verify that there is no erasure, alteration, or another signature under the felt tip signature in the upper left-hand corner. This can be done by a careful examination of the original signature and secondly, by turning over the check and looking for the paper indentation made by the original signer with a ballpoint pen. A felt tip pen leaves no such indentation.

TIME LIMIT ON CASHING

Unlike normal checks, traveler's checks have no expiration date on them. The traveler check companies would prefer that customers save extra checks for the next vacation while they invest the purchaser's money for their own profit.

SUSPECTED COUNTERFEIT CHECK

Each traveler's check company has security features built into their checks. However, American Express has a unique one. Each check is printed in two different inks. To verify if one of their checks is legitimate, turn the check over. With a damp finger, wipe the left side denominator. It should easily smear the ink. Repeat the process with the right side and it should not smear. On counterfeit checks either both or neither denominator would smear.

One easy counterfeit verification technique is to understand the name of the issuing company. America Express Company issues their traveler's checks in many different currencies, including Canadian currency. However, a past counterfeiter has taken advantage of retail clerks by printing up counterfeit Canadian Express Traveler's checks in Canadian currency. Some U.S. businesses readily accepted the checks only to find them later returned as fraudulent.

Traveler's check companies do offer free training materials to assist the retailer in identifying fraudulent checks. A search on the Internet will direct the researcher to the relevant sites with instructions on how to procure these materials.

Summary

Much of the check fraud in America can be directly attributed to business owners failing to give proper training to their sales clerks. Investing a small amount of time in this area would reap huge returns in the form of identified and rejected forged and counterfeit checks.

How to Spot a Bad Check

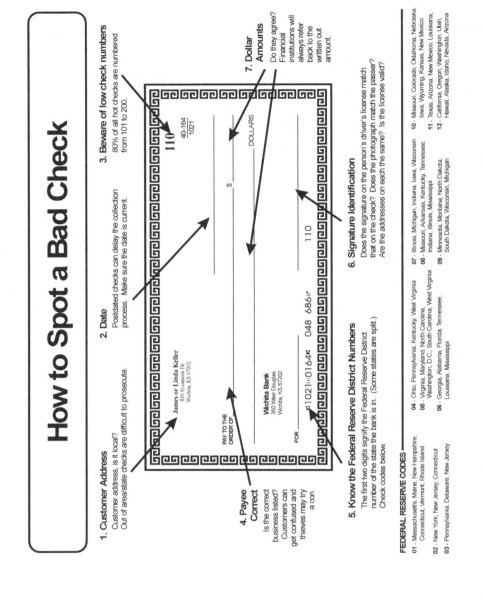

1. Customer Address
Customer address, is it local?
Out of area/state checks are difficult to prosecute.

2. Date
Postdated checks can delay the collection process. Make sure the date is current.

3. Beware of low check numbers
80% of all hot checks are numbered from 101 to 200.

4. Payee Correct
Is the correct business listed? Customers can get confused and thieves may try a con.

7. Dollar Amounts
Do they agree? Financial institutions will always refer back to the written out amount.

5. Know the Federal Reserve District Numbers
The first two digits signify the Federal Reserve District number of the state the bank is in. (Some states are split.) Check codes below.

6. Signature Identification
Does the signature on the person's driver's license match that on the check? Does the photograph match the passer? Are the addresses on each the same? Is the license valid?

FEDERAL RESERVE CODES

01 - Massachusetts, Maine, New Hampshire, Connecticut, Vermont, Rhode Island
02 - New York, New Jersey, Connecticut
03 - Pennsylvania, Delaware, New Jersey
04 - Ohio, Pennsylvania, Kentucky, West Virginia
05 - Virginia, Maryland, North Carolina, Washington, D.C., South Carolina, West Virginia
06 - Georgia, Alabama, Florida, Tennessee, Louisiana, Mississippi
07 - Illinois, Michigan, Indiana, Iowa, Wisconsin
08 - Missouri, Arkansas, Kentucky, Tennessee, Indiana, Illinois, Mississippi
09 - Minnesota, Montana, North Dakota, South Dakota, Wisconsin, Michigan
10 - Missouri, Colorado, Oklahoma, Nebraska, Iowa, Wyoming, Kansas, New Mexico
11 - Texas, Arizona, New Mexico, Louisiana,
12 - California, Oregon, Washington, Utah, Hawaii, Alaska, Idaho, Nevada, Arizona

References

Fraud Magazine, Now You See It, Now You Don't, August 2011; Company Check and Credit Card Fraud ROBERT TIE

Amount of Check Fraud Rose Substantially in '93 : Crime: 'The banking system is under attack,' authorities say. Desktop publishing is one reason.; December 1, 1994 | From Associated Press

US News and World Report, May 19, 2008; 5 Ways to Avoid Being a Check-Fraud Victim
The real-life inspiration for "Catch Me If You Can" offers five ways to keep from being victimized
By LUKE MULLINS

Construction Business Owner, March 2007; Fight Payroll Check Fraud; Written by: Bob Howe

eWeek.com 2010-07-28; Massive Check Fraud Operation Run by Hackers Revealed at Black Hat
By: Brian Prince

ACFE, January/February 2012 ;'Check 21' Can Make Fraud Easier; BE ALERT TO CHANGES IN CHECK-IMAGING TECHNOLOGY; Linda Lee Larson, DBA, CFE, CPA, CISA

Sarbanes-Oxley Compliance: Laying Plans for Check Fraud Prevention Controls
Written by Jessica Andrews, AP Technology, 2004

Winning the War Against Check Fraud; Why Is Positive Pay Necessary?
Written by Rich Love, CEO of AP Technology, 2000

FBI Financial Institution Fraud and Failure Report - Fiscal Year ending Sept. 30 2003.

CSO Physical Security, April, 2, 2012; How to fight check fraud; By Mary Brandel

https://www.jpmorgan.com/cm/BlobServer/2014_AFP_Payments_Fraud_Survey.pdf?blobkey=id&blobw here=1320639355606&blobheader=application/pdf&blobheadername1=Cache-Control&blobheadervalue1=private&blobcol=urldata&blobtable=MungoBlobs

http://www.stopcheckfraud.com/statistics.html

http://www.nw3c.org/docs/research/check-fraud.pdf?sfvrsn=10

http://www.ckfraud.org/index.html

http://www.checkguarantee.com/check-fraud.php

http://www.afponline.org/fraud/

http://abcnews.go.com/Business/check-fraud-thing-past-criminals-adapt-debit-fraud/story?id=15964217

http://www.niceactimize.com/blog/index.php/2014/05/the-checking-fraud-paradox-checks-may-be-going-away-but-check-fraud-isnt/#.VQjXxI54pcQ

Chapter Nine

Bank Card Fraud

Bank card fraud performance objectives:

- Explain who owns and issues bank cards; credit and debit
- Describe the typical transaction process of a bank card purchase
- Explain the various types of bank card fraud
- Describe the security features on a VISA bank card
- Describe the security features on a MasterCard
- Explain the concept of bank card skimming
- Identify the fraud prevention measures taken by bank card companies
- Identify typical characteristics of a counterfeit bank card

Introduction

Credit cards and debit cards, like checks, were developed as an easy way for consumers to leave large amounts of cash at home and lower their risk of loss to robbery or theft. However, crime involving the use of bank cards has created its own set of problems. This unit will address those issues and potential solutions.

Extent of the Problem

The Visa and MasterCard companies alone account for approximately 65 percent of all outstanding revolving credit (consumer credit card debt.) Given this large percentage it is not surprising that most substantive fraud cases are centered on one or both of these bankcard companies. In response these two companies also put out the greatest number of fraud prevention training kits and materials for businesses. Additional information on these materials can be found at their respective web sites.

Exact bank card fraud statistics are difficult to determine with any certainty. Newly created scams, on-line fraud and international commerce continually alter the amount of money lost to banks and businesses. However, an August 2013 Nilson Report indicated that in calendar year 2012 (the most recent report available in March of 2015) credit and debit card fraud resulted in $11.27 billion in losses. Card issuers (banks, etc.) bore 63% of the fraud liability and merchants assumed the remaining 37%.

Interestingly, when one hears of a credit card 'data theft' from a large retailer like Target or Home Depot, this is normally not due to any fraud against the physical bank cards from bank card companies, like Visa or Master Card. In those situations, the targeted retailer's privately owned internal bank card data systems have been compromised. While the effect is the same - the customer's bank card information has been stolen - it falls back to the retailer for the financial loss. Target's actual dollar losses from their single data hack of December 2013 was reported out in February 2015. Target Corp. lost an actual $162 million. Many more data thefts have occurred in 2016-2018.

The good news is that, at the end of 2017, retailers had reduced bank card fraud by 29%. This decrease was attributed to a combination of internal controls and improved card security features.

Bank Card Transactions

When the customer presents a bank card, either credit or debit, the merchant processes it through a card terminal. It can be either a magnetic stripe or chip card. During the short wait period for approval the card information is sent through a series of checks (dark shaded arrows) to verify that the merchant is a legitimate retailer and that the card has not been reported lost or stolen. It even checks with the cardholder's bank to make sure that the cardholder is up to date on their monthly payments.

Once that process has been verified the approval process is reversed (light shaded arrows) as those permissions are sent back to the merchant to accept the bank card as a legitimate form of payment.

Model Card Transaction

☐ **Authorization**

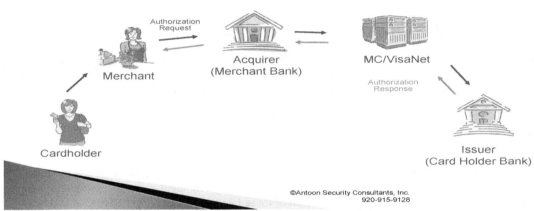

Bank Card Transaction Approval Steps

Types of Bank Cards and Merchant Readers

The card readers used for bank card processing by retailers are of three types. One type reads the magnetic stripe on the back of the card (Mag Stripe Readers) and another reads the embedded microchip for the same information (Chip Readers.) Both the Mag Stripe and the Chip cards must be swiped or inserted into their respective readers. Yet a third type uses a radio frequency signal (RFID Reader) to communicate with a bank card. Reloadable money cards fall into the same bracket as bank cards. E-readers that use cell phone proximity transmitters (no direct contact between merchant reader and payment device) are a separate class as they do not use physical cards. They are addressed after this section in the NFC Section.

Magnetic stripe cards have been around for decades. As a result, criminals have had ample time to figure out how to copy the information on the magnetic stripe and use it to their advantage. The ease of swiping the 'mag stripe' card through a magnetic stripe reader (almost every merchant in America has one) has made this card common in the wallet and purse of every charge/debit card merchandise buying person in the U.S.

The information on these stripes contains the cardholder's name, the account number, the expiration date, and the Card Verification Value (CVV), also known as the Card Security Code (CSC). This is all the information that is needed to process a bank card transaction. The ease of copying and counterfeiting magnetic stripe bank cards has led to the development of the other two forms of cards.

Magnetic Stripe on Rear of Bank Card

RFID (Radio Frequency Identification) cards were introduced in 2006. They operate by reflecting radio waves sent from a merchant's reader to your card and back to the reader with information containing your account number and expiration date. Instead of a three-digit security code RFID (or Smart) cards generate a unique card verification number for each transmission, and no number is used twice. Even if a thief could capture the transmitting signal during a purchase the security code would be invalid on the next transmission.

RFID bank cards are passive in nature. This means that the sensor inside the card remains inactive until it comes within about six inches of an RFID reader. The reader sends out a signal which activates the credit card sensor and begins the transmission process for reading the account information and completing the transaction. Millions of the cards are in circulation but, according to the U.S. Secret Service do not have an impact on fraudulent use. The lack of useful information to be captured is the primary reason. Counterfeiting them won't work, again, because of their design.

There are many articles and videos documenting the capture of RFID information on these types of cards while being carried in purses and wallets. The information is not false. Signals and information from your card can be captured while in your possession. But, as mentioned, the information captured cannot be used to make purchases *at this time*. However, criminals are a creative and inventive people. Given enough time this may change. In the meantime, the cards are currently safe. However, if you still feel violated there are commercial products being sold that are supposed to block the signal from your card. They are made of metal and wrap around the cards and even some that are composed of complete wallets. Not all work as well as advertised. The best solution is common aluminum foil wrapped around your card. But removing it if you needed to use it for a purchase might be bothersome. However, the reality is that while they exist most merchants that accept bank cards do not have an RFID reader to take advantage of this form of bank card, defaulting to either the chip or the magnetic stripe on the back. One more point; for those who are concerned about being tracked by the sensor inside of the card, it is not designed for that purpose and cannot be remotely tracked by your bank.

RFID Chip Credit Card   Card Includes WIFI Symbol

Chip cards (also known at EMV cards - which stands for Europay, MasterCard and Visa) have been around for many years in countries outside of the U.S., but their use inside the U.S. has not taken hold during that time. The basic reason was cost; cost to create new cards and cost to make and buy new readers. That thought has changed as bank card fraud reaches new heights, owing primarily to ease of fraudulent use and counterfeiting of magnetic stripe cards in the U.S. via 'skimming' (detailed later in this chapter.) The change to reduce fraud was finally forced by Visa, MasterCard, Discover and American Express. They made a joint announcement that if merchants don't install chip card payment terminals by October 2015, then any card fraud will be their responsibility. Conversely, they also told financial institutions that if they have not issued new bank cards with chips to their customers by the same date then they will be responsible for any fraud associated with non-chip cards used by their customers. Experts predict that only about half of all merchants will meet this deadline. In fact, as of March 2018 Visa reported that only 60% of merchants are chip reader equipped. Banks are predicted to be at about 70% with their turnover for the same date. Gas stations with pay-at-the-pump terminals are the exception on the date. Originally gas stations had until October 1, 2017. Due to difficulties with complaint hardware that deadline was recently extended to October 1, 2020. However, there is no legal requirement to change; the entire concept is voluntary.

To accommodate customers with a chip card shopping at a merchant without a chip card reader will still be able to make a purchase. Chip cards, for the foreseeable future, will retain the magnetic stripe on the back of the card that retailers will still be able to process. Of course, thieves will then also continue to be able to skim the magnetic stripe and duplicate a counterfeit card.

With all this new chip technology the U.S. will still not match the same technology being used in over 130 countries around the world. Across the oceans chip bank cards for both credit and debit purchases use a PIN (personal identification number) for each transaction. This is called a 'chip and PIN' system. In America we only use a PIN for debit card purchases while a signature is required for credit card purchases. The latter is known as a 'Chip and Signature' system. The decision by the major banks in the U.S. is that even though chip cards can be programmed to only be used with a PIN for all purchases, their chip cards will continue to be 'verified' by the use of a customer signature, thus the 'Chip and Signature' name. The logic, as one bank spokesperson states, is that it would be 'less confusing for the consumer' as we change over to the chip method of payment. As the major bank card networks (Visa, MC, etc.) only manage the processing of the cards, they are not able to dictate to banks as to how to secure their own cards.

This aberration may cause some confusion for customers using their cards. First, chip debit cards will retain the requirement for a PIN for purchases. Most chip credit cards will not. However, to receive a cash advance from an ATM on your chip credit card you will need to have a PIN. But that PIN is not for actual credit card purchases, it only works at ATMs. Additionally, if you travel overseas (and even our foreign neighbors) and attempt to use your chip credit card you may be denied because your card does not have the associated PIN that is required in other countries. Banks assure us that if you simply inform the foreign merchant that your chip credit card is a signature verification form of card that they will then process it in that manner. If the merchant refuses to honor this request you can still go to a foreign ATM and use your chip card and ATM PIN to receive cash. However, note that some banks are creating a 'chip and PIN' card for some or all of its customers. JPMorgan Chase, Target (and their Red Card), Apple Rewards have planned 'Chip and PIN' cards. Some Wells Fargo, Barclaycard, and Sam's Club cards will have the ability to function as 'Chip and PIN' when required. As things quickly progress in this area it is best for customers to check with their financial institutions on the availability of the 'chip and PIN' cards, particularly if you travel overseas.

The security advantage of chip cards over RFID cards is that, while both cards incorporate a single use card verification number, the chip card encrypts that number during the transaction. That simply means that, while the RFID number could be captured during transmission, the chip card does not transfer via radio waves (it is a passive, non-radio wave chip) and, even if captured in some manner, it cannot be read because of the encryption.

Finally, all the best card technology will have no impact on 'card-not-present' transactions. E-commerce business merchants are going to need to find other ways to address fraudulent cards that they cannot see.

Bank Card with Embedded Passive Chip
Usually Gold or Silver Colored

NFC Communication and Transaction

This chapter would not be complete without an explanation of how merchant transactions occur via cell phones and other forms of personal communication devices.
NFC, or Near Field Communication, devices are really devices equipped with active RFID chip sensors. While standard bank chip cards contain passive chip sensors, these active RFID chip sensors contain a battery to power the sensor so that it is always communicating with the outside world. Except for that difference a merchant purchase and payment via either a debit or credit card account would work the same as with a physical card. (See comparison graphic at end of chapter.)

The reason for the existence of NFC enabled devices however, is not primarily for retail purchases. NFC devices allow for smart phone communication as well as shopping mall smart posters that read your phone. Some NFC readers can also read passive RFID sensor tags encased in countless consumer items. While badges and cards may have to be close to the reader to work, other readers overcome that limitation with the use of 'far-field' antennas to read from a distance. NFC can be used for asset inventory, manufacturing tracking of parts, keeping track of young children with tags in their backpacks, tracking attendance of college students, logging in employees via ID badges, paying toll road fees, your car remote, U.S. passports, and any other application that requires active tracking including tracking your airline baggage in the near future.

Bank Card Forms of Fraud

There are many forms of bank card fraud and the types of fraud continue to increase. This module will examine several of the more prevalent forms.

RE-EMBOSSING STOLEN CARDS

There was a time when a thief would steal a bank card and continue to charge purchases on it until it was reported stolen and no longer valid. The thief would then throw the card away as it no longer was of any value. Today, the thief who charges a card to the maximum, or finds that it has been reported stolen, recycles the card in a unique manner. Subjecting it to heat recycles the card by melting down the original embossed information and creating a flat card as it was in its original form. The card is then re-embossed with the legitimate names and numbers of cardholders whose information has been obtained by the means described earlier.

Cards are flattened in one of two ways. Because plastic has a "memory", any original embossed information has been stretched from the basic card. When heat is applied to the plastic card the embossing will revert to its original, flat state. Inserting the card into a cup of very hot water for several seconds will accomplish this. Another method is to place a hot clothes iron on the card covered by a cotton cloth. In both situations the numbers shrink back into the card leaving basically an authentic card with no embossing. The thief now takes the card and places it into an embossing machine (available from an office supply house), and types in the new information. With the re-embossed card, the thief will use it as the legitimate cardholder. This fraud will work only if the clerk is unable to get a read when swiping the card through an electronic reader.

To make sure the card cannot be read the thief de-magnetizes the magnetic stripe on the back of the bank card. By wiping a magnet over the stripe or scratching it with a knife blade the stripe, and associated information, will be destroyed. The clerk realizes that the card reader will not read the stripe and then reverts to manually typing in the re-embossed numbers from the face of the card. Thus, the actual account holder is charged and the card company approves the sale. The true cardholder is unaware of the counterfeited card, in their name, and will not find out about the charges until they show up on the monthly statement. The easiest method of stopping this fraud is for the merchant to ask for identification to go along with the card.

With the advent of chip cards this fraud should no longer be effective. However, some retailers cannot afford to switch over to the chip readers or simply choose not to. They will continue to be affected by this potential fraud.

REPROGRAMMING MAGNETIC STRIPE

In many cases merchants who accept bank cards never examine or even look at the face of the card that is being presented. This lack of proper card acceptance procedures leads to easy fraud at that merchant's location. The thief will take a stolen bank card, and after using it to its limit, will reprogram the magnetic stripe on the rear of the card. This is done by using an easily procured magnetic card swipe reader and attaching it to any personal computer. These card readers are sold through computer magazines and security suppliers as access control card readers. After running the card through the computer, it allows the card to be reprogrammed using a legitimate name and numbers. These cards can be re-used as often as the card holds up. Although the information does not match up with the face of the card, these cards are used where merchants do not normally examine the card anyway.

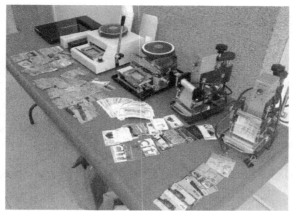
Credit Card Reprogramming Operation

Obviously, the prevention feature is to examine the card while the merchant still has it and compares it with the name printed out on the receipt. Merchants that accept the newer 'chip and PIN' cards but continue to use the signature verification only (rather than using the PIN feature) will continue to suffer losses to this fraud.

FRAUDULENT TRANSACTIONS

The following list of 'card present' transaction points, provided by Discover Cards, is consistent for any merchant accepting bank cards for payment.

Detecting Potentially Fraudulent Transactions
Keep a close eye on the customer who displays the following suspicious behaviors:

- Makes random purchases without paying attention to size, value or price
- Presents you with a credit card taken from a pocket instead of a wallet
- When asked, claims to have left photo identification at home or in the car
- Arrives at or about closing time and tries to hurry you through the sale
- Purchases a large item and refuses delivery
- Displays no interest in the warranty on expensive items
- Is overly slow and deliberate when signing the sales draft, perhaps because the signature is being forged

COUNTERFEITING

Counterfeiting continues to be a growing type of bankcard fraud in both frequency and production of Visa and MasterCard cards. New technology has aided criminals in producing exact replicas of actual bankcards from scratch. Counterfeiting is responsible for the overall increase in bank card fraud.

Holograms were originally created to resist the counterfeiting of bank cards but today are themselves routinely counterfeited. Most large-scale counterfeiting operations occur in Taiwan, Hong Kong, and China. Smuggled into the U.S., holograms sell for between $5 and $15 apiece. Increasingly, the key to quick identification of a counterfeit card lies in the examination of the hologram. True bankcards have the hologram embedded into the plastic. Counterfeit cards commonly contain only a hologram decal that has been affixed to the surface of the card. Using a fingernail, it can be felt as it lies slightly above the surface of the card.

Counterfeit Card Examination

A close examination of bank and bank cards can reveal clues to its authenticity. The four-digit BIN (Bank Identification Number) is always printed on the face of the card and will be located beneath or above the first four digits of the card embossed numerals. These four digits must always match the first four embossed numbers. Counterfeiters don't normally know what numbers will be embossed on the blank card they manufacturer and thus cannot print this BIN on the card. It is frequently missing or is incorrect on counterfeit cards and is the easiest method of detecting counterfeit cards. Even the new 'chip' cards will not prevent this form of fraud if the magnetic stripe continues to be accepted.

NOTE: Bank card examination points for all five of the major card companies can be viewed at the end of this chapter.

Consumer Frauds

While this unit is intended to primarily address business fraud, consumers can be affected by bank card fraud as well. Three common types are addressed below.

ACCOUNT TAKEOVER

Account takeover occurs when a suspect obtains a person's personal information. Often the suspect does not need the actual card number. Once the suspect has the personal information, he or she will contact the bank card company and change the address on the account.

Next, the suspect will call and report this card as lost or stolen and request a new card replacement. The new card is then sent to the new billing address on the account. The suspect has successfully taken over your account - hence the term "account takeover". It doesn't require the technology of a counterfeit card, or the waiting time of a fraudulent application.

Companies often link personal identification numbers (PIN) and other information automatically to the new card. Thus, via an ATM, the suspect can access cash, and sometimes even have access to checking account information that you provided to your bank card institution. Despite all the new security measures that many card companies have initiated, the occurrence of account takeover frauds is on the rise. In the past card receipt verification by the owner was accomplished via calling from the home phone number, which the thief would normally not have access to. However, current card verification can be done via computer log in. This is much more troublesome as thieves are more adept at logging in as you as part of their fraud techniques.

POSTAL INTERCEPT

Postal intercept is when a suspect intercepts your bank card through the mail. Most mailboxes are not secure, and most thieves know this. Thieves will wait for the mail delivery and then check over the incoming mail for new bank cards, stealing them before returning the mail to the box. Whenever possible, a lock should be added to a personal or company mailbox if one is not already in existence.

If a new or replacement bank card is expected via the mail and it is not received, the applicable bank card company must be contacted as soon as possible. Certain delivery companies will leave the package containing the new bank card on the doorstep of a home or business if no one is available to receive it, and it could easily become stolen. Estimated delivery dates of new cards should be ascertained so that a report of the possible theft can be made in a timely manner.

BANK CARD SKIMMING

This form of bank card fraud has been around for many years, but it has recently seen an increase in its use. The process was designed to be used for legitimate business purposes, but unfortunately it is also frequently misused for criminal purposes.

An electronic bank card reader (also known as a "skimmer") is manufactured for the legitimate purpose of being used in conjunction with cash registers and/or bank card machines, as well as for electronic security access control card readers. It is used to gather information that is encoded in the magnetic stripe on the back of access control cards, credit and debit cards. Information that is routinely collected includes such things as the cardholder's name, address, and card number. However, when used with a criminal intent, this same information can be used over the telephone or Internet for unauthorized purchases, to make illegal cash withdrawals, or even in the production of counterfeit cards.

Smart Phone Attached Bank Card Skimmer

There are generally two methods by which this confidential information becomes compromised. The first is at the merchant location itself, during the transmission process used for purchase authorization. When a customer makes a bank card purchase, the card is swiped and the information is collected from the magnetic stripe, and is then telephoned in for approval. It is now that the scam can occur. The skimming device, roughly the size of a small cell phone and hidden from sight, is covertly connected to the phone line between the phone jack and the bank card machine itself. During the purchase authorization process, the electronic skimmer captures the information and stores it in the device itself, which is later downloaded and manipulated by the criminal for a variety of illegal purposes. The customer has no way of knowing that the information has just been captured because they never lose sight of the card and the capture device is hidden.

The second scenario is one in which a portable device, typically a smart phone with an attached card reader - which can usually store up to 100 account numbers at a time - is carried in the pocket of a waiter/waitress in a restaurant. The card is swiped through the legitimate machine for purchase approval of the authorized transaction, and is also run through the cell phone reader for the purpose of stealing the magnetic stripe information.

In both scenarios, the merchant's employee is either the thief, or is paid a flat rate per card by the thief to obtain the information. The skimmer is equipped with a button that can be pressed to immediately erase all the collected data, thereby eliminating any evidence of the crime in the event they are asked for the reader. This makes prosecution extremely difficult even if the thief is caught red-handed.

A similar scam to the one above, and much more popular, relates to the attachment of a fake reader/skimmer on the merchant's point of purchase reader. Thieves purchase dental paste and mold card reading scamming devices that will fit directly over the legitimate reader. Prefabricated readers can also be found for sale on the internet. The homemade readers made from the gray paste matches the typical plastic of ATMs or they color it to match. Inside the mold is a duplicate magnetic stripe reader that captures your personal information. They are attached to gas pumps, ATMs, and surprisingly, even the actual terminals on merchant counters, probably on unstaffed counters. They return later to swap out the readers again and download the stolen data found inside the fake reader. Debit cards are targeted at ATMs using a disguised, hidden camera to record your PIN as you enter it. Some cameras record and others use WIFI or Bluetooth signals to wirelessly send real time video of the ATM keypad view to a nearby parked vehicle containing the thieves. The PIN is then later matched to the account transaction and your card number. In other cases the thieves place their own keypad on top of the real keypad to wirelessly capture your PIN. (See photo below.)

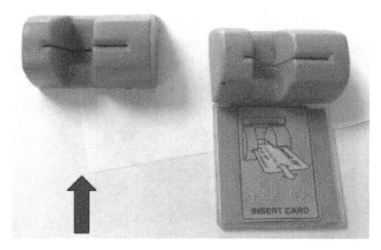

The real card reader slot.   The capture device

The side cut out is not visible when on the ATM.

Fake ATM Reader/Skimmer

Keypad Overlay to Wirelessly Capture PIN   or   Camera Hidden in ATM Brochure Box

Until the production and use of bank cards is via 'chipped' cards only, with the magnetic stripe removed, this fraud will continue to grow. It may take years before we see the mag stripe disappear.
The Secret Service has stated that bank card skimming is the fastest-growing form of bank card fraud in the United States today. Although banks and bank card companies generally absorb the losses generated in these cases, the way they offset the loss is by raising their interest rates and fees. Therefore, it is a crime that affects everyone and it is wise to be aware of the potential for this type of fraud.

Note that the bank card industry has released a handheld wireless bank card processing machine. Don't confuse these for skimming devices. These devices process bank cards right at the table and print a receipt from the same machine. They come in both skim and 'card dip' versions (pictured). The wait staff would not normally walk away with your bank card with one of these devices.

Wireless Chip Bank Card Processing Machine

HIGH TECH SKIMMING

Another form of skimming has hit the streets. It takes advantage of radio frequency technology. Embedded in some bank cards is a radio frequency (RF) chip. As technology continues to evolve the intent of these cards is that the card holder would simply wave the card in front of whatever device accepts the card (vending machine, ATM) and the machine would read the embedded card number and associated data, processing whatever service you are requesting.

The associated fraud relates to the wireless aspect of the card. Already available are mobile radio frequency scanners that can read the radio frequency of your bank card right through a purse or wallet.

Thus, a criminal could walk up to you in a crowded venue, like a sporting event or bus stop, hold the reader (which can be disguised as any mobile communication device) next to the purse or wallet, and grab the card information out of the air from within 12". It would then be used for illegal purchases. At this point the only known deterrent is to wrap the card in aluminum foil, purchase a special card sleeve made from thin metal mesh or purchase a special metal mesh wallet. These solutions block the transmission of radio waves.

Wireless Contact (Chip) Bank Card Indicator
Located on Front or Back of Card

Those readers who have a US passport might already have such technology in their hands. If the cover of the passport has the following image on it, your passport contains an RFID chip. The same issues that relate to bank cards affect passports.

Universal RFID Chip Indicator

Fraud Prevention Technique

There is only one effective method of reducing or preventing bank card fraud at the point of sale. That is identification.

IDENTIFICATION

With the theft and counterfeiting of bank cards, most thieves will not have identification papers with the same name as that listed on the bank card. Requesting a form of identification to match the name on the bank card is an excellent manner of reducing fraud. Simply asking to see a driver's license or state identification card and comparing the picture and signature is one of the most effective methods of reducing fraud. Thieves are aware that this is rarely done and can take strong advantage of this fact. Retailers argue that asking for ID takes time at the register and creates undue irritation for the customer.

Security Advances

Bank card companies continue to create new security features to halt bank card losses. While 'chip cards' were discussed at the beginning of the chapter, more basic security features are described below.

HOLOGRAMS

This technology was created in 1984. Accomplished using laser photography, holograms on VISA cards are in the form of a floating dove and on MasterCard cards in the form of two world globes. Both holograms were highly praised as a method of stopping organized crime from counterfeiting bank cards. Bank card companies spent millions in researching and designing the hologram. However, six months after being introduced a large number of counterfeit cards, complete with respectable counterfeit holograms, were seized in a police raid. Nevertheless, holograms remain as one of the current security features found on bank cards. As referenced earlier, running a fingernail over the hologram should detect a surface applied counterfeit sticker rather than the factory embedded legitimate hologram. Beginning in 2007 VISA altered some of their cards and removed the hologram on the face of the card. Instead they have added a smaller size, 'mini-dove' design on the rear of the card. Details follow.

VISA Card Mini-Dove Hologram
Placement Anywhere in Dotted Line Area

PHOTOGRAPHS

Some bank card issuing banks offer the cardholder the option of having their photograph incorporated on the face of the card. Presumably, the merchant who accepts the card will then compare the photograph to the person offering the card. If in fact this occurs, it will be an effective method of reducing fraud. Security experts are withholding judgment on its effectiveness as the photo images may be altered or the retailer may ignore its presence all together. However, implementation has been slow and seems to have not been taken up by most financial institutions issuing bank cards.

SIGNATURE PANEL

Bank cards have had for some time security on their signature panels. VISA has had the word 'VISA' printed in blue and gold at an angle across the stripe. MasterCard has had their name printed in blue, red, and yellow, also at an angle on the signature stripe. However, some new VISA bank cards will have a high-tech signature panel. It has space age looking horizontal lines with fading breaks in between. Held under ultraviolet light the word 'VISA' can be viewed and is repeated on the stripe. A sample is shown on the next page.

HIDDEN IMAGES

Another security feature makes use of ultraviolet light (black light). When bank cards are exposed to ultraviolet light the card reveals a hidden image on the front surface. VISA cards will show a V over the VISA logo while MasterCard has a large MC in the center. American Express has capital letters reading AMEX across the face of the card while Discover has the word DISCOVER printed horizontally across the card face. The expectation is that because the images cannot be seen without the light, counterfeiters will not retool their own counterfeit operations to incorporate the ultraviolet light image feature.

Merchants can use this little-known feature by purchasing a small ultraviolet (UV) light and installing it under their counters. A simple wave of the card under the light will detect counterfeit cards immediately. Such lights, about 24 inches in length, can be purchased at most lighting stores and many large discount and hardware department stores. They are self-contained and only need to be plugged in. They would not, of course, detect re-embossed or altered cards.

VISA has a different holographic image on their cards. It is a holographic magnetic stripe on the rear side featuring doves in flight that appear in multiple color animation when the card is moved from side to side or up and down. The black dot behind the middle dove appears to move when the card is moved. The word 'VISA' appears in the sun, again, when the card is moved. Also, when the card is moved a ring appears around the sun. Finally, micro text depicting a repeating 'VISA' can be seen on the center line of the holographic magnetic stripe. MasterCard, Discover, and Diner's Club also allow their card issuers to use their own variations of holographic magnetic stripes. EMV/Chip cards may or may not have the holographic magnetic stripe.

VISA Holographic Magnetic Stripe and Signature Panel

FINGERPRINT ON CARD

This new technology, introduced by MasterCard in late 2017, allows the user to simply place their finger on the card to authenticate a payment. Registration is done with the issuing financial institution. Up to two fingers can be registered. The print is stored on the card and matched with the user print during payment. After inserting the card into the reader, the user touches the card for comparison. No PIN is required. It is currently in trial overseas.

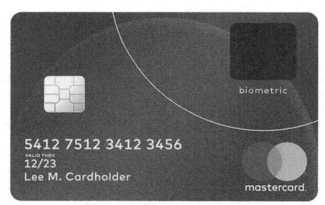

Biometric Fingerprint Card

Industry Updates

In late 2017, MasterCard announced that its newly assigned card numbers will begin with the digit '2' as well as the existing '5'. Officially known as the BIN (Bank Identification Number), it will have no effect on end users except for the examination of fraud or counterfeit card examination procedures.

Also, the credit card industry has recently determined that signatures on receipts and electronic keypads are no longer necessary. As of April 2018, the signature requirement is no longer necessary. Merchants will still have the option of requesting it but it is not needed. The industry says that the underlying security aspects of card payments no longer require it.

Finally, in mid to late 2018, Mastercard continues to offer options to the actual plastic bank card. It announced that it will update its mobile electronic payment options to include biometric facial, fingerprint, and iris authentication for payment services. The other major players are sure to follow this lead.

Summary

For all the technology that bank card companies implement, nothing is as effective as a properly trained sales clerk. An observant and diligent clerk who takes the time to examine the card and the cardholder is still the best security effort that any merchant can use to prevent losses and the resultant higher retail costs for everyone.

Bank Card Examination Points

MasterCard®

All MasterCard account numbers start with 5. The embossing should be uniform in size and spacing, and extend into the hologram.

The preprinted Bank Identification Number (BIN) must match the first four digits of the embossed account number.

The valid date lists the last month in which the card is valid.

Issuers have the option of placing a holographic magnetic stripe on the card back, replacing the Globe hologram or the Debit hologram.

The three-dimensional hologram, which may appear on the front OR the back should reflect light and appear to move.

All new U.S.-issued consumer debit cards must display the Debit hologram.

The magnetic stripe should appear smooth, with no signs of tampering.

The last four digits of the account number appear on the signature panel in reverse indent printing.

The three-digit CVC2 appears to the right of the signature panel.

The word "MasterCard" is printed repeatedly at an angle on a tamper-evident signature panel.

Are you suspicious about a card? Call for a Code 10 Authorization.

Visa®

The Flying Dove Hologram appears on most cards, however its location on the card may vary. It can be in its traditional location on the front of the card, or a smaller hologram may be located on the back of the card.

All Visa embossed, unembossed or printed account numbers start with 4. All digits must be even, straight and of the same size.

The four-digit preprinted Bank Identification Number (BIN) must be printed directly below the account number and match the first four digits of the embossed account number.

The Visa Brand Mark must appear in blue and gold on a white background in either the bottom right, top left or top right corner. A "V" is visible over the Brand Mark when the card is placed under an ultraviolet light.

The signature panel must appear on the back of the card and contain an ultraviolet element that repeats the word "Visa.®" The panel will look like this one, or have a custom design. It may vary in length.

The words "Authorized Signature" and "Not Valid Unless Signed" must appear above, below or beside the signature panel. If someone has tried to erase the signature panel, the word "VOID" will be displayed.

A three-digit Card Verification Value 2 (CVV2) must appear in the white box to the right of the signature panel or on the signature panel.

Many cards have the original Visa Logo design, together with the dove hologram, in the bottom right corner.

If you are ever suspicious about a card or a transaction, call your authorization center and request a Code 10 Authorization.

209

American Express

All American Express® Card Numbers start with "37" or "34." The Card Number appears embossed on the front of the Card. Embossing must be clear, and uniform in sizing and spacing. Some Cards also have the Card Number printed on the back of the Card in the signature panel. These numbers, plus the last four digits printed on the Charge Record, must all match.

Preprinted Card Identification (CID) Numbers must always appear above the Card Number, on either the right or the left edge of the Card.

Do not accept a Card outside the Valid Dates.

Only the person whose name is embossed on a Card is entitled to use it. Cards are not transferable.

AMERICAN EXPRESS

3759 876543 21001   7997

00/00   85

C F FROST

Some Cards contain a holographic image on the front or back of the Card to determine authenticity. Not all American Express Cards have a holographic image.

The signature on the back of the Card must match the Cardmember's signature on the Charge Record, and must be the same name that appears on the front of the Card. The signature panel must not be taped over, mutilated, erased or painted over. Some Cards also have a three-digit Card Security Code (3CSC) number printed on the signature panel.

Merchant Code 10 Authorization
1-800-528-2121
if you are suspicious of a Card transaction

Discover®

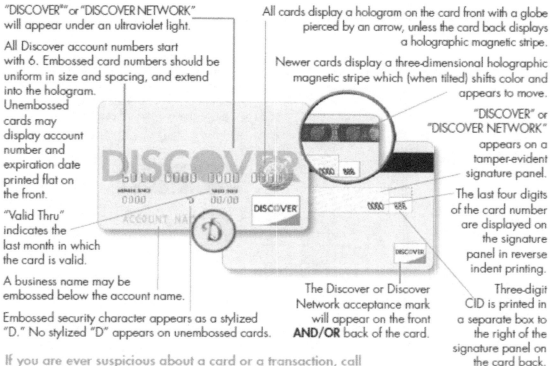

"DISCOVER"® or "DISCOVER NETWORK" will appear under an ultraviolet light.

All Discover account numbers start with 6. Embossed card numbers should be uniform in size and spacing, and extend into the hologram. Unembossed cards may display account number and expiration date printed flat on the front.

"Valid Thru" indicates the last month in which the card is valid.

A business name may be embossed below the account name.

Embossed security character appears as a stylized "D." No stylized "D" appears on unembossed cards.

All cards display a hologram on the card front with a globe pierced by an arrow, unless the card back displays a holographic magnetic stripe.

Newer cards display a three-dimensional holographic magnetic stripe which (when tilted) shifts color and appears to move.

"DISCOVER" or "DISCOVER NETWORK" appears on a tamper-evident signature panel.

The last four digits of the card number are displayed on the signature panel in reverse indent printing.

Three-digit CID is printed in a separate box to the right of the signature panel on the card back.

The Discover or Discover Network acceptance mark will appear on the front **AND/OR** back of the card.

If you are ever suspicious about a card or a transaction, call your authorization center and request a Code 10 Authorization.

Diners Club International®

The Diners Club® split-circle graphic with slash marks will appear under an ultraviolet light.

All Diners Club account numbers start with 30, 36, 38 or 39. Embossed card numbers should be uniform in size and spacing.

"Valid" and "Thru" dates indicate the first and last month in which the card is valid.

Other acceptance marks or logos such as Discover® or PULSE® may appear on the back of the card.

The holographic magnetic stripe contains a repeating image of the logo, name and world map which shift color and appearance when the card is tilted. It should appear smooth, with no signs of tampering. Some cards may have a standard black magnetic stripe.

The Diners Club split circle graphic appears on a tamper-evident signature panel.

CVV2 appears on the signature panel in indent printing.

Full or partial account number may also appear in indent printing.

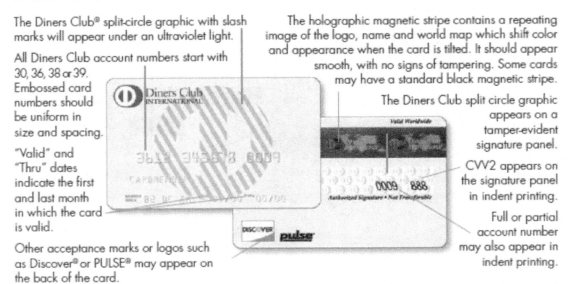

If you are ever suspicious about a card or a transaction, call your authorization center and request a Code 10 Authorization.

How to Validate a Credit Card
By Jess.Net

Take any credit card number:
4417 1234 5678 9113

Now double every other digit starting from left to right.

```
4   4  1 7  1  2  3 4  5  6  7  8  9  1  1  3
x2     x2     x2     x2     x2     x2     x2     x2
_____
8      2      2      6     10     14     18     2
```

Add these new digits to the undoubled ones
 (count two digits numbers as two single digits: 14= 1+4)

8+4+2+7 + 2+2+6+4 + 1+0+6+1+4+8 + 1+8+1+2+3 = 70

If the final sum is divisible by 10 then the credit card number is valid. If it is not divisible by 10 the number is invalid or fake.

Cracking the Credit Card Code
By Jess.Net

Sample Credit Card Number:
4417 1234 5678 9113

The first digit is the Major Industry Identifier. It designates the category of the entity which issued the card.

1 and 2 are Airlines
3 is Travel and Entertainment
4 and 5 are Banking and Financial
6 is Merchandizing and Banking
7 is Petroleum
8 is Telecommunications
9 is National

The first six digits are the Issuer Identification Number (IIN). It will identify the institution that issued the card.
VISA: 4xxxxx
MasterCard: 51xxxx – 55xxxx and 2xxx
Discover: 6011xx; 644xxx; 65xxxx
AMEX: 34xxxx; 37xxx

Thus a card number with an IIN of 376211 is a Singapore Airlines 'Krisflyer', American Express Gold card. A card with an IIN of 529962 designates a pre-paid 'Much-Music' MasterCard.

The 7th and following digits, excluding the last one, are the person's account number. Using the last 12 digits allows for a trillion possible combinations. Many cards only use nine of the digits at this time.

The final digit is the 'check digit'. It is used to validate the credit card number using the Luhn algorithm.

Infographic: RFID vs. NFC

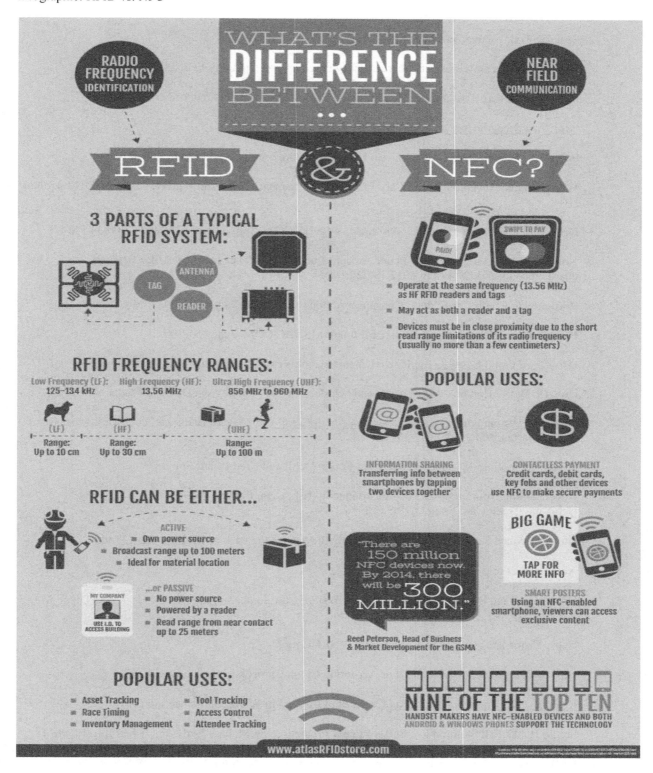

Courtesy: atlasRFIDstore.com

References

Security Today magazine; March 2018

https://usa.visa.com/visa-everywhere/security/emv-at-the-pump.html; Feb. 2018

https://www.chargebackgurus.com/chargeback-blog/how-merchants-reduced-fraud-2017

https://www.bayometric.com/mastercard-fingerprint-credit-card/

https://www.creditcards.com/credit-card-news/signatures-soon-may-not-be-required.php

Where's Banks' Incentive to Cut Card Fraud? Leslie Sarasin, American Banker; MAR 29, 2012 2:16pm ET

Debit card thieves get around PIN obstacle; MSNBC.COM Bob Sullivan; 3/9/2006 2:00:54 PM ET

Now banks are trying to pin the blame for card fraud on you. The Guardian. Miles Brignall ; guardian.co.uk, Friday 4 May 2012 18.02 EDT

Recognizing Credit Card Fraud; Consumer Action, Published: July 08, 2009

Bad guys are getting better at credit card fraud; MSNBC.COM June 15, 2012

Debit Card Fraud Cases on the Rise; HispanicBusiness.com; June 5, 2012 Chelsey Levingston

How Do Banks Handle Credit Card Fraud? chron.com by Valerie Fox, Demand Media

Consumer Action: Questions and Answers About Credit Card Fraud; Bankrate: Your Rights in Case of Fraud; Martha White; May 24, 2011

Wisco Computing: Merchant Credit Card Fraud; Debit and Credit Card Fraud

Understanding your credit and debit card identity risk; Cape Bank
Debit and Credit Card Fraud; CIBC

How to Reduce Your Risk of Credit Card Fraud; Manage the Risk of Business Card Fraud

About.com; From Demir Barlas

Debit card fraud is skyrocketing, is difficult to stop; Cleveland.com; June 03, 2011; Teresa Dixon Murray, The Plain Dealer

Cyber Crime and Bank Fraud; Business IDTHEFT.org

How to Get a Merchant Account For Accepting Credit Cards; businessknowhow.com

Regulation E: Understanding Debit Card Fraud Rules; Jim Wang; Bargaineering.com

Study: Banks Fall Short on Credit Card Fraud Protection; by Melissa Rudy; Published July 18, 2011; CardRatings.com
NMI; Network Merchants Inc.; Combating Faceless Fraud; Nicholas P. Cucci, C.F.E. • Jun 26th, 2012

Social Business Bank. 31 Ways to prevent Chargebacks and minimize Fraud – Part 2; May 24th, 2010

Online Bank Fraud Continues To Plague Small Businesses, Study Says; Infostruction.com; posted by nimda, April 25, 2011

Target Data Hack Loss: The Inquirer (www.inquirer.net), February 27, 2015, by Dave Neal

MW Market Watch (www.marketwatch.com), September 30, 2014 by S. Patel

Banking My Way (www.bankingmyway); What info is stored on your card?

Good Housekeeping; http://www.goodhousekeeping.com/family/budget/smart-credit-cards-safety

U.S. News and World Report: Coming Next Fall: More Chip and PIN Cards in the U.S.; October 28, 2014

The Plain Dealer, Cleveland, Ohio; http://www.cleveland.com/business/index.ssf/2014/10/heres_why_credit_and_debit_car.html

New Republic, January 16, 2014; http://www.newrepublic.com/article/116236/credit-card-magnetic-stripes-are-putting-you-risk-identity-theft

CreditCards.com; Use of Reloadable Cards Surging Among Mellennials; http://www.creditcards.com/credit-card-news/study-use-reloadable-surging-millennials-1701.php

RFID Insider; RFID vs. NFC; October 11, 2013, James Thrasher

RFID Insider: RFID Asset Tracking; March 4, 2015; Suzanne Smiley

Credit Card Forum; Creditcardforum.com; Chip and PIN Credit Cards in the USA for 2015?; January 2, 2015

Chapter Ten

Currency Counterfeiting

Currency Counterfeiting Performance Objectives:

- Cite the two counterfeit currency detection methods
- Identify the various counterfeit currency visual examination points
- Explain what the series year means on currency
- Cite the text contained on the security threads of US currency
- Cite the watermark images embedded in US currency
- Explain the operation of a counterfeit detection pen
- Explain why a detection pen does not always work
- Explain how ultraviolet light may help detect counterfeit currency
- Explain the concept of a 'raised note' in currency counterfeiting
- Describe the procedure for retailers in discovering a counterfeit note

Introduction

Counterfeiting, by definition, is the duplication of anything of value. It is normally associated with money but can involve a variety of other items as well. Clothing, art, jewelry, prescription drugs, coupons and even shampoo have all been counterfeited. The methods, control and investigation of these counterfeit items could be the focus of a course by itself. The problem is severe enough that many private companies affected by this crime hire their own investigators to track down the bogus products. This position might offer the student a possible career track that is usually unknown. However, our concentration will be limited to education relative to U.S. currency to assist businesses in identifying counterfeit currency before they accept it.

Distinguishing Features

Money Handling

There are two specific measures that a businessperson can implement to identify real currency from counterfeit currency. The first is <u>tactile</u> and the second is a <u>visual</u> inspection. Characteristics of both are discussed here.

TACTILE

This method of detecting counterfeit currency works best for those persons employed in cash handling businesses. When all you do is receive and hand out cash, a person can develop a skill in detecting the difference between an authentic bill and a counterfeit one. The primary reason for this is that 'paper' money is not paper at all. U.S. currency is actually made of cloth. It is composed of 75% cotton and 25% linen. That is the reason you can leave money in your pants pocket, run it through the wash, and it will come out fully intact. Treasury and Secret Service agents closely guard the finished product that is to be used to print money. Any off-site paper production by private vendors is monitored by the Secret Service and even paper scrapes confiscated.

Counterfeiters will attempt to duplicate the consistency of actual currency by using heavy cotton bond paper such as 25% rag bond. However, the texture is not the same to the tactile trained person and counterfeits are frequently discovered by touch as the cash handlers count out received money.

VISUAL

This is the area that can have the greatest detection opportunity. Many aspects of currency lend themselves to visual examination. These visual examination points can be learned by anyone and easily incorporated into a retail clerk's money acceptance procedure training program.

Series Date

A discussion on the various visual characteristics of US currency must first address the varying forms of currency in circulation. Unlike minted coins the date on a bill does not reflect a printing date. Dates on bills are prefaced with the word SERIES. This date reflects the last design change made on that denomination of bill. In the past minor changes not noticed by the public might have necessitated a new series date. As an example, depending on the personality, a new Secretary or Treasurer of the United States has, in the past, dictated a new series date. More importantly, the introduction of completely re-designed bills also creates a sequence of new series dates, the first major change being in 1996 with enlarged and offset portraits. Each revision from that first major change results in a new series date printed on the bill.

An interesting side note to series dates is that the 'old' currency is not removed from circulation. As a result, people might find themselves, for example, holding three different, yet valid, forms of $20 bills in their hand with different dates and looks. The old bills, like the new ones, will only be withdrawn from circulation when they are worn out.

Colored Fibers

The first aspect is the colored fibers that are embedded in each bill. A close examination of an individual bill will reveal tiny red and blue cloth fibers of varying lengths that were mixed in with the raw pulp material and thus are pressed into the bill during the manufacturing process. These fibers are made of Dacron synthetic fibers and can be literally picked off a bill with a sharp object. Counterfeit bills simulate these fibers by printing red and blue lines onto the paper. Photocopied bills may not be able to pick up these small colored lines and so they would be completely absent from the bill. To better view the actual colored fibers a real bill should be examined. Note, however, that the fibers are less than 1/4" long.

Colored Fibers

Portrait

The second item to be examined is the portrait on each bill. The engraving plate used to print currency is used on an intaglio press. Each bill is subjected to 20 tons of pressure which leaves a three-dimensional effect. Because of this pressure the entire bill, with the portrait being most obvious, is raised on the surface while the reverse side is slightly indented. Looking at the portrait is intended to give the viewer a three-dimensional effect. Standard printing and copying methods simply apply a flat dimension to the portrait. Additional examination should be given to the facial and hair lines, as these fine lines may appear broken in counterfeits.

Post 1996 series bills will have an enlarged portrait on the bill. The examination points are the same, however. The difference in the bills is the size and location of the portrait. The portrait was enlarged to allow a greater visual identification of a specific denomination of bill and was moved off center to eliminate the center 'billfold crease' that occurs when people fold their bills in half. Enlarging the portrait also allowed for the addition of concentric lines around the portrait. These fine concentric lines are visible to the naked eye but are supposed to distort the focus mechanism on a color photocopy machine. However, post 2003 series bills have discontinued the concentric lines around the portrait.

Some counterfeiting and fraud efforts can be prevented by simply knowing whose portrait is on which bill. They are referenced below.

$1-Washington
$2-Jefferson
$5-Lincoln
$10-Hamilton
$20-Jackson
$50-Grant
$100-Franklin

Old and New Portraits

Border

The borders on currency are an intricately woven series of scrolling lines. The lines are computer engraved onto the printing plate by a spirographic computer program. The result is very sharp, evenly spaced lines along all the borders. Photocopy duplicating attempts can create wavy lines visible to the naked eye.

Ink Color

U.S. currency has two main colors of ink on it. The face of the bill is primarily black ink while the reverse is primarily green ink.

The green ink is a proprietary color and the exact formula of pigments required to achieve the green color is a closely guarded secret. As a result, one of the prevention techniques is to hold up a different bill to the suspected counterfeit bill and compare the colors. Unless it has been heavily washed or faded in the sun the colors should be the same from one series of bills to the next.

The black ink on the face is of a generic color. However, it is still unique. All U.S. currency is printed with ink on its face side that has a magnetic content. When the currency eventually rotates through the Federal Reserve System it is checked for legitimacy by scanning each bill for its magnetic signature. Counterfeit money has no reason to be printed in the more expensive and somewhat restricted special ink making it easy to electronically find during the scanning process.

In November of 2003 yet another change was made to US currency. The Treasury Department printed a new series 2004 $20 bill featuring subtle background colors of green, peach and blue on both sides. All the new series of bills will feature different symbols of freedom. The $20 note features a large blue eagle in the left background and a small metallic green eagle and shield to the right of the portrait. The words "Twenty" and "USA" show in shadow on the right side of the bill. One more change is the addition of tiny yellow 20s scattered on the background of the bills. Finally, the oval around the portrait and the fine lines to deter photocopying have been removed.

The $50 bill, released in October of 2004, contains subtle background colors of red and blue on both sides. A field of blue stars is located to the left of the portrait of Grant, while three red stripes are located to the right. A small metallic silver-blue star is located on the lower right side of Grant superimposed on the lower red stripe. Continuing with micro printing, the words "United States of America" appears on Grant's collar, under his beard, and the words FIFTY, USA, and 50 can be found in two of the blue stars to the left of the portrait. You can also find the word FIFTY repeated within both side borders of the note. As with the $20 bill, the oval border and fine lines around the portrait on front and the Capitol on the reverse have been removed. Finally, tiny yellow 50s dot the reverse. The embedded security thread remains. A $100 note has followed with similar changes. All these changes are being driven by high tech counterfeiters. The Department of Treasury expects to introduce new currency designs every seven to ten years to foil currency counterfeiters.

Seals

Each bill has two seals on the front side. The Federal Reserve seal on the left is printed in black ink. Pre-1996 series seals had a pointed perimeter, like a gear wheel. Post 1996 bills have a smooth perimeter.

Old Style Seal   **Current Style Seal**

The Treasury Department seal is on the right side of the bill and can be different colors. The primary color is the standard green (as are the serial numbers), found on all bills that are identified as Federal Reserve Notes along the top of the bill.

Treasury Seal

Standard Bill with Federal Reserve Note on Top

However, two previously common colors, red and blue, are not seen too often as collectors usually pull them out of circulation when they surface in daily money transactions, albeit, infrequently now as time progresses.

The red colored seals (and their serial numbers) are actually called United States Notes. That phrase is stated at the top of the bill. Originally issued in 1862, it was the first national currency in the U.S. and existed before the Federal Reserve System was created in 1913. Upon creation of the Federal Reserve System new notes bearing the words Federal Reserve Note were created. Because both notes served the same purpose the United States Note was discontinued in 1971. However, like other currency, they can remain in circulation until pulled for wear and tear.

Blue colored seals (and the serial number) are called Silver Certificates. They were issued to the public in 1878 and could be exchanged for silver dollars. Subsequently this redemption policy was revoked in 1968 and these bills were no longer issued. Both U.S. Notes and Silver Certificates are still considered legal tender at face value.

Additional colored seals that have been issued over the years may create some confusion about whether they are real or counterfeit. Printed in very limited numbers they have rarely been seen in public and would certainly draw attention to themselves. The following are some unique items.

Gold colored seals were printed on bills called Gold Certificates. They were used exactly like silver certificates (except for the exchange of gold) but were much less common.

Brown colored seals, called Hawaii Overprints, were special notes printed during World War II. These notes, actually both Silver Certificates and Federal Reserve Notes, were printed with brown seals and serial numbers to prevent Japanese spies from infiltrating Hawaii and putting counterfeit money into the hands of U.S. soldiers. U.S. soldiers would send their payroll cash home to the U.S. mainland and, without their knowledge, could be sending counterfeit money to the U.S. mainland. The intent of the Japanese was to create havoc with the American economy in such a way that Americans would lose faith in their own money. Such a plan was actually uncovered prior to its implementation. The solution was to quickly change the appearance of currency being issued to soldiers stationed in Hawaii and then restrict its importation off the island. Besides the brown seal, each note was imprinted with the word 'Hawaii' on both ends of the face and across the entire reverse side. The importation restriction was implemented in July of 1942 and was not lifted until October 1944.

About the same time that the Hawaii notes were being printed the same issue arose in West Africa in our war with Germany. Again, currency that was issued to our soldiers in that area was changed in appearance. Silver certificates used for payroll payments were printed with blue serial numbers but with yellow Treasury seals.

These out of circulation notes are now considered collector's items, with the red and blue seals being the most common. The other bills are considered rarer and can be found on money collector's (numismatic) web sites as well as at online auction sites. An excellent visual source of currency is Google Images, and search for U.S. Currency.

Detection Techniques

The best method of detecting counterfeit currency bills is via a close examination as has been discussed up to this point. The 1996 series notes set the new standard for counterfeiting resistance. This has continued with the 2004 series notes, and the $100 2009 series note issued in 2013. The Treasury Department states that it will continue to update US currency as needed. The intent of all these changes is to make it easier for retailers and others to distinguish authentic currency from counterfeit currency. Let's examine some of the changes.

PORTRAIT

The enlarged portrait is easier to recognize and the added detail is harder to duplicate. It is off center to reduce wear and tear on the portrait and to make room for a watermark on the right (and sometimes the left) side. The $100 note is no longer contained in an oval frame. The head and full shoulders reach from the top of the bill to the bottom.

CONCENTRIC FINE LINES

The fine lines printed behind both the portrait and the building on the reverse side are difficult to replicate and were designed to prevent copying on photocopy machines. However, this feature has been removed from the 2004 series bills as they no longer have a portrait frame.

Concentric Fine Lines

SECURITY THREAD

A polymer thread embedded vertically in the paper to the right or left of the portrait (depending on denomination) indicates the denomination of the bill. The words 'USA 50' can be seen on a $50-dollar bill, as an example, from both sides of the bill when held up to the light. Similar numerals would match other denominations of new bills. Additionally, this thread glows in different colors depending on the denomination when held under an ultraviolet light. An interesting side note to this feature is that it originally was designed to assist the Federal Reserve Banks in optical sorting of currency and was later claimed as a security feature by the U.S. Secret Service.

Security Thread

WATERMARK

A watermark, identical to the profile portrait on the bill, is located to the left or right of the portrait when viewed from the front or the rear. The placement changes with the denomination of the bill. It is clearly visible when held up to a light source. This is a very valuable security feature. It will be difficult for a counterfeiter to replicate. Retailers and other examiners should first look to see if it is present. Then, it should be carefully examined to make sure that the portraits match. Counterfeiters will sometimes 'wash' a bill, removing some or all the ink on the bill and then re-print it as a higher denomination. The portrait, in these bills, would not match. Merchants who simply glance at the bill under light to verify a 'portrait' have accepted counterfeit bills as a result.

The newer $5 bill (series 2006) is the exception to the portrait watermark. Instead it has a large number 5 watermark on the right side of the bill and three smaller 5s on the left side of the portrait. The $5 bill from the 1999 series does contain the portrait watermark to the right of the printed portrait.

Watermark

Compare the Watermarks for the Counterfeit

COLOR-SHIFTING INK

The number in the lower right corner on the front of the note looks green when viewed straight on, but appears black when viewed at an angle. The $10 bill changes from green to copper. This is not featured on the new $5 bill. Its value is questionable. The color change is subtle and may not be obvious to the average person. The most recent $100 bill has a 'bell in the inkwell' icon. This icon also color shifts from copper to green which is supposed to make the bell disappear inside the inkwell. The same note color shifts the 100 denomination in the lower right with the same colors.

LOW VISION FEATURE

The larger numeral on the right rear of the note is easier to read for the sight impaired. While this is not technically a security feature it was introduced with and is grouped with other security features. This feature appears on all the new bills.

Low Vision Numeral

MICRO-PRINTING

Because they are so small, micro-printed words are hard to replicate by a counterfeiter. On the front of the $100 note, "USA 100" is printed on the numeral 100 in the lower left corner and the words "The United States of America" is on Franklin's coat collar.

On a $50 note, "Fifty" is repeated within the end borders and "The United States of America" is on Grant's shirt collar.

A $20 note has the words "USA20" in the numeral 20 in the lower left corner of the front of the bill and the words "The United States of America" on both sides of the bottom of the portrait.

A $10 note has the word "Ten" repeated in the numeral located in the lower left corner and "United States of America" on the lower edge of the portrait.

The $5 note contains the words "Five Dollars" in the side borders on the front and, as with previous bills, "United States of America" at the bottom of the portrait.

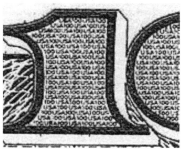

Micro Printing Feature

SECURITY FEATURES VISUAL AIDS

As this textbook is printed in black ink the visual effect of looking at the currency samples is not as effective as looking at real currency or color images of currency. With that said a quick and simple internet site will give you much greater clarity and detail than can book pages. I would encourage you to visit moneyfactory.gov and check out this government site for full color examples of every denomination in U.S. currency. Training materials, free of charge, are available for both police and retailers.

3-D SECURITY RIBBON

The 2009 series $100 bill introduced the 3-D Security Ribbon. The purple tinted ribbon runs from top to bottom to the right of the portrait of Franklin. The ribbon contains images of bells that change to the numeral 100 when the bill is moved.

$100 Bill with Changing Image of Bells

RAISED PRINTING

Also new to the $100 bill is raised printing. If you move your finger up and down Franklin's shoulder you will feel it rough to the touch.

FEDERAL RESERVE INDICATORS

As referenced earlier, a new universal seal represents the entire Federal Reserve System. A letter and number beneath the left serial number identifies the issuing Federal Reserve Bank as follows:

A1 – Boston, MA
B2 – New York, NY
C3 – Philadelphia, PA
D4 – Cleveland, OH
E5 – Richmond, VA
F6 – Atlanta, GA
G7 – Chicago, IL
H8 – St. Louis, MO
I9 – Minneapolis, MN
J10 – Kansas City, KS
K11 – Dallas, TX
L12 – San Francisco, CA

SERIAL NUMBERS

An additional letter is added to the serial number. The unique combination of eleven numbers and letters appears twice on the front of the note and is printed in green ink to match the Treasury Seal.

Additional Detection Methods

Besides a visual examination of bills there are other ways of reducing the chances of accepting counterfeit money. They are as follows.

DETECTION PEN

This device, called a counterfeit detection pen, is similar in appearance to a felt tip pen. The pen is used to make a small mark on the face of the bill. If the ink creates a dull yellow or brown line the bill is usually genuine. If the mark is black it means the bill is usually counterfeit. There have been cases where the quality of the counterfeit bill was such that the pen left a brown mark. Likewise, black ink marks have been left on genuine bills that have been laundered in bleach. The bleach apparently changes the characteristics of the cloth bill making the pen record a black mark. Also, if a genuine note has been altered to read to a higher denomination, the counterfeit pen will show an authentic bill as it cannot determine one denomination from another. While these aberrations can occur, the counterfeit detection pen serves a purpose and is a great tool for retailers. Counterfeit detection pens can be purchased at larger office supply outlets. However, these pens should never substitute for visual examination of currency notes.

Counterfeit Detection Pen

ULTRAVIOLET LIGHT

These lights detect the standard paper typically used in counterfeit money. When genuine currency is illuminated under ultraviolet ('black') light it appears as a very dull green color. When regular bond paper, such as that used by counterfeiters is illuminated under this light it will appear as a much whiter color. This is true because genuine currency is made of cloth, not paper. Again, false positives can be created when currency is laundered in a bleach solution as it might be when left in a pocket of a pair of pants. Ultraviolet/black lights can be purchased as a complete 24-inch plug-in unit at larger hardware, department and lighting stores. Attached under a counter, they would make checking a suspicious bill quick and easy.

A much more effective use of a UV light might be in merchant locations with low lighting that makes examining security features difficult. Each U.S. currency from the 1996 series forward contains an illuminating security thread with unique colors for each denomination. This would help to quickly identify the legitimacy of a bill as well as the denomination with just a glance. Note, it would not assist in spotting 'washed' bills as previously discussed.

The bills and related fluorescing light colors is as follows:

$5 - Blue
$10 - Orange
$20 - Green
$50 - Yellow
$100 - Pink

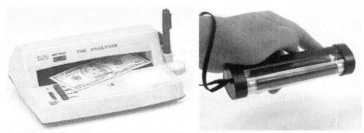

Ultraviolet Light Detector - Desktop and Portable Versions

An interesting side note relates to bright white spots that will fluoresce under black light and appear on genuine currency. These spots are likely protein based stains. Such protein stains standout as small, bright, white marks or splotches under black light. One likely source of the stains is cocaine residue. Some experts state that traces of cocaine have touched at least half of the U.S. currency in circulation in America. Of course, protein based bodily fluids may also contribute to the staining.

MAGNETIC INK DETECTORS

The final device that can assist in detection of counterfeit money is a magnetic ink detector. As previously discussed, genuine currency is printed with magnetic ink. This detector accepts the suspicious bill and will respond to the magnetic qualities in the ink on the bill. If it does not contain magnetic ink it identifies the bill as counterfeit. These detectors are most easily found via the Internet. However, they are the most expensive of the three detection devices listed here.

Magnetic Ink Currency Detector - Desk and Hand Held

Rapid Examination Techniques

While all the counterfeit detection points listed above are valid and helpful the novice examiner may find themselves questioning their ability to accurately determine a counterfeit bill and perhaps question a customer. This is true whether the person is a law enforcement officer or the manager of a local fast food restaurant. Until counterfeiters put more effort into their products there are two methods of examining a bill with almost 100% certainty.

REMOVE A FIBER

The first rapid examination point is to attempt the removal of any of the blue or red fibers embedded into the bill. By using any small, sharp object the examiner can pick at any of the visible fibers on the bill. If the fibers are *not* present anywhere on the bill (compare it to another bill) it should be considered counterfeit. Should the visible fiber scratch off, as ink would, the bill is counterfeit. If, however, the fiber can be loosened and physically lifted from the bill it would be an indicator that the bill is authentic. However, this test must also be coupled with an examination of the watermark portrait as explained next. Make sure you conduct BOTH examinations on a bill.

WATERMARK EXAMINATION

This second examination point focuses on the watermark portrait. First it must be present in all post 1996 series bills. Its absence would indicate a counterfeit bill. However, further examination must still occur. It is important to carefully compare the visible watermark portrait to the portrait printed on the bill. A failure of the portraits to exactly match profiles is another indicator of a counterfeit bill.

While technically not a counterfeit this is what the criminal is doing. Using readily available chemicals they are partially 'washing' the ink off a bill. A $10 bill is a common example. Having washed parts of the ten-dollar bill it is set aside. The counterfeiter now color photocopies a $100 bill onto very thin tracing paper, called onion skin paper. Cutting out the relevant parts of the onion skin $100 bill he glues the cut-out parts onto the washed $10 bill. The glue that is used is very thinned wallpaper paste. When dried, the $10 bill almost replicates the $100 bill and feels like real currency because it is. A counterfeit detection pen will not detect the alteration because the base is still real currency. A retailer who examines the bill for a confirming watermark will see a watermark portrait but does not actually *compare* the portraits. This allows the counterfeiter to pass off these $10 bills as $100 bills. (Other denominations can be used). Note that these bills would still have the red and blue fibers embedded in the bill because they are genuine bills but have been altered to a higher amount. Therefore, checking the watermark should be done along with checking for fibers. Further note that the $5 bill does not have a portrait but, instead, has the numeral 5 as its watermark in two different locations. (See the previous section on 'Watermarks' in this chapter.) This form of watermark would make this bill an unlikely candidate for washing by a counterfeiter.

Washed Ten Dollar Bill - Note the 'Ten'

The other related detection method, still reliable until the counterfeiter's technology catches up, is to view the written-out amount over the US Treasury Seal. Because of the overlapping printing the counterfeiter must leave the word TEN printed on his altered $100 bill. However, retailers have not been trained to read or look for this discrepancy. Taking the time to do both examination points could save $100.

A low tech, but highly effective, method of increasing the value of a bill is as follows. In this example the con artist would use a $1.00 bill and two $10.00 bills. One of the ten's is laid over the one-dollar bill. Once lined up over each other the artist would simply cut the corners or side off one side of the bills. The $1 digits would be thrown out. The $10 digits or ends would be taped in place on the back side. The process would be repeated with the opposite end and a second $10.00 bill. The altered $1.00 bill is now presented as $10.00. This is highly effective in taverns, gas stations, any place where there is a rapid exchange of money and the cashier does not examine the bill. Incidentally, the torn off $10.00 bills are presented to an unwitting retail clerk in exchange for a purchase of merchandise with an explanation of that is how they were received.

Altered One Dollar Bill

Receiving Counterfeit Money

When counterfeit money is received retailers are not sure what to do with it. Here are some guidelines.

First, if the note is even suspect, do not return it to the passer. Call a supervisor and explain the situation. You will have a pretty good idea if the passer is also the counterfeiter by noting if the passer remains at the business while the note is being examined and the police called or if he/she hastily exits. If the person exits the business note a vehicle description and license plate, if this can be done safely, as well as a description of the passer.

Next, the clerk who accepted the bill should write their initials and the date on the border of the bill.

Finally, do not handle the bill any more than necessary. If this is an original counterfeit then only the clerk and counterfeiter's fingerprints will be on the bill. Immediately put the bill into an envelope or paper bag and give it only to the responding police officer. A receipt should be requested.

Currency Reader for the Blind

For those businesses that would like to offer a unique service to your visually impaired customers the U.S. Bureau of Engraving and Printing is offering a Federal Note Currency Reader. It is being offered free of charge to blind or visually impaired individuals.

These readers will denominate all U.S. Currency Federal Notes in circulation. It will identify the denomination in one of three modes: a clear natural voice, a pattern of tones, or a pattern of vibrations for privacy considerations. For more information go to: www.moneyfactory.gov/uscurrencyreaderpgm.html

To receive a reader, download an application for verification of eligibility from the BEP's website at: http://www.bep.gov/uscurrencyreaderform.html

For those wanting to use the camera on their smart phones, two apps are available. For Apple devices use the EyeNote app. For Android use the IDEAL Currency Identifier app.

Summary

With the increasing popularity of computer printers and color copiers the threat of counterfeit currency is no longer from the professional printer, but much closer to home. In fact, counterfeiting by persons using personal computer printers accounts for the largest increase in counterfeiting ever seen by the U.S. Secret Service. Because counterfeit money attributed to a specific business bank deposit is deducted from that business's deposit it is important to spot and stop the counterfeit bill at the point of purchase.

Training materials to assist retailers is available from the Treasury Department and are free in limited quantities. Visit www.uscurrency.gov/educational-materials for more information.

References

How Counterfeiting Works; HowStuffWorks.com; Marshall Brain

Currency Design in the United States and Abroad: Counterfeit Deterrence and Visual Accessibility
Marcela M. Williams and Richard G. Anderson
Federal Reserve Bank of St. Louis Review, September/October 2007

Funny money no laughing matter in recession; MSNBC.COM M. Alex Johnson 8/7/2009

How to Spot Counterfeit Money; wisebread.com; Philip Brewer 9/20/2007

Fake money a growing problem for small businesses; Los Angeles Times; July 05, 2010 Cyndia Zwahlen

How the U.S. Could Pressure North Korea Tomorrow: Quit the $100 Bill
business.time.com   DAVID WOLMAN | February 24, 2012

Preventing the Counterfeiting of the U.S. Dollar; GoCurrency.com

The TOP TEN Ways to Detect Counterfeit U.S. Currency; voices.yahoo.com   Phillip W. Chambley, Jan 2, 2009

How Peru Became the World's Counterfeit Capital; Time.com; By LUCIEN CHAUVIN /
LIMA Thursday, Nov. 25, 2010

UPDATE 1-New US $100 note aims to deter counterfeiters; Reuters.com
By David Lawder WASHINGTON, April 21 | Wed Apr 21, 2010 2:39pm EDT

U.S. Bureau of Engraving and Printing

Chapter Eleven

Retail Theft Prevention

Retail Theft Prevention Performance Objectives:

- Cite the types of shoplifter categories
- Describe professional shoplifter theft devices
- Identify commonly shoplifted items
- Describe common methods of shoplifting
- Explain methods to prevent shoplifting
- Cite the suggested shoplifting apprehension procedure

Introduction

Retail theft is defined as the taking of retail merchandise while lawfully on the property of a merchant, without the merchant's permission, and with the intent to permanently deprive the storeowner of the property. Retail theft and shoplifting are synonymous terms while loss prevention refers to overall inventory shrink or loss of merchandise through all possible means.

Extent of the Problem

Results from 2017 National Retail Security Survey (NRSS), which were released just before the National Retail Federation's (NRF) PROTECT conference in June 2017, report that inventory shrink accounted for 1.44 percent of retail sales, or $48.9 billion, in 2016. This is up from 1.38 percent ($45.2 billion) in 2015. In addition, nearly 49 percent of retailer participants reported an increase in inventory shrink in 2016.

While different states will have different population bases, according to a recent report, in general, U.S. retailers lose $35 million *a day* to shoplifting equating to about $30 billion a year. There are approximately 20 million shoplifters in the U.S. and, on average, only 1 in 50 is ever apprehended.

According to a 2018 report, for every $1 recovery made by the retailers that responded to a survey, $12.82 was lost to retail theft. Hayes International consultants, the author of the study report, calculates that only 7.8 percent of total retail theft losses resulted in a recovery.

Loss Prevention Statistics
- Inventory shrink cost the US retail industry $48.9 billion. (Source: NRF Survey 2017)
- The average shrink rate is 1.44% (Source: NRF Survey 2017)
- Nearly half of retailers surveyed reported increases in overall inventory shrink. (Source: NRF Survey 2017)
- The average cost per shoplifting incident doubled to 798.48. (Source: NRF Survey 2017)
- The average costs of return fraud was $1,766.27, with a median of $171. (Source: NRF Survey 2017)
- 36.5% of shrink is external, due to shoplifting and ORC, outpacing shrink caused by employee theft, vendor fraud and administrative errors. (Source: NRF Survey 2017)
- 1 out of 11 Americans (approximately 27 million) shoplift. (Source: NASP)
- US grocery stores allocate only 0.36% of sales to reducing shrinkage. (Source: NRF Retail Study)

Shoplifting Statistics
- More than 10 million people have been caught shoplifting in the last five years. (Source: <u>NASP</u>)
- Habitual shoplifters steal an average of 1.6 times per week. (Source: <u>NASP</u>)
- 57% of adults convicted of shoplifting say it is hard for them to stop shoplifting. (Source: <u>NASP</u>)
- 33% of juveniles cannot stop shoplifting after getting caught. (Source: <u>NASP</u>)
- Most non-professional shoplifters don't commit other types of crimes. (Source: <u>NASP</u>)
- Drug addicts, who have become addicted to shoplifting, describe shoplifting as equally addicting as drugs. (Source: <u>NASP</u>)

Types of Shoplifters

Shoplifting is committed by a cross-section of people. Different levels of income, types of education, gender and race are all well represented in the arrest records of shoplifters. Moreover, shoplifters can generally be classified by type. Common examples are as follows.

JUVENILE

Almost all juvenile shoplifters take merchandise for personal use. Examples of stolen items are video games, audiotapes, CDs, clothes, jewelry, and cosmetics. Some juveniles steal because of peer pressure and others for the thrill of the experience. Juveniles rarely consider the experience a crime. A few are even coached by their parents and, if caught stealing, the parent pretends to discipline the child for the theft, hoping that the police will not be called.

Studies have shown that:

- One in ten juvenile shoppers in a retail establishment will steal.
- The most common juvenile shoplifting incident involves a teenage girl taking cosmetics.
- Most juvenile shoplifters prefer to steal in department and discount stores.
- Juvenile offenders are frequently accompanied by three or four fellow shoplifters or accomplices.
- Juvenile shoplifters generally do not have a criminal history.

Although juveniles normally steal items of small monetary value, the frequency of their crimes, along with the large number of offenders involved, causes juvenile shoplifting to be a substantial security problem with high losses.

HOMEMAKER

Next to juveniles, this population is the most frequent type of shoplifter. This is true because, as a group, they are the most frequent visitor to a retail establishment, particularly food stores. This group includes both males and females. Like juveniles, homemakers typically have no criminal background. This class of thief mentally rationalizes the theft based on:

- Unemployed spouses
- Personal financial problems
- Limited food budgets
- Rationalization against perceived high food prices
- A feeling of deceptive advertising
- A belief that retailers earn huge profits (in fact net profit is an average 3-5 cents on the dollar).

Numerous studies have shown that, when apprehended, most homemakers have had enough money on their person to pay for stolen items. Also, one out of ten homemakers admit stealing from a retail establishment. When apprehended these shoplifters had concealed their stolen merchandise in items they brought in with them. These items include purses, umbrellas, shopping bags, or coats. A few parents attempted to use their infant children by concealing merchandise under the child in a stroller. Visual surveillance and apprehension are the only preventative measures to these shoplifters.

Even the Elderly Will Shoplift

EASY ACCESS SHOPLIFTER

This shoplifter is not a customer or employee of the store but enjoys a unique relationship with the retailer. Included in this category are:

- Vendor salespersons
- Delivery persons
- Visiting buyers
- Former employees
- Repairpersons
- Government inspectors

These people have access to areas of retail establishments that the general public does not. Merchandise is stolen from behind counters and in stockrooms and is not generally seen by security personnel on the floor or detected by electronic equipment. While difficult to measure, this type of theft can be substantial. Covert video equipment and escorts while on the premises can reduce this type of theft.

DRUNKS/VAGRANTS

Due to their appearance, this type of potential shoplifter is easy to detect. They usually shoplift for their immediate needs or wants such as food, liquor, or warm clothing. Many times, these thieves are under the influence of alcohol and as such can be violent and should be approached with caution. The only method of preventing this crime is to call the police when these types enter the store.

DRUG ADDICT

This shoplifter is extremely dangerous. He/she is desperate for drugs and this desperation can lead to violence. The property they steal will be given to an intermediary fence in exchange for either drugs or money to purchase drugs.

The drug addict is generally a young person who may be wearing a long sleeve shirt on a hot day to conceal needle marks. They may also appear to be in a daze because of being under the influence of drugs and can become violent if approached. The use of some drugs can also temporarily increase the strength of these individuals. These thieves may openly steal from the merchant and then flee. They are dangerous people and security personnel should normally not attempt to apprehend them alone. If possible, they should be followed after calling law enforcement for assistance.

KLEPTOMANIAC

Kleptomania is defined as the persistent, neurotic impulse to steal. It is classified as a mental illness. While some shoplifters, when apprehended, wish to have the store and police believe that they are kleptomaniacs, the truth is that this type of shoplifter is rare. Additionally, a true kleptomaniac would not normally admit to being one.

Kleptomaniacs will frequently have a past criminal record for shoplifting. This is because they do not have the same mental intent to steal as other shoplifters and thus do not practice the same level of caution used by other shoplifters. This means that they are more frequently observed and apprehended.

This type of thief shoplifts without considering the value or personal use of the item they are stealing. In fact, many times they seem to want to be caught. They will steal in any type of retail establishment and criminal prosecution has no deterrent effect. Some spouses of kleptomaniacs have actually made arrangements with department stores to have a bill sent to them for items observed to have been shoplifted by their spouse. The only deterrence to kleptomaniacs involves physical and surveillance preventative measures and subsequent apprehensions.

PROFESSIONAL SHOPLIFTER

Professional thieves make a living stealing from stores. These thieves account for only 1% of apprehended shoplifters. However, the actual dollar value of their thefts accounts for a much higher value than their low numbers would suggest. The low number of apprehensions may be due to their skill in avoiding detection or it may reflect a lower number of shoplifters in this category.

This type of thief is more likely to have a criminal record and steals strictly for the monetary gain made by fencing all stolen items. He/she steals only expensive items. Increasingly they operate in teams to streamline their operations and make a greater profit. A recent FBI statistic indicates that organized retail crime (ORC) operations now steal an annual $30 billion dollars. This figure includes credit card fraud, retail theft, gift card fraud, and price tag switching.

Professional shoplifters utilize special theft devices in their quest to avoid detection yet allow them to steal the most they can. These devices include:

Booster Boxes

These are empty boxes that are wrapped as gifts or large purses can also be used. On one end, or on the bottom, there is a hinged cap. The thief walks through a shopping mall area with the gift box and enters a store with the "gift". Placing the gift box next to the merchandise to be stolen, the thief quickly inserts the item into the booster box and out of sight. Because this is done so quickly, it is almost impossible to detect. The loss prevention officer must actually see the item disappear inside the box to be certain that the crime even occurred. Such an absolute observation is difficult without the assistance of video recording equipment.

Hollowed Out Book   **Foil Lined Purse to Bypass Electronic Security System**

Drapery Hooks

Drapery hooks are sewn or hooked to the inside liner of a long trench coat. The thief picks up an item of clothing, jewelry, etc., and with a quick flick of the wrist throws the item inside the slightly open coat and onto a drapery hook. With practice, the thief will be 100% successful with their aim and the theft. The number of hooks is limited only by the size of the coat. Awareness of this theft method is the key to prevention and apprehension.

Elastic Band

This homemade theft device involves a length of sewing elastic that is pinned inside the thief's shirtsleeve at the shoulder. The opposite end, still inside the sleeve, is cut off about two inches above the wrist. This end is affixed with an electrician's wire alligator clip. Just prior to the theft the elastic is stretched down and over the palm of the hand and the clip is clipped to a ring worn on the thief's hand. With the hand turned down the clip is not visible. The thief will then ask to see expensive jewelry and will attempt to have three or more pieces laid out on the counter. Then below the level of the counter the thief will move the clip between the fingers of one hand. Drawing the clerk's attention to a piece of jewelry with one hand, the thief will use the fingers of the other hand to attach the clip to the targeted piece and let go of the clip. The elastic will instantly pull the piece up the sleeve and out of sight while the thief's hand never moves. When the puzzled clerk reacts to the missing piece the thief will present the empty hands and act indignant. The clerk recognizes the loss but without the action of moving hands that were never out of sight, cannot press the issue. The only way to verify this theft is by watching a video recording of the crime in slow motion.

Leg Concealment

Some female professional thieves practice a unique method of stealing items. They steal by lifting their long dress, placing the stolen item between their thighs and walking out of the store. It is accomplished by waiting for a private moment in the store, taking the item, bending down, placing the item between the legs and then simply letting the dress drop, re-covering her legs. The entire action is done very quickly and smoothly. With practice the thief can walk out of the store with a normal stride. These thieves have been known to walk out with coats, boxes, appliances and even large frozen hams. Visual recording for later identification and prosecution is the only deterrent to a repeat visit by the shoplifter.

Stealing a Flat Screen TV by Slipping it Between Legs and Walking Away

Foam Pet House

This shoplifter will pretend to be pregnant by wearing a pet cat house made of foam. These commercially manufactured pet houses are shaped like a beehive with a hole in the front. When elastic is sewn to the sides and strapped around the abdomen under a maternity top these thieves do resemble a pregnant woman. With this guise, the thief will simply push stolen merchandise under her shirt and into the hole in the pet house. An enormous amount of merchandise can be stolen in this manner. Prevention, in this case, is simply awareness. Even "mothers-to-be" must be observed.

Foam Pet House

Girdles

While not frequently worn today, girdles can still be purchased. Professional female shoplifters use them by pulling them up under long dresses, but only to the knees. With the sewn in crotch they make a natural depository for stolen merchandise. The thief simply lifts her dress and drops the items into the girdle. Visual recording equipment may detect the theft for later identification of the suspect.

Retail Theft Techniques

Besides the professional shoplifter methods, there are various other techniques used by the different classes of shoplifters. Some of these methods follow.

GRAB AND RUN

This technique simply means that the shoplifter walks into a store and takes an item from a display counter or rack and runs out the door. Merchandise located near the front entrance is the most likely to be stolen. This technique is most often used by drug addicts, juveniles and increasingly by gangs. Prevention methods dictate that only inexpensive or prop displays be set up next to the entrances of the store.

Grab and Run

CARTON THIEVES

These shoplifters are so brazen that they walk out the door with the merchandise in the original box in which it is sold. One of the reasons that this works in some stores is that these stores give out their empty boxes as a courtesy to the public. This easily occurs during busy stocking hours when store is open. Prevention dictates that all boxes be broken down and stored out of public access. In some cases, thieves will walk out with display items. Making sure that all display items are electronically secured will detect this.

Display Walk Out   **Cart Pusher**

Stolen Merchandise Inside Bins Walk Out

STOCKROOM THIEVES

These are shoplifters who enter stockrooms to carry out boxes of goods, sometimes out a rear exit. If challenged in the rear storeroom they plead ignorance of the proper exit or indicate that they are looking for the restroom.

To legally restrict public access the store needs to identify all private room doors with "Employees Only" signs. Putting up international "no entry" and "no bathroom" signs may be necessary as a defense against the one-quarter of the U.S. population that is illiterate.

TICKET SWITCHERS/PRICE CHANGERS

Some thieves change price tags from a less expensive item to a more expensive item. This specific activity is frequently addressed in state retail theft statutes. Prevention considerations include stick-on price tags that are of the self-destruct type when peeled off. If the item is to be marked down, never use pen ink on the price tag. Writing in the marked down price makes it too easy to compromise prices by both dishonest employees and shoplifters. Whenever possible use the pre-printed packaging UPC symbols for pricing. However, the clerk should be instructed to look at each UPC symbol to verify that it is the original one. Thieves have been known to cut out a cheaper priced product's UPC symbol and tape it over the original code.

DESIGNER LABEL THEFT

This thief will enter the store and cut out the brand label from a piece of clothing. The thief then approaches a sales clerk for a discount or simply points out the defacement and returns later to purchase the garment from the reduced sale rack. This form of theft is difficult to deter. Overt camera systems in the area of high priced merchandise may stop this thief from bringing out a cutting instrument in public view.

TRAVELING GROUPS

These thieves come into a store in a large group of 10 to 20 people. They will openly steal merchandise and pass it from member to member within the group. Soon the merchandise is out of sight and out the door. Detaining the original shoplifter will not work because the stolen no longer present. The only defense is to call out all employees to watch them closely. Discourage the thieves by obviously watching them. Videotaping of the incident will assist in any potential prosecution. Law enforcement should be called as soon as possible to assist in dealing with the situation and any possible personal searches that may take place.

The retailer should be made aware of the fact that this same group may not be shoplifting at all. Sometimes these thieves enter a store and intentionally cause diversions by fighting among themselves or feigning illness. They know that this will attract all the management personnel and many of the sales associates in the store. Their goal is to try and create such a disturbance that everyone in the main office will leave the office empty to observe or respond to the crisis. Two accomplice thieves will then enter the empty offices with the sole intent of locating the safe. Frequently they will find the safe unlocked or even standing open. It is then a simple matter to empty the safe contents and casually walk out the door. A spotter will then signal the other group members that the theft has occurred and they all walk out together. By the time the money is discovered missing they are gone and cannot be prosecuted without the money in their hands as evidence.

REFUNDING

This thief enters a store, removes new merchandise from the shelf and boldly walks it to the front desk for a refund, claiming a lost receipt. Accurate records on repeat customer returns help to prevent this. If a single customer has too many returns, the store has the right to refuse to refund. Also, if a camera recording system is in place it can be reviewed while the customer is being delayed. Customers should be asked to present a photo identification and telephone number. This information is cross-referenced with an internal database. False identifications can be verified with a published national identification manual. Phone numbers can be checked through a reverse phone directory for customer name comparison. Implementation of these procedures will rebuff the repeat refunder thief.

UNATTENDED DRESSING ROOMS

When dressing rooms are not attended, a retailer makes it easy for thieves to put on clothing and walk out wearing it. Dressing rooms should either be attended or the doors be locked and a sales clerk should need to be summoned to try on clothes. Even then, customers should be limited to three items at a time to keep track of what is going in and what is coming out.

CART PUSHER

This brazen shoplifter will simply walk out of the store's front door with a single large item or a shopping cart full of merchandise. Store employees are so successfully trained to be customer service oriented that sometimes they have been known to hold open doors for shoplifters with large boxes in their hands. Retailers must be trained to attach a special tape to all large un-bagged customer merchandise and to then look for that tape as shoppers exit the store. Customers pushing carts out the door from the wrong side of the store or carrying merchandise without shopping bags should be asked to produce a receipt.

Photographed Cart Pusher

Prevention Techniques

CLOTHING ATTACHMENTS

A large plastic type of clothing attachment, that can only be removed via a store demagnetizing device, is a deterrent to some. The intent is simply to discourage even considering stealing the item. However, with some shallow wire cutters the pin can be severed.

The more traditional item is simply a loop of wire that is passed through the clothing and attached to the hanging rack. It is effective at preventing an easy theft.

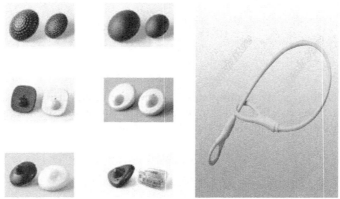

Security Clothing Attachments   Clothing Security Loop

INK TAGS

Ink tags are another device attached to clothing items. When the tag is forcibly removed by the thief the internal dye capsules break staining the attached clothing article and making it unusable. However, a common defeat technique, discovered by thieves, is to put the clothing article in a freezer which solidifies the dye.

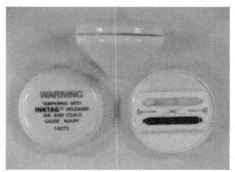

Ink Tags

ELECTRONIC ARTICLE SURVEILLANCE (EAS)

This electronic theft detection system uses a pair of stanchions placed on either side of the store exit. Any merchandise that has been 'tagged' with an EAS sensor will trigger the detection to sound an alarm.

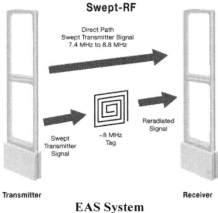

EAS System

The EAS sensors come in an array of configurations. They can be attached at the store with, typically, no tools needed. Some sensors can be attached to the product or enclosed inside the packaged box. However, this involves working with the manufacturer and would require bulk purchases.

Manufacturer Provided EAS Inside Packaging Tag

UPC Store Applied and Attached EAS Sensors

POINT OF SALE (POS) ELECTRONIC THEFT DEVICES

Non-clothing items, in their original packaging, can be protected with electronic devices attached directly to the package. They can be adapted to detect motion or a cut wire.

POS Electronic Theft Sensors

NEW POS THEFT DEVICES

Sweep Hook: a new item, introduced in 2017, demonstrates a spiral anti-sweep hook. It requires the customer to turn a knob to release a single product. This makes 'sweeping' of all products at once impossible. Of course, as mounted a thief could steal the entire display unit!

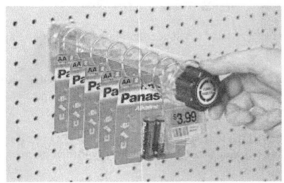

Anti-Sweep Hook Display

Product Keeper: clear plastic boxes, called product keepers, with specialized electronics are being marketed to protect high cost, small items such as razor blades and cosmetics.

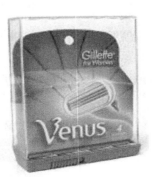

Product Keeper

Density Tag: available in early 2018 this item is attached to the exterior of a package and operates by 'sensing' the presence of the packaged merchandise through the box. Called a StrapLok, if a shoplifter attempts to open the box and steal the contents, this device will trigger a 95-decibel alarm and flashing LED. The device will attach to the existing box strapping.

StrapLock Density Anti-Theft Device

Suggested Shoplifting Apprehension Procedure

When a shoplifter has been observed and detained, the following procedure is recommended for the proper processing of the person.

➤ Escort the individual to an office secluded from the general public. Whenever possible, another person should be called to witness the proceedings. If the suspect is a female another store employee, preferably a female, should be present at all times.

➤ Inform the individual of the reason for his/her detention. DO NOT accuse the individual of shoplifting. Tell him/her you *suspect* him/her of shoplifting. Remember, you are not the police, judge, or jury.

➤ Immediately call the respective police department to report you have detained an accused shoplifter. Document the time detained and time called.

➤ Do not leave the person unattended.

➤ Do not detain the person for an unreasonably long time. This is subject to interpretation, but if the police have not responded within 30 minutes it would be advisable to document the identity of the person and then to release them. You can photograph the person.

➤ Allow the individual to make a phone call. If the person is a juvenile, store officials should call the parents immediately.

➤ Complete the necessary detention report in duplicate. One copy will accompany the police and the other copy will stay in the store files.

➤ Do not search the individual. Only a police officer can perform this function and then only based on the information provided by the detaining official.

Industry Updates

In a 2017 study about the effectiveness of electronic alarm tags and detection pedestals, they were proven effective. One retailer removed all tags and pedestals from ten stores. Shrink loss in all stores went through the roof. In another study, often due to pressure to remove unsightly shoplift deterrents, retailers shifted to soft tags and hidden tags sewn into garments. Again, shrink skyrocketed. Most experts agree that EAS (Electronic Article Surveillance) is strictly a deterrent and most agree that it is here to stay.

Another development with EAS relates to the issue of failing to deactivate the tags at the point of sale. Still under development, but successfully tested, is a system of automatically deactivating EAS tags from a distance using Bluetooth-type technology.

Some stores will have ATM machines in their stores. A chain of stores using them conducted a study on their use. While it does not relate to loss, it did demonstrate how to increase sales. By moving the ATMs to the rear of the store, people who did not purchase anything at the front of the store were more likely to make a purchase while walking through the store.

Another recent study involved a panel of actual shoplifters who shared their thoughts on what served as a deterrent to shoplifting. The number one thing cited was an attentive salesperson who approached them, sought to assist them, and continued to monitor them.

This same group discounted cameras in a store. They would scout out the camera locations first. Then, removing an item from a display they would simply walk to an area out of view of the cameras to conceal it. As far as on product deterrents, ink tags were the item that would most deter them.

Finally, a concept called CPTED (Crime Prevention Through Environmental Design) has now been applied to shoplifting. The recent studies on this are too involved to detail in this chapter. However, readers are encouraged to study CPTED and Retail Security or Shoplifting to identify concrete examples to apply in a retail setting.

Summary

Proper training and procedures are the keys to successful deterrence efforts. However, if a shoplifter is still encountered then the following rule of thumb should always be followed.

There should be no doubt in the mind of the detaining person that an act of shoplifting has just occurred. This means that the taking of property was witnessed, the apprehending person saw it being concealed, the subject was never of out sight (they did not drop the property), and the subject has either passed the last point of purchase opportunity or has exited the doors of the store. If these rules are followed then the liability risk inherent in any detention situation will have been reduced dramatically.

Tips for Retailers on Spotting Shoplifters

<u>General Appearance and Actions</u>

- ➢ Extremely fast walking or in a hurry.
- ➢ Looking without interest in size, price, or color.
- ➢ Crowding into racks.
- ➢ Shabbily dressed; looking at and handling expensive merchandise.
- ➢ Shabbily dressed teenagers wearing expensive accessories (cashmere sweaters, etc.).
- ➢ Looking, handling – but refusing service.
- ➢ Selecting and putting aside merchandise.
- ➢ Rolling and folding merchandise.
- ➢ Carrying merchandise to secluded spots.
- ➢ Matching merchandise.
- ➢ Behind a crowd or walking around with merchandise in hand.
- ➢ Pushing or dropping merchandise on the floor.
- ➢ Examining stock under counters or in drawers.
- ➢ Watching other customers – "cutting eyes."
- ➢ Holding merchandise below counter.
- ➢ Two customers huddling at counters.
- ➢ Folding or closing up open merchandise.
- ➢ Watching salesclerks – or in an uncovered department.
- ➢ Ill-fitting clothes: extremely loose or bulky, slit pockets.
- ➢ Still-legged walk, indicating merchandise possibly between legs.
- ➢ No purse, coat, hat, gloves, etc., in a department selling such items.
- ➢ Masquerading as an employee in back areas.
- ➢ Lingering after store closing.
- ➢ Leaving the store and re-entering by another door.
- ➢ Sudden change of mind at elevators.
- ➢ Using stairwells.
- ➢ Handling boxed merchandise instead of adjacent open stock.
- ➢ Plain loitering.
- ➢ Unnatural looking in mirror.
- ➢ Switching tickets.
- ➢ Trying on and leaving on merchandise while "looking at" other items.
- ➢ Pushing merchandise up sleeves.
- ➢ Teenagers in groups – riding elevators or escalators.
- ➢ Using tissues or handkerchiefs in jewelry section – palming.
- ➢ Diverting clerk's attention: asking for items not on display.
- ➢ Intoxication.
- ➢ Evidence of narcotic addict.
- ➢ Reports or pointing out as being suspicious refunder.
- ➢ Disguises such as wigs or dark glasses (increasingly difficult to detect now).
- ➢ Wearing eyeglasses one day and not the next.
- ➢ Carrying folded newspapers, folded bags, new or rumpled.
- ➢ Shopping bags with unwrapped merchandise.
- ➢ Empty shopping bags, own or other stores.
- ➢ "Double-header," one bag in another.
- ➢ Open bag held at edge of counter.
- ➢ Any bag, blown up and empty or stuffed with newspapers or other bags.
- ➢ Trap boxes – generally tied, with one end or side contrived to be a trap door.
- ➢ Bags, boxes, shoe boxes, etc., carried into fitting rooms.
- ➢ Any type of box or bag placed on counter.
- ➢ School books, satchels, or briefcases, particularly if with folded newspapers or bags.
- ➢ Knitting bags, diaper bags.

> ➢ Large pocketbooks, flight bags.
> ➢ Folded coat or sweater.
> ➢ Umbrella when sun has been shining.
> ➢ Unwrapped merchandise between bags.

Fitting Room Activity

> ➢ Going into fitting rooms unattended.
> ➢ Taking two identical items into fitting room.
> ➢ Going into fitting room with part of merchandise on hanger and part off hanger.
> ➢ Taking excessive number of items to fitting room.
> ➢ Multiple occupancy, particularly by teenagers.
> ➢ Evidence of "lookouts," one person inside and one outside.
> ➢ Holding curtains.
> ➢ The gentle sound of rustling bags.
> ➢ Removing tickets while in fitting rooms.
> ➢ Excessive movements between floor and fitting rooms.
> ➢ Changing fitting rooms with, or without, merchandise.
> ➢ Hurried taking of merchandise to room, no apparent selection of size or color.
> ➢ Refusing of service.
> ➢ Ostensibly leaving room with merchandise in it and returning.

Shoplifting (The Cause)

> ➢ Inadequate control over merchandise, greater opportunity for theft.
> ➢ Poor merchandise display.
> ➢ Modern merchandise display concept.
> ➢ Insufficient sales coverage.
> ➢ Inefficient sales coverage.
> ➢ Improper training.
> ➢ Lack of involvement.
> ➢ Indifferent attitude.
> ➢ Lack of respect for the property of others.
> ➢ Permissiveness of parents.
> ➢ Drug related problems.
> ➢ Financial pressures.

Shoplifting (The Cure)

> ➢ Controlling merchandise and reducing opportunity for theft.
> ➢ Prevention measures.
> ➢ Adequate sales coverage.
> ➢ Improved training and continuing training program.
> ➢ Getting people involved.
> ➢ Motivation, Incentives, Rewards.
> ➢ Improved attitudes.
> ➢ Community involvement programs.
> ➢ The program in the schools.
> ➢ The program for the parents.
> ➢ Prosecution.

References

LPM Insider, March 21, 2018

Loss Prevention, Magazine, June 2017

http://www.shopliftingprevention.org/what-we-do/learning-resource-center/statistics/

EAS: Retailers' first line of defense; Checkpointsystems.com

Shoplifting Prevention 101; Identify and Prevent Retail Theft; From Shari Waters, former About.com

Shoplifting Facts: Retail Theft of Merchandise; By Chris E McGoey

Recession Sparks Global Shoplifting Spree; Time.com; By Bruce Crumley / Paris Wednesday, Nov. 11, 2009

Retail Theft Decreased in 2011; Shoplifting accounted for approximately 35.7% of total losses
CSP Daily News | July 9, 2012

Retail theft rate eases but remains a $34.5B problem: Analysis; Business Insurance
Rodd Zolkos; June 21, 2012 - 2:38pm

Organized Retail Theft; A $30 Billion-a-Year Industry; FBI 01/03/11

The State Of The Loss Prevention Industry: 2012 Update; SecurityInfoWatch.com
BY MARK DOYLE CREATED: JUNE 5, 2012

Countering Organized Retail Theft: Reducing Economy-Related "Shrinkage"
Franchising.com; By: Rollie Trayte And Gary Widman

Protecting Your Merchandise and Bottom Line; RBC Retail Security LLC

How Do I Prevent Retail Theft?; smallbusiness.chron.com; by Maggie McCormick, Demand Media

New Strategies to Combat Organized Retail Theft; CheckpointSystems.com

Stop Losing Inventory and Start Boosting Profits Today; Loss Prevention Systems, Inc. 2012

What is an EAS System?; Retailtheftprevention.com (how stuff works)

Retail Theft And Its Link To The Recession; ABCarticledirectory.com;
By: Andrew Cameron

Preventing Retail Theft; You can't make a profit if your merchandise is free. Implement these tips for minimizing employee and shoplifter theft. entrepreneur.com; July 18, 2007

Top 5 Retail Theft Prevention Tips; Balluun.com; by ALLEN on JUNE 28, 2012

Surveys Show Retail Theft Increasing; stores.org; Jul 2009

Top 4 Sources of Shrinkage; retail.about.com; Shari Waters

Security: Retail Theft Prevention; MRstarfinancial.com

Retail security: Critical strategies; CSOonline.com; By Derek Slater 9/13/2011

Retail Theft Prevention Tip #4: Say Goodbye to Opportunity; balluun.com; by ALLEN on JUNE 21, 2012

5 top tactics in retail theft today
Technologies that offer convenience to shoppers also assist criminals (including employees) with retail theft; CSOoline.com Physical Security; by Joan Goodchild, Senior Editor; April 30, 2010

The Most Effective Retail Loss Prevention Methods; The Profit Experts (rgroupint.com)
Romeo Richards

Chapter Twelve

Crime Prevention Through Environmental Design (CPTED)

CPTED Performance Objectives:

- Define CPTED
- Explain the concept of CPTED
- Cite and explain the four strategies of CPTED
- Cite examples of each of the strategies
- Cite examples of CPTED crossover situations

Introduction

Crime Prevention Through Environmental Design, frequently identified by its acronym CPTED, is the study and design of the built environment with the intent of reducing the fear and incidence of crime, thereby improving the quality of life. Practitioners of CPTED will study a given area or space, ranging from a single building to an area as large as a neighborhood and even an entire new planned community. The study is done with the intent of identifying unsafe design characteristics with subsequent explanations and recommendations for solutions. CPTED also involves identifying safe passages for both vehicles and pedestrians through a city or neighborhood, thereby addressing roadways and their design.

CPTED requires the involvement of a variety of community laypeople and leaders to be successful. Architects, landscapers, law enforcement, city planners, and interior designers all play roles in the success of CPTED in any community. The participants understanding of the basics of CPTED is essential to the building of an effective CPTED team.

The design of a building or other area can attract or deflect criminal elements simply by its design. Criminal offenders consciously recognize a particular space as being an advantage to them to commit a property or personal crime. They view these spaces with the mindset of desiring to commit the crime as effortlessly as possible by taking advantage of the environment. The rest of the population - the potential victims of these crimes, the residents or guests of the area - may consciously or subconsciously feel uncomfortable in the same area but may not be able to identify exactly what is causing the level of discomfort. It is understood that the environment is not a welcoming place and people will either avoid it or go through it as quickly as possible in order to get in and out safely. This attitude begins the cycle of community deterioration. When residents and normal users avoid an area, it begins the first stage of death for that area. This unit of instruction is designed to give the reader a better understanding of exactly why individuals feel uncomfortable in some environments, and what can be done to correct the poor design that is the root of the discomfort, leading to a safer space and increased use by legitimate users.

CPTED Strategies

There are four key strategies that comprise CPTED:

- Territoriality

- Natural Surveillance
- Access Control
- Activity Support

TERRITORIALITY

The concept of territoriality relates to people's willingness to protect territory and property that they feel is their own. These same people have a certain respect for the territory of others and are more likely to challenge trespassers and abnormal users of that territory. Items that express ownership would include: fences, pavement treatments, artwork, signs, landscaping, and good maintenance.

Fences have never been designed to effectively keep people out; they have merely represented a specific property line. Fences can be friendly or unfriendly. Chain link, split rail, picket, and garden fences are all considered friendly fences. The key to both friendliness and territoriality is the ability to see through or over them. Unfriendly fences are solid walls of wood or concrete over six feet in height. They effectively turn away neighbors and do not contribute to the overall concept of CPTED.

Metal Fence Gives Ownership

Split Wood Rail Fence Gives Ownership

Fences clearly communicate to the casual observer that the property on the other side is private. Normal users who approach the area or are walking next to it understand and accept this. Abnormal users have two issues with fences. First, their presence on the other side of a fence negates the 'accidental trespass' explanation. Secondly, their mere presence on the other side of a fence is an indicator to local area observers that there is a trespasser. This observation may cause the police to be called or can later result in a description or identification of the trespasser or criminal. A fence need not be elaborate to work in CPTED. Indeed, a two-foot-high split rail fence is just as clear a boundary marker as is a six-foot chain link fence. However, a fence in obvious neglect and disrepair similarly communicates to the abnormal user that ownership has been abandoned and local user observation will be minimal or non-existent.

Pavement treatments guide both cars and pedestrians in safely traversing streets and even sidewalks. When vehicles approach an intersection with a red light or stop sign there is sometimes an indeterminate line as to exactly where to stop and where pedestrians should walk. At times pedestrians are forced to walk into the opposing lateral traffic flow to walk around stopped vehicles. Cities that have implemented CPTED understand that creating a contrasting colored crosswalk in the intersection designating a formal crosswalk results in fewer conflicts between vehicles and pedestrians. Colored crosswalks have been achieved by using paint and even colored cobblestones or bricks. Both drivers and pedestrians are naturally drawn to respect the barrier by stopping before it or walking within it.

Inlaid pavement designs in public areas, courtyards, sidewalks, and any place that pedestrians gather, shows ownership and discourages abnormal users. Such pavement designs are usually hosted by the local government but can also be sponsored by a neighboring corporate business. The attraction of normal users typically justifies the extra expense on the part of all parties.

Pavement Clearly Indicates Pedestrian Crossing

Artwork demonstrates ownership and pride. Art in any location usually represents a caring, responsible neighborhood. Art also tends to draw normal users to admire it, thus offering a number of eyes that drives away the abnormal user. However, when graffiti appears, as it is inclined to do, allowing the graffiti to remain on the art work tends to accomplish the opposite goal of attracting the abnormal user who is attracted to what appears to be an abandoned or forgotten space.

Attractive Attraction

Signs giving specific direction to users (and rules for abnormal users) make the normal user feel more comfortable in traversing unfamiliar streets or neighborhoods. However, these signs must be friendly in design and direction. Park-like signs work best in directing people while not being obnoxious in their intent. Violation of the clearly stated rules on the signs easily identifies the abnormal user. In a vibrant community normal users will challenge the abusers and police can more readily identify and make contact with them, thus driving them away.

Clearly Marked Directions/Rules

Landscaping offers a unique opportunity for territoriality. Landscaping is a symbolic barrier. While easily trampled upon and passed over, it also clearly marks the transition between public and private areas. Flower beds, gardens, ground cover plants, and shrubbery are clear indicators of the boundaries of the public areas. Without the need for signs or fences, landscaping universally identifies the beginning of a private space where intruders are not welcome and are easily identified when they trespass. When a stronger message is to be sent, thorny shrubbery can be planted that will also act as a physical barrier.

Landscaping Offers Territoriality

One of the side benefits to landscaping is the aesthetics. An attractive environment creates a sense of pride and ownership for the property owner and, by default, for the immediate neighborhood.

Maintenance is another aspect of territoriality. Normal users can quickly determine if an area is safe to traverse by viewing the degree of home and yard maintenance in a neighborhood. Real estate agents have recognized this fact for decades. Homes and yards that have not been maintained are harder to sell and will sell for less money. Obvious cues of a poorly maintained area are homes in need of exterior paint or new siding. Additionally, such conditions as broken and hanging screen doors; broken lawn furniture; a worn-out roof; discarded newspapers; lawns full of weeds; uncut grass for several weeks; dog feces lying all around; shower curtains in windows and patio doors; or disabled cars parked in the street demonstrate a lack of ownership and uncaring residents. The neighborhood decay is present and obvious. Such conditions allow abnormal users to feel comfortable as they will not likely be recognized as interlopers.

One of the interesting applications of territoriality is neighborhood schools. Such schools are obvious government buildings. However, when the neighborhood feels a buy-in with the school the residents are more watchful and caring of the property and users of the school at all hours. School officials who work with the neighborhood experience far fewer incidents of vandalism at their schools than do schools whose administrators do not foster local relations. A few simple things can make the difference: offering complimentary tickets to the neighbors to all school functions; hosting student neighborhood clean-up patrols; conducting neighborhood interest and concern surveys with appropriate responses. These activities will help to ensure that the school is being watched over at all hours.

NATURAL SURVEILLANCE

The intent of this principle is that criminals don't want to be seen. If potential intruders feel as though they can be observed before or during a criminal act then they very well might perceive the risk of apprehension as being unacceptable. Most criminals are least likely to act when there is a high risk of their actions being observed. Thus, by placing physical features, activities, and people in ways that maximize the ability of normal users to see what is happening criminals may be deterred from committing crimes. However, people frequently, albeit inadvertently, create vision barriers that offer concealment for criminals. Things like overgrown bushes, sheds and garages, solid fences, shadows due to poorly designed lighting, building wall recesses, decorative entrance pillars, and decorative false walls (inside and outside of buildings) lead to concealment and criminal behavior by abnormal users.

Surveillance of an area can come about through several different methods. People offer surveillance by their presence. Abnormal behavior in an otherwise normal location is quickly identified and registered. Indeed, in this day and age of terrorism society is encouraged to be vigilant in their observation of abnormal behavior. Personal cell phones have made the reporting of abnormal behavior a much easier task, and more likely to be undertaken.

Signage Creates Warning to Abnormal Users

Electronic surveillance systems are becoming common in urban environments. Video cameras, operated by both private owners and governments, watch over streets, building entrances, parking lots, and sidewalks. Individuals monitoring these cameras can identify aberrant behavior and notify the proper authorities.

Windows in buildings have always been a natural means of monitoring the outside. The size and number of residential windows have remained intact over the years and continue to allow property dwellers to monitor their territory. However, business windows are becoming smaller and fewer in numbers. This is in response to environmental efficiencies. The disadvantage is that there are fewer eyes to watch over adjacent parking lots and pedestrian walking areas. The result of this design characteristic is a more comfortable setting for the abnormal user and a less safe area for the normal user. For criminals the lack of windows is a potential sign of a related lack of surveillance.

Unobstructed sight lines deter the abnormal user from committing criminal acts. Landscaping plays a part in this to the point where a 'rule' has been created: The Rule of 7-2. The rule states that the lowest canopy of a tree must not be lower than seven feet and the highest growth of a shrub should be two feet. Abnormal users are prevented from concealing themselves among tree branches or hiding in bushes when these measurements are recognized and enforced. Another landscaping issue can be solid shrubbery lines. When normal users cannot see through a line of bushes abnormal users feel more comfortable on the 'hidden' side. All too often that hidden side is a parking lot where criminal acts occur. A better solution is to break up the shrub line with a tree spaced every 20 feet or so. Around the tree trunk should be an open space of at least four feet on either side of the tree. This allows people driving by to observe aberrant behavior, reducing the likelihood of criminals loitering in the area.

Rule of 7-2

Fencing should have see-through slats, and earthen berms must allow for natural viewing breaks like that suggested for shrub lines and trees. Pedestrian and bike paths must be evaluated for hidden attack locations. Exterior stairways and patio areas should have see- through supports.

ACCESS CONTROL

In the access control area users are controlled in their movements so that normal users can fully enjoy their surroundings. Appropriate fencing may have to be used for remote areas to deter abnormal users. Proper landscaping will direct users into the correct and safe path. Signage can remind users not to take shortcuts for their own safety. Lighting on these paths directs the normal user while illuminating and discouraging the abnormal user.

Lighting of Paths Makes Safer Walking

The implementation of active neighborhood watches can be very effective in observing abnormal activities. Fostered and supported by the police, neighborhoods can watch out for themselves. In some cities volunteer citizen patrols are issued police radios and walk or drive patrol beats in their communities. Urban communities with parking problems issue parking stickers to residents to park on the streets. This eliminates abnormal users from parking in these neighborhoods and ensures the residents ownership of their streets and recognition of intruders.

When additional fortifications are needed physical hardware can be implemented. Locked doors, electronic card access systems, cameras, security systems, stairway mirrors, and staff identification cards all assist in deterring the abnormal user.

ACTIVITY SUPPORT

Generally, people feel safe and comfortable in the presence of other people. Designing activities that foster that concept continues the positive cycle. Food vendor carts at night on the main street bring people together. Benches adjacent to wide sidewalks accommodate walkers and loungers.

Community Sponsored Activities Make People Feel Safe

Allowing schools to open their doors and illuminate their exterior basketball, soccer, and other ball courts at night brings the neighborhood together. People will naturally be attracted to the area and watch over the normally dark and seemingly unsafe area. Regularly scheduled evening picnics on closed off streets will bring out the neighbors and build a sense of community and support for the neighborhood.

The creation of basketball courts under bridges and interstate overpasses, as is done in Sacramento, California, brings a safe activity to a formerly unsafe area and gives residents a recreational outlet in the middle of a developed, urban area.

Effective Use of Lost Space Under Highway

CPTED Considerations and Examples

The four CPTED concepts can be clearly defined. However, the implementation of one concept can and does cross over into other conceptual areas, in effect having a dual impact on crime control. The following examples will help to illuminate the CPTED principles.

NATURAL SURVEILLANCE

In older school buildings, there have typically been fewer crimes against children around the school. The reason is a basic CPTED concept, although it was not designed with this in mind. Old school buildings were built with large classroom windows all the way around the building. These large windows overlooked the entire school property and allowed teachers and staff to see what was happening in the area. Child abuse perpetrators could never be sure that someone was not looking out and spotting them. That made loitering around the property hazardous for them, and so they were either discouraged from harming children around the school or were forced to take their activities elsewhere.

New schools of all grade levels have far fewer and smaller windows creating less natural surveillance opportunities and giving a criminal a greater level of confidence at not being observed. However, it should be noted that due to energy efficiency concerns, older buildings of all kinds are being retrofitted with smaller windows to reduce the loss of energy, surrendering the natural protective surveillance that larger windows once offered.

Buildings that are open to the public or that do not have controlled entry are an inviting environment for criminals. Large public buildings, hotels, and conference centers all share the design of blind corners in long hallways. Once inside a building a criminal can freely walk around, entering vacant rooms or offices to steal, dealing drugs in the restrooms, or potentially assault building occupants. Assaults may be accomplished by waiting around a corner for an unsuspecting victim to approach and be taken by surprise. The suspect can hear the unaware person approaching and may have a good indication of the gender of the person based on the sound of the footsteps and type of shoe being worn on hard floors. The victim has no advance notice as he/she walks around the corner. A mirror mounted on the opposing wall will discourage this type of loitering and allow occupants to see around a corner before walking into danger.

TERRITORIALITY

Symbolic property barriers may give trespassers and criminals pause for thought before choosing to enter private property. Such barriers give indication that the owner/occupant cares about the property and might have greater interest and observation. Items such as a split rail fence, low cut decorative bushes, a border flower garden or rock garden, or even a plastic chain attached to 4"x4" posts indicate ownership and access control. Territoriality is about ownership of the property.

Excellent Example of Outdoor Patio Ownership

Planting trees in front of a house in a publicly owned terrace suggests home dweller interest in their property right up to the street and even beyond. Cities frequently will provide and plant the trees with the understanding that the adjacent homeowners take responsibility for them. Indeed, if you park your car at the curb on a city owned street in front of someone's cared for home, the homeowner sitting on the porch or watering the lawn is likely to give you a long stare that clearly implies you are parking on his property. Some will even challenge you as to your business. This is Territoriality at its extreme.

Unsafe Bus Stop - No Ownership

Directional maps in a downtown area give a safe feeling to a visitor and demonstrate ownership by the government. There is usually a much greater comfort level for a person in a new city when they can find their location on a posted tourist map and identify their destination. Anyone who has ever been lost in a new city without a map understands the feeling of frustration at not knowing where you are or how to get where they want to go. Clearly delineated bus routes on large city maps also bring back tourists and their spending dollars. Seattle has large public city maps with colored bus routes to guide the visitor. Washington, D.C. does the same thing with their metro system, making it a more pleasant experience for tourists navigating the streets.

Downtown Street Directory

Debate continues on the installation of emergency phones in a downtown area. Detractors will say that such phones advertise a crime ridden area. Supporters point out the comfort level that tourists will have knowing that assistance is simply a pushbutton away. The truth is that if a visitor or resident is ever accosted or simply feels threatened the availability of an emergency phone is a practical solution to quickly summon assistance. Like many crime control items, the mere presence of an emergency phone may deter the criminal element from that area. When such a system is combined with a security video system, criminals are even less likely to present themselves on the streets knowing that their faces may be recorded and identified. The hoped-for goal is a safer street and area for both residents and visitors.

Police and Fire Call Box
To Assist Downtown Shoppers

Benches that are placed in either parks or along streets provide the opportunity for visitors and shoppers to take a break, and then continue their shopping rather than leaving the area. However, they also can be used as makeshift beds by the homeless in large cities. This can be alleviated by designing the park bench with a cross bar in the center. It deters people from sleeping on the benches and encourages strangers to share the space with the 'territorial' bar offering separation of seating spaces.

Benches Lead to Comfortable Shoppers Who Return to Shop

Benches with Dividers Allow Strangers to Share   **Dividers Also Discourage Abnormal Behavior**

A Lack of Territorial Ownership Leads to Abnormal Activity

A Lack of Territorial Ownership Leads to Abnormal Activity

ACTIVITY SUPPORT

One 'activity' that is always safe but typically hidden is a shopping mall security office. Because this space does not generate an income for the mall the security office is almost always positioned in an out of the way corner and can even be moved from location to location when a rent paying vendor comes forward, making it difficult to find a safe haven in an emergency. Placing the security office in a central area is an optimal situation for the mall, customers, and the security department. It allows rapid and visual access to the shoppers and, as this is who they serve, should always be in a high visibility location.

Centralized Mall Office

Public restrooms are not typically located in the main shopping corridors of malls. Restrooms space does not bring in income and thus are designed and placed in out-of-the way locations in most malls. These locations are what draws in criminals and, specifically, pedophiles. Sexual assaults and/or the abduction of children through adjacent emergency exits are the result of these ill-placed locations. For the safety of shoppers restrooms must be located closer to main shopping areas.

Mall Restrooms Located Out of Sight

Bus shelters can be a haven for homeless people, discouraging tourists and residents from riding public transportation. However, a public entity with the foresight to pipe in recorded classical music will find that complaints about harassment at a bus stop, or the feelings of not being safe, are reduced.

Lighting in bus shelters is another important consideration. Adequate lighting to see inside the clear, plastic sides before a person enters is important. But caution must be exercised that not too much light illuminates the interior. If the bus shelter occupants cannot clearly see out because of the bright light, a feeling of vulnerability may result. The addition of security cameras can greatly reduce both the feeling and reality of criminal activity. However, the cameras must be monitored to make them effective with prompt response when warranted. Furthermore, they must be contained in vandal resistant housings. Appropriate signage indicating the presence of cameras further deters crime.

Clear Visibility and Lighting for Safety

Food kiosks are always a draw for hungry patrons. Kiosks are an excellent example of a safe activity in both safe and unsafe areas. Because they draw in groups of people the area is made safer for all users thus attracting even more people. Sidewalk food kiosks located on busy streets after bar hours helps to calm intoxicated people and further contribute to a safe environment. However, city requirements and licensure affect the viability of food kiosks.

Mobile Food Carts Bring in Crowds   **Sidewalk Tables Contribute to Safe Behavior**

Cities impose operating license requirements and license fees on food kiosks. The local Health Department may require inspections and additional licensing. Sometimes the Sanitation Department has yet more regulations with their own inspections and licenses. City councils worry about crowds and impose limitations on location and hours. Further resistance comes from established storefronts that do not want the competition during their open hours and do not care what happens to the neighborhood after they close at night. All this can make it very difficult to implement a safe activity and will only change with a greater appreciation and education of government officials for CPTED concepts.

ACCESS CONTROL

Traditional buildings can be entered through any natural hole built into the walls; doors, windows, vents. All are access points for trespassers and the criminal element and, most cases, can be approached at night without clear observation. However, a new CPTED concept of surrounding a building with water allows better control of personnel and vehicles. Designing a pond completely around a building offers many benefits. The water is esthetically pleasing to employees and visitors. It offers a calming effect which can be further enhanced by the presence of wildlife. A pond can be used as a fire water source and also can be used as a cooling source for heating/ventilating/air conditioning systems. Control of pedestrians and vehicles is easily accomplished with appropriate bridges and access points. Companies may also use these ponds to enhance community goodwill by sponsoring such events as model boat racing upon them.

Ponds Control Access and Allow Supportive Activities

One of the concerns regarding these ponds is the possibility that a vehicle that might slide into the pond. Two options exist to prevent this from happening. The first is a cable vehicle barrier system found on some interstate system highways. Planting low growing bushes under the cable will block the view of the protective system. Another option is the creation of a protective earth berm around the pond. At three feet high, the berm does not inhibit any views. Installing a sidewalk on top of the berm further protects the pedestrian and encourages its use as a scenic recreation trail.

Another creative approach to access control relates to bridges. Graffiti taggers, vandals, and thrill seekers often use the undersides of bridges as their playground. Installing a fence on the side of a bridge has proved not to be an effective deterrent. However, a design change in fencing appears to work. The new design is to place the fence out from the side of the bridge about three feet. Low hedges planted on the *inside* of the fence keep casual climbers from approaching the fence. More determined climbers may be further deterred by thorny vines that grow along both sides of the fence and extend three feet out and away from the top of the fence via a chain link trellis overhang.

When fencing is called for in access control the use of welded wire or ornamental steel fencing should be used rather than the more common chain link fence. It is more appealing to the eye, structurally more sound, and can be much more difficult to climb over.

Trespassers might be inclined to walk through areas where communities or companies are encouraging the natural growth of prairies and landscaping to conserve water or re-create the natural environment. Sometimes all that is needed to hinder trespassers is the perception of danger. One unique concept is the installation of a sign with a deceptive message, such as 'Caution – Rattlesnakes'. Adding a graphic of a rattlesnake can impart the requisite visual fear of entering the property. The signs would be posted at a height just above the vegetation in locations where natural egress by trespassers might occur.

Signs to Discourage Entry

As in many CPTED cases the ability to be a creative thinker coupled with the "Think like a criminal" philosophy can deter crime and take back a neighborhood or business community.

CPTED Crossover Examples

Government ordinances or codes have frequently been implemented to reduce the opportunity for a crime to be committed. These codes can coincidently mirror CPTED concepts. However, uninformed officials can inadvertently create opportunities for crime with these codes.

Examples of what could be called 'positive' codes include cutting grass around a home or property, litter control, weed control, and requiring property owners to remove graffiti within 48 hours. These types of codes all contribute to an orderly, caring society and neighborhood. Enforcement is needed, however, and residents may have to call to make sure the codes are enforced.

There are some codes that are put into effect that could be called 'code hazards'. These codes are passed with good intentions but are not completely thought out and did not have someone with CPTED training review them.

One common example is solid wood or block fencing erected around apartment and business trash receptacles. The intent, to block unsightly garbage bins, is valid. The unintended consequence is two-fold. First, garbage that might fall into the walled enclosure is likely to remain there. Employees may not be of the mindset to pick up fallen garbage, when closing the doors will block the problem from sight. Paper products are not the more significant problem in this situation. Fallen food or plant products will rot in warm temperatures, saturating the surrounding area with a foul odor. The non-vented, solid block or wooden structure will then act as a furnace compounding the unpleasant problem.

The second issue is more serious. Frequently, employees who must take out the trash do so at the end of a work day. If the business is open until late in the evening the employee must exit the building, usually from the rear and into the night, and walk to the property boundary where the trash containers are kept. Criminals may take advantage of this situation by hiding behind the solid walls and then attacking the unsuspecting employee.

Enclosures with Solid Walls and Doors
Conceal Potential Attackers

The solution to both issues is what is called 'psychological' barriers. Such a barrier gives the appearance of a fence, but actually allows a person to see through and past the barrier. Examples would be slatted boards, diamond patterned wood or vinyl panels, or boards mounted with 3"- 4" inch spaces between them. Visually, one perceives a wall. But the potential victim approaching it would be able to see through the boards and detect the presence of a person loitering behind them. Trash enclosures of this style have a dual advantage. First, they offer the same psychological barrier effect, in essence concealing the existence of the trash bins. More importantly, because they have natural venting, free flowing air tends to dry out any rotting substance on the ground reducing odors and attracting fewer rodents. Employees are also more cognizant of falling debris that might blow away and are more likely to pick up any fallen trash.

Good Psychological Design   **Poor Security Design**

Another example of a code hazard is inappropriate earth berms. These are sometimes created between businesses and residences, and around parking lots. The intent is to visually block an 'unsightly' piece of property from the neighboring property. Parked cars in a large parking lot are sometimes viewed as a 'visual blight' by government officials. A frequent solution to has been to create a 5' or 6' earthen barrier around the perimeter to block out the parked vehicles and then to plant trees and bushes on the berm to make it look attractive. While the motive is certainly reasonable the increased potential for crime may not have been considered. Criminals who would not have broken into vehicles or stolen them outright because of the fear of natural surveillance have now had that threat removed. Patrons returning from their shopping experience may now be assaulted behind the blocked view. As referenced earlier, a more appropriate response would be to build a lower, three-foot-high earthen berm, cover it with low growing low maintenance vegetation, build in natural 6' to 8' breaks every 20' and plant tall growing trees in the breaks.

Landscaped Berm
Does Not Allow Natural Surveillance of Shoppers Above

Another solution to the problem of acres of parked cars and the creation of berms to block them out has been popular in Florida for quite some time. All commercial parking lots around businesses must have a certain percentage of their surface covered with traffic islands planted with trees. Entering these parking lots is almost like driving in a park. Trees are planted everywhere and create the psychological barrier effect of not seeing the business and rows of cars as much as green trees. Yet, patrons can clearly see and be seen under the trees for natural surveillance.

Summary

Effective pre-design planning can reduce both the incidence and fear of crime in buildings, neighborhoods, subdivisions, and entire communities. Engaging the services of a certified CPTED expert will ultimately reduce future crime related losses.

References

Crime Prevention through Environmental Design: CPTED 40 Years Later
By Captain Ed Book, District Commander, Gainesville, Florida, Police Department; and Professor
Richard Schneider, Urban and Regional Planning, College of Design, Construction, and Planning,
University of Florida, Gainesville, Florida; The Police Chief;
July 2012

CPTED Basics; Everett Police Department, Everett, WA; Officer S. Praxton

Crime Prevention Through Environmental Design (CPTED); landlordassoc.org

Crime Prevention Through Environmental Design Planning to Prevent Crime
about.com Business Security; By William Deutsch

Crime Prevention through Environmental Design, 1994
popcenter.org; By Timothy D. Crowe and Diane L. Zahm

Crime Prevention Through Environmental Design (CPTED)
Author Palace; By AlfredLancer ; Submit on 08/30/10

Crime Prevention Through Environmental Design (CPTED)
Article-niche.com Home Repair; Jay Stockman, January 30, 2006

CPTED For Parking Lots And Garages; SecurityInfoWatch.com
CREATED: JANUARY 27, 2009

Does It Look Safe to You?; School Planning & Management; peterli.com;
by Scott Berman

A lesson on Crime Prevention Through Environmental Design (CPTED)
ICMA.org; 30 May 2008; Julia Warren, City of Lake Oswego

The Continuing Evolution of CPTED; LandscapeOnline.com

Why CPTED Still Requires a Mixture of Professional Security Services
ezinearticles.com; January 26, 2010; Richard Baggaley

CPTED, still the exception; thefreelibrary.com
COPYRIGHT 2003 American Society for Industrial Security

Crime Prevention Through Environmental Design; crimewise.com; By Robert A. Gardner, CPP

CPTED: Safer Communities by Design; securitymagazine.com; Sarita Hill Coletrane; December 1, 2011

Appendices

- Residential Security Survey
- Business Security Survey

Note: Purchasers of this book may request copies of the most recent survey forms to be emailed to them at no cost. This would give you an updated and a 'master' copy of the surveys for photocopy purposes.

Please email the author at Jerry.Antoon@gmail.com with your request and indicate which form you desire.

**Residential
Security Survey**

Confidential Document

Address:

City:_____State_____Zip_____

Contact Person: (optional)_____

Conducted by:

Name:_____

Agency:_____

Date:_____On-Site Escort:_____

Structure type: Single story_____   Two story_____ Tri-level_____

                         Single family_____   Duplex_____ Apartment_____

                         Other _____

      S = Satisfactory   U = Unsatisfactory   NA = Not Applicable

Note: 'U' indicators require written explanations

	S	U	NA
1. Landscaping			
A. Bushes below window – 2 feet high maximum (or thorn bushes)	☐	☐	☐
B. Trees above window – 7 feet high minimum	☐	☐	☐
C. Tree branches at least six feet away from roof edge	☐	☐	☐

Comments:

	S	U	NA
2. Lighting			
A. Rear yard: 35 or 50watt H.P.S. with dusk/dawn sensor. (High Pressure Sodium Light)	☐	☐	☐
B. Front porch dusk/dawn screw-in sensor adapter	☐	☐	☐

Comments:

	S	U	NA
3. Door Locks - All			
A. Rekeyed when moved in	☐	☐	☐
B. Caregiver/child sitter training on locking/unlocking locks	☐	☐	☐

Comments:

4. Front Door

	S	U	N A
A. One inch minimum throw deadbolts	☐	☐	☐
B. High security (four hole) strike plates	☐	☐	☐
C. Three inch strikeplate screws (remove to verify)	☐	☐	☐
D. With glass within 40" – double cylinder deadbolt w/high security strikeplate (and emergency key on string in area)	☐	☐	☐
E. Without glass - single cylinder deadbolt w/high security strike plate	☐	☐	☐
F. Solid core construction	☐	☐	☐
G. Without glass - door viewer	☐	☐	☐
H. Child height door viewer	☐	☐	☐
I. Out swinging door has security hinges	☐	☐	☐

Comments:

```
┌─────────────────────────────────────────────────┐
│                                                 │
│                                                 │
│                                                 │
│                                                 │
└─────────────────────────────────────────────────┘
```

5. Attached Garage – Residence Entry Door

	S	U	N A
A. One inch minimum throw deadbolts	☐	☐	☐
B. High security (four hole) strike plates	☐	☐	☐
C. Three inch strikeplate screws (remove to verify)	☐	☐	☐
D. Solid core construction	☐	☐	☐
E. No glass in door (fire codes)	☐	☐	☐
F. Single cylinder deadbolt w/high security strike plate	☐	☐	☐
G. Door viewer	☐	☐	☐
H. Child height door viewer	☐	☐	☐
Out swinging door has security hinges	☐	☐	☐

Comments:

```
┌─────────────────────────────────────────────────┐
│                                                 │
│                                                 │
│                                                 │
│                                                 │
└─────────────────────────────────────────────────┘
```

6. Attached Garage – Direct Basement Entry Door (no window)
    A. One inch minimum throw deadbolts
    B. High security (four hole) strike plates
    C. Three inch strikeplate screws (remove to verify)
    D. Solid core
    E. Single cylinder deadbolt w/high security strike plate
    F. Out swinging door has security hinges (Garage level)
    G. Out swinging door has latch guard plate (Garage level)
      (Basement level doors are normally in-swinging)
Comments:

7. Rear Door – Hinged Patio Door

    A. One inch minimum throw deadbolts
    B. High security (four hole) strike plates
    C. Three inch strikeplate screws (remove to verify)
  * If entire door is one single pane of tempered safety glass:
    D. Double or single cylinder deadbolt w/high security strike plate
  * If door is composed of individual panes of glass:
    E. Double cylinder deadbolt (spare key) w/high security strike
      plate
    F. Out swinging door has security hinges
Comments:

8. Rear Door - Sliding Door

    A. Lift barrier strip or protruding screws in upper track
    B. Auxiliary sliding door bolt
Comments:

	S	U	N A

9. Rear Door – Standard In-swing
    A. One inch minimum throw deadbolts
    B. High security (four hole) strike plates
    C. Three inch strikeplate screws (remove to verify)
    D. Solid core construction
    E. With window/glass within 40"-
       double cylinder deadbolt (spare key) w/high security strike plate
    F. Without glass – single cylinder deadbolt w/high security strike
       plate
    G. Without glass – door viewer
    H. Child height door viewer
Out swinging door has security hinges

Comments:

	S	U	N A

10. Garage, Attached - Doors
    A. One inch minimum throw deadbolts
    B. High security (four hole) strike plates
    C. Three inch strikeplate screws (remove to verify)
    D. Solid core construction
    E. Exterior entry doors w/ windows w/double cylinder deadbolts
    F. Exterior entry doors w/o windows w/single cylinder deadbolts
    G. Out swinging doors with security hinges
    H. Overheard door w/electric garage door opener or hardware lock

Comments:

	S	U	N A

11. Exterior Cellar - Ground Level Doors
    A. Hinges in good condition
    B. 3" Hinge frame side screws
    C. Carriage (round head) bolts on exterior side of hinges
    D. Locking mechanism carriage bolts (if visible to exterior)

    E. Inside lock present/good repair
    F. Doors in good condition
Comments:

	S	U	N A

12. Windows – Single/Double hung
    A. Auxiliary keyed lock
    B. Wireless alarm sensor for ventilation to 4"   ☐   ☐   ☐
Comments:

>

13. Windows – Casement (crank out)   S   U   N A

    A. Locking latches in working order
    B. Verbal instruction to always latch for best security   ☐   ☐   ☐

   Comments:

>

     S   U   N A

14. Windows - Sliding
    A. Auxiliary keyed locks -- top and bottom
B. Wireless alarm sensor for ventilation to 4"   ☐   ☐   ☐
 (Required if window can be lifted out of frame).

Comments:

>

     S   U   N A

15. Windows - Tilt /Turn (tilt in and swing in)
Locking hardware working order   ☐   ☐   ☐

Comments:

>

S   U   N
                A

16. Windows - Louvered
 Superglue put into glass frame to lock in glass panes(or)   ☐   ☐   ☐
Expanded steel mesh screen screwed into door frame on inside   ☐   ☐   ☐
Comments:

S   U   N
                A

17. Windows - Basement
    A. Security bars installed   ☐   ☐   ☐
    B. Lock on security bars   ☐   ☐   ☐
    C. Security bars escape key located on same plane minimum 40"   ☐   ☐   ☐
        and maximum 64" away (or)
    D. Glass block/expanded steel mesh screen installed (or)   ☐   ☐   ☐

    E. Glass replaced with 3/8" polycarbonate (steel straps on inside   ☐   ☐   ☐
        and behind plastic, screwed into wood frame to prevent
        kicking out window)
Comments:

S   U   N
                A

18. House Numbers
    A. Are they visible from street   ☐   ☐   ☐
    B. Are they a minimum of three inches tall   ☐   ☐   ☐
    C. Are they illuminated or reflective at night   ☐   ☐   ☐
    D. If alley, are they visible on rear of house   ☐   ☐   ☐
Comments:

	S	U	N A

19. Window Air Conditioner
Is it secured on the outside with a eyebolt screwed into
bottom of carrier/case

    B. Is there an eyebolt screwed into the wall stud below the AC and
        attached to the AC with a locked chain pulled tightly

Comments:

	S	U	N A

20. Telephone access box
   No central alarm monitoring system
     A. Is there a padlock on the phone box lock hasp to prevent line
        tapping and unauthorized toll calls

Comments:

   Central monitoring system is present in home

	S	U	N A

     B. Are the phone wires inside solid metal conduit tubing or half
        pipe

C. Does the conduit extend into the ground 18 inches for
underground utilities or above 8 feet for overhead lines

     D. Is the conduit securely attached to the wall studs
     E. Is there a secure auxiliary metal box attached to wall around
        phone box

Comments:

21. Home Safe

	S	U	N A

Is the safe covered by a non-descript general type of cardboard
box so as to conceal its presence, in a hall closet or storage area
Comments:

NOTE: Survey recommendations, if implemented, should substantially reduce a criminal opportunity but are not to be construed as a guarantee that a crime will not occur on the premises.

Additional security issues not included on this form but observed during survey should be included below as a part of this survey.

Additional Recommendations for Improvement

PROBLEMS   and   RECOMMENDATIONS:
(add additional pages as needed)

Crime Prevention Photos for Clarification

Barrel Bolt on Interior Sliding Glass Door

Barrel Bolt on Exterior Sliding Glass Door

Screws in Upper Sliding Door Track

Wireless Window Alarm Sensor
(to detect opening of either closed or 4″ ventilation of window)

Phone Box Without Lock

Single Cylinder and Double Cylinder Deadbolts

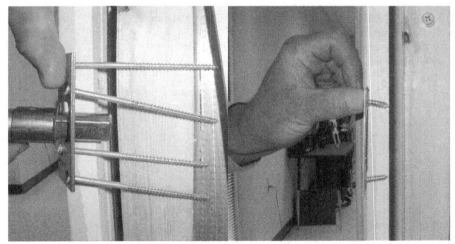

Four Hole and Two Hole Standard Strike Plates

285

**Business
Security Survey**

Confidential Survey

Organization Name:
Address:
City:_____State_____Zip_____
Contact Person: _____

Conducted by:
Name:_____
Agency:_____
Date:_____

S = Satisfactory   U = Unsatisfactory   NA = Not Applicable

Note: Items checked as "U" are referenced at end of report with recommendations for improvement.

	S	U	NA
1. Fencing and Barriers			
A. Minimum height of 8'	☐	☐	☐
B. Fence construction of at least 9 gauge chainlink or similar material so as to provide security while permitting surveillance of activity within the fenced area	☐	☐	☐
C. Lockable gate of same material as fence at all pedestrian or vehicle openings	☐	☐	☐
D. All the gates are secured with a U.L. approved lock	☐	☐	☐
All debris and foliage which might diminish visibility or hide intruders kept clear of fences and gates	☐	☐	☐
Are glass door entries and window fronts protected by adequate bollards	☐	☐	☐
	S	U	NA

	S	U	NA
2. Landscaping and Ground Maintenance			
A. All shrubbery of the "spread" or "ground cover" variety; or trimmed to less than 2 feet so that an intruder will be denied concealment and to make it difficult to secrete stolen property; tree branches trimmed to 7' height	☐	☐	☐
B. Trees, utility poles, dumpsters, vehicles or any other objects that could facilitate climbing are cleared to a point at least 6 feet from building or fences	☐	☐	☐
C. All outbuildings, sheds, boxcars, trailers or any other storage facility containing items of value locked in a manner to that stipulated for main buildings housing similar items of value	☐	☐	☐

3. Parking Areas
   A. Segregated parking for employee, visitor, company operated and shipping and receiving vehicles provided ☐ ☐ ☐
   B. Employee and visitor vehicles prohibited from parking adjacent to any exit door or loading dock ☐ ☐ ☐
   C. All specific parking areas clearly and conspicuously marked and checked for compliance by a specifically accountable individual ☐ ☐ ☐
   D. All parking areas are fenced and gated ☐ ☐ ☐
   E. All gates either locked or monitored by human or electronic surveillance at all times ☐ ☐ ☐
   F. Parking areas designed to facilitate surveillance ☐ ☐ ☐

4. Doors, Pedestrian
Solid Core ☐ ☐ ☐
       (or)
   B. Metal clad hollow core ☐ ☐ ☐
   C. Outswing doors fitted with security hinges ☐ ☐ ☐
   D. Lock bolt protection plate (Latch Guard) ☐ ☐ ☐
   E. Door viewer peephole (no window) ☐ ☐ ☐
   F. Polycarbonate or acrylic installed in window frame with reinforced edging ☐ ☐ ☐
       (or)
Expanded steel wire mesh bolted over window frame w/carriagebolts ☐ ☐ ☐

5. Door, Overhead
Steel panel, solid core ☐ ☐ ☐
       (or)
Solid wood ☐ ☐ ☐
   C. Secured in channels so as not to be pried out ☐ ☐ ☐
       If containing windows:
   D. Minimum 1/4" polycarbonate or 3/8" acrylic in window with reinforced edging ☐ ☐ ☐
Expanded steel wire mesh bolted over window frame w/carriage bolts (round headed bolts) ☐ ☐ ☐

S   U   NA

287

6. Door Locking Mechanisms - Pedestrian
   A. Single deadbolt cylinder with 1" hardened bolt 5-6
      pin tumbler and exterior revolving collar   ☐ ☐ ☐
   B. Double Doors: Sliding or Barrel bolts on top and bottom ☐ ☐ ☐
   C. Door brace of 2"x4" wood or 1/1/4" metal pipe held by
      metal brackets of at least 1/4" steel secured by through-
      the-door carriage bolts (check local fire code applicability) ☐ ☐ ☐
   D. All strike plates and hinges attached to inner doorframe
      with 3" wood or metal screws (wood frame doors only) ☐ ☐ ☐
   E. All outswing pedestrian door lock latchbolts protected with UL
      approved bolt latchguards ☐ ☐ ☐
   F. All unnecessary handles, knobs, etc. removed from exterior
      doors not used for ingress ☐ ☐ ☐
        Deadbolts not allowed:
   G. Clutch type lever locks ☐ ☐ ☐
   H. Emergency exit hardware with non-exposed bolt ☐ ☐ ☐

7. Windows
   A. All windows securely anchored in solid wood or metal frames ☐ ☐ ☐
   B. Any windows not involved in any evacuation plans or
      required for ventilation permanently secured by means of
      screws, nails, wire mesh, bars, or locks ☐ ☐ ☐
All first floor windows professionally installed with 1/4"
      polycarbonate glazing (or)
          3/8" acrylic glazing professionally installed (or) ☐ ☐ ☐
   D. Professionally installed security film over plate glass (or) ☐ ☐ ☐
   E. Laminated security glass (burglary resistant glass) ☐ ☐ ☐
   F. Operable windows equipped with supplemental keyed locks ☐ ☐ ☐

8. Other Openings
   A. All other openings such as roof hatches, skylights, air shafts,
      vents, or coal chutes welded or otherwise permanently secured
      if not used; or affixed with grates, padlocks and hasps if
      opened occasionally (96 square inches or larger) ☐ ☐ ☐

9. Building - Interior Barriers
   A. High Risk Areas
     1) Doors, windows, and other openings of any area within the
       building(s) of extraordinary vulnerability such as: money
       handling rooms, document file room, computer room, or
       high value inventory rooms: secured in the same manner as
       those on the building exterior ☐ ☐ ☐
   B. Normal Risk Areas
     1) Areas of less, but still substantial vulnerability such as:
       offices, general production or merchandising areas and
       storage rooms housing medium risk inventory or tools, are
       secured by at least a steel hollow core or solid wood core
       door and deadlatch lockset protected by a latchguard plate ☐ ☐ ☐
                               S   U   NA

10. Safes and Vaults
    A. If money is being stored on site, is it kept in a U.L. rated
       money safe □ □ □
    B. Does the monetary content match the U.L. rated safe as
       identified in Appendix A □ □ □
    C. Is the safe located in a place visible from a public street to
       discourage burglary □ □ □

Is there an evening security light illuminating the safe □ □ □
                    or
    E. Is the safe protected by at least one intrusion alarm sensor □ □ □
    F. Are irreplaceable company paper records kept in a U.L. rated
       fire safe or vault □ □ □

Is the fire safe/vault of the proper type and classification for the area □ □ □

    H. Are computer data records kept in a U.L. rated data safe □ □ □
    I. Is the data safe correctly classified for the contents and hours:
       i.e. tapes in a 150 and discs in a 125 with hours of rating □ □ □

Are the manual safe/vault combinations changed on an annual
basis □ □ □
    K. Are the safe/vault combinations changed after employees with
       knowledge of the combination leave the company or is their
       personal PIN removed from electronic safe combinations □ □ □

11. Lighting
    A. Is lighting sufficient in all areas of property to alleviate
       shadows and allow sufficient illumination to recognize shapes
       and colors □ □ □
    B. Is lighting sufficient around all windows and non-traditional
       burglary points of entry to recognize shapes and colors □ □ □
    C. Is lighting sufficient at all entrances, in all parking lots, at all
       gates and other locations where people would normally walk
       to allow the discernment of individual facial features from at
       least 20 feet away by the average person □ □ □
D. Is there a luminaire maintenance policy in effect that replaces
  lamps at 75% of the effective lifespan of the lamp □ □ □
    E. Are all lamps currently functioning □ □ □
    F. Has the local electric utility company been invited to perform
       a lighting survey-or has a consultant completed a survey □ □ □
                                                    S   U NA

12. Intrusion Alarm Systems
    A. Are all exterior perimeter doors contact switched ☐ ☐ ☐
    B. Are operable perimeter windows contact switched ☐ ☐ ☐
    C. Are higher security interior rooms protected by a motion
  sensor (computer room, safe room, R&D room, executive
      offices) ☐ ☐ ☐
D. Are non-conventional burglar entry points protected by an
      intrusion sensor (vents, roof hatch, skylight, A/C ducts, floor
      manhole covers) ☐ ☐ ☐
    E. Are high value rooms with exterior walls protected with
      either wall vibration sensors or motion sensors ☐ ☐ ☐
    F. Is there any object blocking the view of any motion sensor ☐ ☐ ☐
Is each sensor tested for proper 'catch' ability on a monthly
    basis ☐ ☐ ☐
H. Is the entire alarm system tested for outgoing signals on a
    monthly basis ☐ ☐ ☐
    I. Is the security force trained on the operation of each sensor,
      so as to discover evidence of internal sensor tampering ☐ ☐ ☐

NOTE: Survey recommendations, if implemented, should substantially reduce a criminal opportunity but are not to be construed as a guarantee that a crime will not occur on the premises.

Appendix A – Money Safes and Storage Values

UL Classification	Risk Classification	Maximum Values
TL - 15	Low	$150,000
TL - 30	Low	$200,000
TL - 15x6	Moderate	$300,000
TL - 30x6	Moderate	$400,000
TRTL - 30*	Moderate	$500,000
TRTL - 15x6	Moderate to High	$750,000
TRTL - 30x6	High	$1,000,000
TRTL - 60x6	High	$2,000,000
TXTL - 60x6	High	$2,000,000

* When the body of the safe is encased in reinforced concrete or constructed of a material equivalent to steel and reinforced concrete.

Above table is courtesy of Central Station Alarm Association,
1701 Wisconsin Avenue, Bethesda, MD 20814 www.csaaul.org

Appendix B – Money Safes vs. Record Safes

Money safes, also known as Burglary safes, are specifically designed for the storage of valuables and to resist and deter entry attempts by a burglar. Storage contents in a money safe can be precious metals, precious stones, bearer bonds, or cash. Money safes are not fire resistant unless separately stated on a label inside the safe door. Money safes are rated at different levels depending on the value of the contents and the anticipated expertise of the thief. Recipients of the survey should check with the person conducting the survey for more information on the various ratings and their meanings.

Record safes, also known as Fire safes or containers are specifically designed to protect paper records and computer media storage devices from the threat of heat associated with a fire. These safes are not burglary resistant unless so rated on a separate label inside the door of the safe. These safes also come in different types and ratings. The different safes accommodate businesses that might not have full time fire department response or that house the safe on an upper floor that might collapse during a fire. More details can be obtained from the person conducting this survey.

Safes that provide both fire and burglary protection (composite safes) are rare and expensive. If dual protection is needed it is suggested that a Money safe be purchased that is large enough to contain a separate Fire safe placed inside of it.

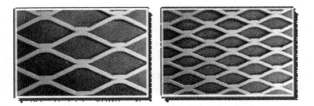

Examples of expanded steel mesh

Latch and Dead Bolt Plate

RECOMMENDATIONS FOR IMPROVEMENT

NOTE: Survey recommendations, if implemented, should substantially reduce a criminal opportunity but are not to be construed as a guarantee that a crime will not occur on the premises.

Additional security issues not identified on this form but observed during the survey should be included as additional items at the conclusion of the recommendations portion of this survey.

ITEM #   **ISSUES and RECOMMENDATIONS:**   **(add photos and pages as needed)**

Made in the USA
Monee, IL
01 September 2020

40039392R00168